¡OBÁMANOS!

ALSO BY HENDRIK HERTZBERG

Politics: Observations & Arguments

¡OBÁMANOS!

THE BIRTH OF A NEW POLITICAL ERA

Hendrik Hertzberg

THE PENGUIN PRESS

New York

2009

THE PENGUIN PRESS
Published by the Penguin Group
Penguin Group (USA) Inc., 375 Hudson Street, New York, New York 10014, U.S.A. •
Penguin Group (Canada), 90 Eglinton Avenue East, Suite 700, Toronto, Ontario, Canada
M4P 2Y3 (a division of Pearson Penguin Canada Inc.) • Penguin Books Ltd, 80 Strand, London
WC2R 0RL, England • Penguin Ireland, 25 St. Stephen's Green, Dublin 2, Ireland (a division of Penguin
Books Ltd) • Penguin Books Australia Ltd, 250 Camberwell Road, Camberwell, Victoria 3124, Australia
(a division of Pearson Australia Group Pty Ltd) • Penguin Books India Pvt Ltd, 11 Community Centre,
Panchsheel Park, New Delhi – 110 017, India • Penguin Group (NZ), 67 Apollo Drive, Rosedale,
North Shore 0632, New Zealand (a division of Pearson New Zealand Ltd) • Penguin Books
(South Africa) (Pty) Ltd, 24 Sturdee Avenue, Rosebank, Johannesburg 2196, South Africa

Penguin Books Ltd, Registered Offices:
80 Strand, London WC2R 0RL, England

First published in 2009 by The Penguin Press,
a member of Penguin Group (USA) Inc.

The contents of this book first appeared in issues of *The New Yorker* and on the magazine's Web site.
Copyright © Condé Nast Publications, 2007, 2008. Reprinted by arrangement with
Condé Nast Publications.

LIBRARY OF CONGRESS CATALOGING IN PUBLICATION DATA

Hertzberg, Hendrik.
Obamanos! : the birth of a new political era / Hendrik Hertzberg.
p. cm.
Includes bibliographical references and index.
ISBN 978-1-59420-236-0
1. Presidents—United States—Election—2008. 2. Obama, Barack.
3. United States—Politics and government—2009–. I. Title.
JK5262008 H47 2009
324.973'0931—dc22
2009025014

Printed in the United States of America
1 3 5 7 9 10 8 6 4 2

DESIGNED BY MEIGHAN CAVANAUGH

For Wolf Hertzberg

CONTENTS

INTRODUCTION

My Barack Obama

The presidential election that put Barack Obama in the White House has been variously called the most important, the most exciting, the most surprising, the most significant, the most consequential, and the most expensive in the modern history of the United States. The most expensive it certainly was, as was the one before and the one before that. What about the rest of the mosts?

I've been counting, and it turns out that this presidential election was the fifteenth since I started paying attention. The *fifteenth*! More than one-quarter of all the fifty-six presidential elections in all of American history! And I've been a participant of sorts in every single one of them, beginning as a nine-year-old fourth grader in 1952 (when I "helped" my mother stuff envelopes and pass out buttons at a storefront Stevenson headquarters in our bucolically Republican suburban village) and then, every four years since, as a volunteer, a reporter, a speechwriter, or a purveyor of observation and opinion. I can honestly say that this one—the campaign and election of 2007 and 2008—was, whatever its historical importance and the rest, the most nerve-wracking I've ever experienced. Also, in the end, the most satisfying.

I cast my first vote in 1964, for Lyndon Johnson, and have voted for every Democratic nominee since. It's never been a difficult call—not even in 1968, when, like a lot of people my age (I was in the Navy at the time, but stationed in lower Manhattan and spending evenings doing dogwork at Bobby Kennedy's midtown headquarters), I hated the Vietnam War and loved R.F.K. I looked upon Hubert Humphrey with a mixture of contempt and pity, but come November I voted for him anyway; I felt sure there was still a good heart under all that cringing, and I thought he'd probably make a decent president. Also, remember his Republican opponent.

I value political liberty and political rights (freedom of thought, speech, conscience, and the press, the right to vote, civic equality) more highly than economic liberty and economic rights (property rights, freedom of enterprise, freedom from want, economic equality). I'm in favor of progressive taxation and generous public provision of education, pensions, and health care. I think people should have enough to eat and a roof over their heads, even if they haven't done much to deserve it. I reject the idea that the market is the singular bedrock of society while everything else is a parasitical growth. I want government to do something about environmental degradation and gross social and economic inequality. I'm a secularist and a supporter of equal rights for women and gays. And when it comes to wanting World Peace I'm practically a Miss America contestant. So I'm a liberal.

I also believe in taking account of political reality, though I'm not completely without sympathy for those who don't. My father, who cast his first vote in 1932, and my mother, who cast hers in 1940, never voted for anybody except Norman Thomas until 1952, when the Socialist Party nominated someone else and Mom and Dad finally got around to taking a dip in the mainstream. I don't fault them in the slightest, because (a) Norman was their dear friend (in 1941 he attended their wedding; two years later, he sent me a letter welcoming me into the world and complimenting me on my choice of parents), (b) he was a great man and a moral paragon, and (c) there was no danger he would inadvertently hand the White House to the Republicans, F.D.R. being a perennial shoo-in. (Nineteen forty-eight is a tougher case, but it wouldn't have been the end of the world if that *Chicago Daily Tribune* headline had turned out to be accurate. Thomas E. Dewey, though a stiff with a silly mustache, was a moderate and an internationalist.)

Nevertheless, as my folks eventually came to see, there are less risky, equally effective ways to introduce the public to progressive ideas than mounting third-party potential spoiler candidacies for president. As long as our elections are plurality-winner-take-all affairs, we are going to have—and we're better off having—two big parties that square off against each other after choosing their nominees in a free-for-all. It's like the National League and the American League: you've got to win the pennant if you want a shot at the Series. In the United States, in other words, if you want to participate in the kind of electoral politics that, potentially or actually, has something to do with governmental power, you're either a Democrat or a Republican.

So I'm a Democrat. For fifteen straight elections I've always wanted the Democrat to win, and I've always ended up trying to do my part to make that happen. But how deeply my emotions get invested in the effort has depended, now that I think about it, on three things. First, the apparent scariness, dangerousness, or wickedness of the Republican nominee—a big factor in 1960, '68, and '72 (Nixon), 1980 (Reagan), and 2004 (Bush *fils*), a less important one, for me, in 1952 and '56 (Eisenhower), 1976 (Ford), 1984 (Reagan), 1988 and '92 (Bush *père*), 1996 (Dole), and 2000 (Bush *fils*, whose lineage and "compassionate conservative" prattle, along with the relatively stable national and international outlook Clinton left behind, offered few hints that he would be either willing or able to inflict historical levels of national and global destruction). Second, the talents or potential transformativeness of the Democratic nominee—for me, an unusually important factor only in 1960 (J.F.K.), 1992 (Clinton), and, to a lesser extent, 2000 (Gore). Third, the closeness of the race: when defeat is a foregone conclusion, as it was in 1956, 1972, 1984, and, well before the end, 1988, one more or less automatically fortifies one's emotions against shock and despair.

The 1980 campaign was, for me, a special case. Four years earlier, I would have been disappointed but not devastated if Jimmy Carter had lost to President Ford, who wasn't such a bad fellow. I had no idea that, out of the blue, I would soon be recruited for the White House staff and that, in consequence, my life would be permanently divided into two periods: B.C.E. and A.D.—Before Carter's Election and After (his) Defeat. I had been deeply interested in politics B.C.E., but, from my perch as a gallivanting young reporter for the *New Yorker*'s "Talk of the Town" section, I wrote mostly about other things: rock music, oddball Manhattan characters, baseball, what have you. (For a brief spell I moonlighted as *Rolling Stone*'s first movie critic.) A.D., it was pretty much all politics.

The four years I spent as a presidential speechwriter were the most intense of my working life, with the highest highs and the lowest lows. It would have been hard for a person to be more involved in a presidential campaign than I was the campaign of 1980, the final weeks of which I spent crisscrossing the country aboard Air Force One, a five-second walk from the president's compartment. That campaign, it would seem, met all three of my criteria for emotional commitment. The Democratic candidate was no superhero—his feet of clay were as familiar to me as his toothy smile—but his conscience was resolute and his integrity beyond doubt. I respected him deeply and very much wanted him to win. His opponent was a thoroughly alarming character, the kind of conservative who keeps *National Review* on the coffee table but reads (and clips) every issue of *Human Events*. Ronald Reagan was the only supreme leader of the Republican Party's ideological-right faction ever to win the presidential nomination, except for Barry Goldwater, whose general-election chances in 1964 had been on a par with Norman Thomas's in 1936. Finally, while the end result in 1980 was a solid win for Reagan, the race was remarkably close going into the closing days. Inside the Carter bubble, up in the sky, we actually thought we had a chance right up until election eve. The letdown was correspondingly severe.

In 2008, by contrast, none of the four leading Republican candidates, who together would account for more than ninety percent of the primary vote, was an unalloyed, career-long, hard-right "movement" conservative. Mitt Romney was the favorite by default of the Washington-based conservative establishment. But he was a chilly technocrat who, as a Massachusetts politician, had been (as he put it) "effectively pro-choice" and, as governor, had helped enact a health-care reform aimed at achieving universal coverage. Mike Huckabee, an ordained Baptist minister and former governor of Arkansas, appealed to a lot of aisle-and-pew evangelicals but not, on the whole, to the leaders of political Christianism, who suspected him, correctly in my opinion, of being soft on certain features of liberalism—reserving somewhat more compassion for the poor than for the rich, for example. He didn't even know the name of the approved ideology: he always called it "conservativism." Rudolph Giuliani belatedly ticked the orthodox ideological boxes after his 9/11 heroics opened what he thought was a sure path to the presidency, but his core conservatism, such as it was, consisted mostly of warmongering. Notwithstanding the enthusiasm for his candidacy in certain sectors of the cable-news-host community, his history as a cross-dressing, wife-dumping, mistress-marrying, gay-friendly, pro-choice, pro-gun-control New Yorker made his nomination improbable from the start.

I thought all along that the fourth occupant of the Republican first tier, John McCain, would be the hardest for any Democrat to beat. But if, despite everything, a Republican was fated to end up in the White House, then for the country's sake I hoped it would be McCain. As best as I could tell, so did most Democrats and liberals of my generational and political cohort.

I thought I had a handle on John McCain. Back in 2000 I had spent time on his "Straight Talk" bus in New Hampshire. Being as susceptible as the next journalist to the novel pleasure of being treated like a fellow human being—and by a Republican! a Republican with a sense of humor! a Republican with a sense of humor who was also a war hero! a Republican who sometimes made naughty or mildly subversive remarks!—I liked him. I knew that his voting record was overwhelmingly conservative, despite his well-cultivated (and sometimes deserved) image as a "maverick." I knew he had actively supported Bush in 2004, even after the disgusting smears leveled by Republican privateers against his friend, colleague, and Vietnam comrade John Kerry. But hadn't he denounced those smears? Hadn't he flirted with the idea of joining Kerry's ticket? Didn't his mavericky meanderings consistently carry him in a vaguely leftward direction? Whenever he confessed to some political sin, wasn't it always having adopted a position he didn't believe in to appease a right-wing constituency, as when he dropped his objections to the Confederate flag prior to the 2000 South Carolina primary?

Of course, I couldn't help noticing, beginning in 2004, that the moment McCain set his sights on the 2008 Republican nomination he began to shed his apostasies (of which there had always been fewer than people like me assumed). By the time he had secured the prize he had committed himself to just about every verse in the conservative catechism, from Bush's tax cuts for the rich, which he had originally opposed, to mandatory caps on carbon emissions, which he had originally favored. He came out against heretical legislation he himself had sponsored, including immigration and campaign finance reform. His general-election campaign, dominated by Sarah Palin and the pitchfork-brandishing forces she represented, was shockingly squalid. He displayed a temperament—erratic, moody, quick to anger—that was more worrying than his mutable policy positions. The Senate had cushioned the consequences of his impulsiveness; the presidency would have magnified them. Even with all that, though, I was still inclined to group him with the relatively less threatening sorts of Republicans, the Fords and Doles and Bush Seniors, rather than with the truly scary ones. At the very least he would have been an improvement on Bush Junior.

The point I'm circling around is that the 2008 election should not, logically, have turned out to be the one that engaged my emotions more than any of the previous fourteen—including the one that occupied my every waking hour, cost me my alcove in the corridors of power, and propelled America and the world into the three-decade-long Age of Reagan. John McCain was a less than normally deplorable Republican. Viewed with a cold eye, the race was not as close as either of the previous two. Objective conditions—the economy, the Iraq war, the horrendous record and impressive unpopularity of the outgoing Republican administration—pointed to a Democratic victory. So did the opinion polls, which showed Obama with a consistent lead for all but a few late-summer weeks of the campaign. That leaves the quality of the Democratic nominee: one out of my three intensity factors. Or maybe one and a half out of three, because if the election wasn't "objectively" close it certainly *felt* that way, right up until the final weekend.

There was at least one other factor behind the unexpected urgency of my emotions. Since one month before the 2008 Democratic Convention I've been, astoundingly, a senior citizen, entitled to a half-price MetroCard, Medicare, and an "Old Guys Rule" T-shirt. I don't feel especially different, but I have become acutely aware that I don't have fifteen more elections to look forward to. After '68 or '80 I could say to myself, "Never mind, wait eight years or at worst till the twenty-first century." But 2008 felt like now or never, or close to it. The dubious pleasure of having, one more time, a president older than I am would have been small consolation for never knowing what it would be like to see the White House occupied by someone I admired with fewer reservations than I had harbored about anyone who had sought the office since Robert Kennedy.

Just about everyone—supporter or detractor—remembers when he or she first became fully aware of Barack Obama.

Among people I know more than casually, the first to take notice was my wife, Virginia Cannon. In 1990, two years before we met, Virginia was a young editor at *Vanity Fair.* For the magazine's June issue front-of-the-book "Fanfair" section, she assigned a one-page featurette on the first black president of the *Harvard Law Review.* The top half of the page was a black-and-white photograph, taken by John Goodman. Obama is wearing a silk tie. The cuffs of his white shirt show at the wrists, accentuating his dark suit and dark skin. He is perched on a bench in the sunlight, legs splayed, right hand on right knee, left elbow on his left knee, chin resting on left hand. The effect is casual with a formal edge, at once jaunty and thoughtful, without a trace of awkwardness. He is twenty-eight years old. He looks almost exactly the same as he does today.

The accompanying short piece, by Elise O'Shaughnessy, is full of hints that the young man does not envision a lucrative future for himself in corporate law. Obama, she writes, "wants to tackle the quagmire of America's inner cities." The problem, he tells her, is that "those communities are unorganized." He is readying himself to do something about it:

> For preparation, Harvard Law School is a "perfect place to examine how the power structure works. It gives you a certain language." When he's fluent, he'll be able to translate the language of the streets ("which I can speak") into the language of the Establishment, and vice versa. The sense of mission derives in part from his experiences in the Third World. He saw brutal poverty while growing up in Singapore with his mother, an anthropologist, and his half-brothers and -sisters in Kenya still live hand to mouth at times. Obama says that his late father's experience in the Kenyan government left him a broken and bitter man, and he responds warily to the assumption that he himself will run for office. "If I go into politics it should grow out of work I've done on the local level, not because I'm some media creation." Though, as media creations go, he'd be a pretty good one.

O'Shaughnessy and the *VF* fact-checkers missed one detail: Obama's mother took him to Indonesia, where the poverty is indeed brutal (and which has the world's largest Muslim population), not to pristine, regimented Singapore (which has more Christians than Muslims and more Buddhists than either). Except for that, this little piece summarized many of the elements of a story which Obama would eventually tell, more than once, in his own words.

Along with tens of millions of other Americans, I first heard some of those words and saw the man who spoke them on the night of Tuesday, July 27, 2004, at the Fleet Center in Boston, when Barack Obama delivered the keynote address of the Democratic National Convention. The surest political instinct John Kerry ever had—and the most consequential move he ever made—was entrusting the task of kicking off his general-election campaign to a mere state senator, a man who said of himself that night, with perfect truthfulness, "Let's face it, my presence on this stage is pretty unlikely."

The moment of Obama's speech that sticks in most people's memories came about three-quarters of the way through:

> There is not a liberal America and a conservative America—there is the United States of America. There is not a black America and a white America and a Latino America and an Asian America—there's the United States of America.
>
> The pundits like to slice and dice our country into red states and blue states; red states for Republicans, blue states for Democrats. But I've got news for them, too. We worship an awesome God in the blue states, and we don't like federal agents poking around in our libraries in the red states. We coach Little League in the blue states and, yes, we've got some gay friends in the red states. There are patriots who opposed the war in Iraq and there are patriots who supported the war in Iraq. We are one people, all of us pledging allegiance to the stars and stripes, all of us defending the *United* States of America.

It's worth savoring the rhetorical precision of these lines.

In the wake of terror in New York and Washington, and in the midst of carnage in Iraq and political viciousness at home, there is a widespread yearning to recapture the solidarity of the weeks after September 11, 2001. For Democrats, there is anger and frustration at being somehow shut out of a patriotic consensus. In this speech, Obama comes riding through the smoke and scoops up his audience like a hero sweeping a stranded damsel onto his horse. He reformulates patriotism in a way that's bursting with energy yet free of either rancor or defensiveness. He frames his examples in ways that soothe every hurt and suture every wound.

An awesome God. Millions of people—even people like me, crusty skeptics fed up with the browbeating of "Christian" busybodies—heard this phrase as simple, comforting sweetness: "awesome" is a kid's word, a word we hear from our children every day in praise of everything from an ice cream cone to a really cool teacher. Millions of others heard it as a different kind of praise, a thrilling echo of a modern church anthem:

> *Our God is an awesome God,*
> *He reigns from heaven above*
> *With wisdom, power, and love,*
> *Our God is an awesome God.*

We don't like federal agents poking around in our libraries in the red states. Suspicion of "federal agents" is a staple of right-wing crankiness; fear of witch hunts in libraries is a staple of the left-wing variety. Matter meets antimatter, producing light rather than heat. *We coach Little League in the blue states and, yes, we've got some gay friends in the red states.* Coaching Little League ties together sports and family into a universally unthreatening package of communitarian volunteerism, but "we've got some gay friends" is the truly brilliant touch. In a casual, non-defensive way, it identifies the speaker ("we") as reassuringly, matter-of-factly heterosexual—but without defining homosexuals as "they": gays have gay friends, too. It casts gayness not as an "issue" but as an everyday human reality. It plants a premise flattering to nearly everyone: that at some level, all of us are tolerant. It subliminally urges "anti-gay" people to look past abstractions and think instead of some gay friend or relative, while urging "pro-gay" people to think of the other side almost affectionately, as mistaken rather than cruel. Obama puts "patriots who opposed the war in Iraq" and "patriots who supported the war in Iraq" on an equal footing, instead of consigning the antiwar patriots to some "also" or "us, too" or "just as much" category. Of course, the conventions of English sentence structure being what they are, one or the other set of patriots has to be mentioned first. Obama's choice is a subtle corrective to eight years of Bush administration slurs. By the end of the passage—"the *United* States of America"—a lot of people were on their feet and, not for the last time while listening to Obama, crying.

Obama was responding to, and sharing, a yearning for unity, but not with split-the-difference mush. Even in this most unifying passage, the underlying political direction is plain: against racism, for civil liberties and gay rights.

As a former speechwriter, I was impressed. But it wasn't just the words. It was equally the aura of mastery. The only other time I had witnessed a comparable performance at a convention was in 1984, in San Francisco, when Governor Mario Cuomo's keynote address instantly made him a national figure. Both men took hold of the audience, in the hall and at home, with preternatural confidence, playing the murmurs and cheers of the crowd like a musical instrument. Both made Democrats, haunted for decades by a phantom of themselves as losers who are weak and glum, suddenly feel like winners who are strong and joyful. Cuomo was grand opera and Obama was the rebirth of the cool, a jazz formalist, but both were virtuosi. Their very names were music.

Touching on Obama and his speech a couple of weeks later in the piece that opens this collection, I wrote, thinking myself rather daring, that it was "not hard to imagine circumstances under which, a decade or two hence, he might represent the future of the country." A decade or two? Well, in my defense, he was young, he had no government experience except being a state legislator, he was black, and he was (as he had put it) "a skinny kid with a funny name."

I caught another glimpse of him the following night, as I was leaving MSNBC's makeshift outdoor studio, set up outside Faneuil Hall. He was on foot, presumably on his way to the studio I had just left. He was tall, slender, and purposeful, and, except for a few swiveling heads, he went pretty much unnoticed.

Fourteen weeks later, unlike the man he had come to praise at the convention, Obama won his election and took his place as the sole African-American member of the United States Senate. I finally met him and his wife, Michelle, six months after that, in the crowded courtyard of the Washington Hilton, at one of the overlapping cocktail receptions that precede the annual dinner of the White House Correspondents' Association. I told him how much I admired his 1995 book *Dreams from My Father*, still the only one he had published. (A half-truth, or half-lie: I had a copy, but hadn't yet done more than dip into it.) He told me that he and Michelle were big fans of the *New Yorker*. He said that he had read some of my stuff and that he didn't think of my work as being knee-jerk liberal. As I stood there wondering where on earth he could have gotten *that* idea, he mentioned a recent piece of mine in a way that suggested to me—and on this point I was extremely suggestible—that he had actually read it.

Naturally, I was pleased. Later, I decided not to obsess too much over this little exchange. In Norman Mailer's famous *Esquire* piece about J.F.K.'s presidential campaign, "Superman Comes to the Supermarket," Mailer reports that Kennedy, on meeting him, said, "I've read *The Deer Park* and . . . the others" instead of the usual "I've read *The Naked and the Dead* and . . . the others." As I remembered the piece, which I hadn't read since it came out, shortly before Barack Obama was born, Mailer makes much of this, speculating on the meaning of Kennedy's preferring his steamy Hollywood novel to his muddy war novel. But when I reread the piece, it turned out that Mailer actually makes very little of it, even though J.F.K. as movie star is one of his themes. He just suggests obliquely that Kennedy was good at flattering a chronicler and leaves it at that. I'll do the same.

My wife, who is now a senior editor at the *New Yorker*, was there too. When I explained to the Obamas that Virginia was my editor at the magazine, and Virginia said dryly, "You should see his copy when it comes in," Michelle shot her a thumbs-up. My wife returned the gesture of solidarity and, once we were alone, made another of her astute early calls: she told me firmly that Michelle was as much a powerhouse as her husband—that the Obamas were a star couple.

Back in New York, I picked up *Dreams from My Father*, and by the time I put it down again I was a supporter of Barack Obama for President. One might dismiss this as professional solidarity—Writers for Obama, the equivalent of Haberdashers for Truman or Peanut Farmers for Carter. But Obama is not just a good writer, or a good writer for a politician. The author of *Dreams* is something rarer in the world of politics: the maker of a genuine work of literature.

The library of books by men who later became president is not large, and little of merit can be found there. The important exceptions before the end of the nineteenth century are Jefferson's *Notes on Virginia* (1787) and Theodore Roosevelt's voluminous works of natural and naval history; in the twentieth the standout is Kennedy's *Profiles in Courage* (1955), though the extent of its author's authorship is disputed. In recent decades a ghostwritten autobiography has become as normal a part of laying the groundwork for a presidential campaign as a quick trip to Israel. Some are entertaining in a mild way (Reagan's *Where's the Rest of Me?*, 1955) and some are simply stupefying (W.'s *A Charge to Keep*, 1999), but as pieces of writing none could truly be called good. Carter's *Why Not the Best?* (1975), which he wrote without professional assistance, is an outlier of sorts—a homely, sturdy construction, like one of the tables he makes in his home woodworking shop. But there's never been anything quite like *Dreams from My Father*.

Written when Obama was around thirty, *Dreams* is an

autobiographical bildungsroman, the story of the author's search for a usable past and a livable identity. It has a young writer's occasional purple overreach. But it is beautifully paced. It is full of vivid setpieces and sharply drawn characters (including the character of the narrator), all of whom have voices of their own and the breath of life. And it has a fine-grained lyricism. Writing in the *New Republic*, Andrew Delbanco pointed to Obama's account of playing basketball in prep school, a passage "which starts with short sentences, each ending in a percussive or sibilant monosyllable, then moves into a run-on sentence that mimics the flow of the game":

> By the time I reached high school, I was playing on Punahou's teams, and could take my game to the university courts, where a handful of black men, mostly gym rats and has-beens, would teach me an attitude that didn't just have to do with sport. That respect came from what you did and not who your daddy was. That you could talk stuff to rattle an opponent, but that you should shut the hell up if you couldn't back it up. That you didn't let anyone sneak up behind you to see emotions—like hurt or fear—you didn't want them to see.
>
> And something else, too, something nobody talked about: a way of being together when the game was tight and the sweat broke and the best players stopped worrying about their points and the worst players got swept up in the moment and the score only mattered because that's how you sustained the trance. In the middle of which you might make a move or a pass that surprised even you, so that even the guy guarding you had to smile, as if to say, "Damn . . ."

Of course, the qualities that make a writer are not the same as the qualities that make a presidential candidate, let alone a president; if they were, Mark Twain might have written his own White House memoir instead of serving as editor and publisher to Ulysses S. Grant. But the qualities of this particular writer, it seemed to me, were not wholly unrelated to the task of national leadership. In both *Dreams* and the more conventionally "political" *The Audacity of Hope*, Obama is acutely self-aware. His authorial confidence never degenerates into egotism or arrogance, and when he writes of moments when he behaved egotistically or arrogantly he calls himself to account. He learns. From the extraordinary hybridity of his life, he distills an extraordinary, and always highly specific, empathy. He has a feel for the texture of American (and not just American) life, both in its complexity and in its grand themes, and he has an understanding of the American past that does justice to many kinds of historical experience. If Obama's virtues as a writer proved to have their equivalents in his actions as a politician, I reasoned, then he might have the makings of a very rare kind of leader.

The next—and, so far, the last—time I got within handshaking distance of Obama was in Chicago, in August of 2007, at the annual gathering of liberal bloggers known then as YearlyKos. (It's since been renamed Netroots Nation.) I used the occasion to start a blog of my own, some of the fruits of which are in this book. The highlight, I wrote in my brand-new blog, was

> when seven of the eight Democratic presidential candidates (all but Biden) came striding and grinning and waving out of the wings, all of them looking astoundingly like themselves. And so well groomed!
>
> The YearlyKos crowd got to its feet, cheering and applauding as one. The applause had a warmth kindled by equal parts of ideological solidarity, partisan pride, self-congratulation, and amazement.
>
> The self-congratulation and the amazement were two sides of the same coin. Four years ago, YearlyKos did not exist. Ditto three years ago and two years ago. One year ago it did exist, but it was viewed and (I gather) viewed itself as marginal, a sideshow, an aspiration— the political equivalent of a Star Trek convention. Now it was being paid court to by (in all probability) the next president of the United States. Here was proof—proof that as a component of "the media," the liberal blogosphere is as important to the Democratic Party as CNN or MSNBC. Alternatively (or complementarily), here was proof that

the l.b. has, with unprecedented speed, achieved full recognition as a constituency of the Democratic Party. It swings as much weight as the teachers' union or the NAACP—maybe more.

During the "debate"—a group question-and-answer session, really—that followed, Obama did not particularly distinguish himself—he was a bit too diffident, and he was the only one who didn't look out at the audience when it was his turn to talk—but no one else stood out, either. Later that afternoon, Obama's staff blogger, Josh Orton, arranged a meeting with about a dozen bloggers. Even though my blogging career was only four days old, I was one of them. We sat on folding chairs in a big, empty box of a room. Obama, in shirtsleeves and tieless, straddled his. Our questions—complicated ones, about things like the details of health-care policy, and flammable ones, about things like gay marriage—were not particularly easy, but the meeting felt like a conversation, not an interrogation. He was relaxed, gently humorous, succinct, frank, and curious. The discussion was off the record, but it violates no confidence to say that, as I suppose we all expected, he made a favorable impression on us.

From the beginning, I bet (nothing huge: a few bucks, a meal, a bottle of wine) that Obama would win. This was not always exactly the same as being more than half sure that it would happen. Before Iowa, I could always get some sort of odds against the field; after, when the only opposition was first Hillary Clinton and then John McCain, the stakes were even. Whenever I was called upon to predict, on some cable TV show or in one of the writer forums the magazine puts on for advertisers or at its annual festival, I predicted that, at the end of the day (to use one of the season's catchphrases, as unavoidable as "going forward" and "robust"), it would be Obama. And I meant it. But that didn't keep my autonomic nervous system, with its associated neurotransmitters, from reacting violently to the ups and downs of the campaign.

The more I became convinced that Obama's candidacy represented a once-in-a-generation opportunity to make many previously improbable good things happen at once, the more the needle on my emotional seismometer jerked this way and that. This way when two hundred thousand Berliners gave Obama a rapturous welcome, when Colin Powell came through with his passionate, powerful endorsement, and when Obama's patient, far-seeing strategy yielded an insurmountable delegate lead in places Hillary neglected to look. That way when Hillary roared back to take the New Hampshire primary, when the video of Obama's old pastor Jeremiah Wright shouting "God damn America!" surfaced, and when McCain's post-convention bounce briefly put him ahead in some of the polls.

Once in a generation? Once in a lifetime, and not just the lifetimes of those of us who started voting in the nineteen-sixties. The chance to elect a black president—more than that, a black president who would also be a progressive president, the most progressive since Lyndon Johnson at his domestic best—might not come around again even for those who were casting their first votes in 2008. The odds on a woman in the foreseeable future are a lot more favorable. Women are still grossly underrepresented in the skyboxes of American government; in 2008, sixteen of the one hundred U.S. senators and eight of the fifty state governors were women. But those numbers were a lot bigger than the numbers for African-Americans—one and one, respectively—and they grow at each election. Combine that with (a) the fact that the electorate is more than half female but only about an eighth black, (b) the ongoing, increasingly rapid collapse of all forms of sexism, reflected in the astounding rise in acceptance of same-sex marriage, and (c) the shattering of the topmost glass ceiling, which Hillary Clinton accomplished even in defeat, and you have a strong case that the nomination of a woman for president is practically a certainty at some point in the next half-dozen cycles. If there were no such person as Barack Obama, or if Obama had chosen not to run this time, does anyone seriously doubt that Clinton would have made short work of John Edwards, Joseph

Biden, and the rest of that stageful of white males, won the nomination, and, most likely, won the election, too? And does anyone seriously doubt that if the "black candidate" this time had been a more conventional sort of African-American politician, he too would have been swept away by Hurricane Hillary?

John F. Kennedy was able to break through the (comparatively weak) prejudice that stood in his path partly because he was so distant from the stereotype of the Irish Catholic politician. Among the things he wasn't: an up-from-the-people, working-class or middle-class scrambler; the product of a Catholic education; a hearty, red-faced, backslapping singer of "O Danny Boy"; a pious regular at Mass; a proponent of "decency" in movies; a lover of beer, baseball, and skittles; a prude, hypocritical or otherwise; the creation of a big-city political machine. Among the things he was: dashing; polished; aristocratically upper-class and entitled; hereditarily rich; a product of Groton and Harvard; intellectually, socially, and sexually sophisticated; unintimidated by and unresentful of "elitists"; a lover of martinis and sailing. Catholics knew very well that he was a Catholic and saw him as an embodiment of their hopes, but to non-Catholics he didn't seem "Catholic" in some vaguely threatening or disturbing way. Besides all that, of course, he was an extraordinarily talented individual. He was highly intelligent; he was cool, calm, collected; he was unflappable. He was impatient to be president, but as a strategist he was very patient indeed. He was Jack No Drama.

The parallels are obvious—apparently, they were obvious to Caroline Kennedy and her uncle Ted—but Obama took the pattern several steps beyond. By an unlooked-for alchemy, his wildly various, exotically unstereotypical background somehow added up to an iconically "American" story and somehow came across as sturdy rootedness. He was an African-American—not because of a recent alteration in racial terminology but because his father was an African and his mother was an American. Kansas, Hawaii, Chicago, Kenya, the Ivy League, Indonesia; a thoroughly "white" family circle as a child, a thoroughly "black" one (thanks to his marriage) as a mature man—he was impossible to slot into ready-made categories, yet he was thoroughly comfortable in, well, in his own skin. His long apprenticeship as a student of himself— which is to say, of racial, cultural, national, and class identities—made him pragmatically conscious of their perils as well as their strengths. But, like Kennedy, he had to be an unusually talented individual to turn all this to his advantage. He displayed no fear of, and no confusion about, seeming to be either "too black" or "too white."

And he was centered. John Kerry's sport was windsurfing, at which he excelled, and which was as natural to who he was as sailing was to John Kennedy; but Kerry allowed it to become toxic to him. Obama's game was basketball—a "black" sport, and he excelled at it, too. But as part of the magical Obama mix, it was anything but toxic. Remember that three-pointer.

America's loopy, accident-prone system of electing presidents is famous for making big money talk loud and for turning most of the country—the forty or so "spectator" states, as distinct from the ten or so "battleground" states—into a political dead zone. Obama pushed back against these realities and, for one election cycle at least, made them less destructive than usual. His campaign became an exercise in something like participatory democracy. When the head office in Chicago sent paid staffers out to open campaign offices in new states, they found that local volunteers, without being asked, had already done the groundwork.

Citizens of the dead zone picked up and traveled in unprecedented numbers to the states that were "in play," not just once but several times, to knock on doors, register voters, and drive people to the polls. Many friends of mine, people who had never done anything like this before, got into their cars (or rented one) and drove to Pennsylvania or Ohio to join their college-age children in the campaign.

But you didn't have to go there to be there. The Obama campaign used the revolution in communications technology to annihilate distance—to enable people to work in the places that count even if they couldn't go there or vote there. If you had a spare hour after work or after class and some minutes left on your cell phone plan, you could sign on to barackobama.com and before you knew it you were talking to a carefully targeted, thoroughly researched undecided voter in Missouri or Colorado. Millions of people signed up by text message. The campaign's social networking Web site, mybarackobama.com, instructed them how to campaign and canvass, and, in the case of the FISA electronic surveillance bill, which Obama supported against the wishes of many of his supporters, to argue with the candidate. By the end, the campaign was in regular e-mail contact with ten million people.

Obama was the first national party nominee to refuse federal general-election cash since 1976, the first year the system of matching funds paired with spending limits was used. He did so, breaking an implicit promise in the process, because he calculated, correctly, that he could raise a good deal more on his own. But his unvirtuous act had the virtuous effect of adding a new and positive meaning to the dread phrase "money in politics." Much of his campaign's financial backing came from the usual big givers, some of whom, however sincere (or nonexistent) their belief that an Obama presidency would be in the national interest, knew that they were buying access, believed that they were buying a better shot at a longed-for government post, or imagined that they were buying influence over future government policy. But most of Obama's money came from small- and moderate-size donations from millions of people—nearly four million by the end—who expected nothing more than a feeling of participation and a sense that they had done something for their country. The big-donor well dried up quickly, because big donors "maxed out"—gave the legal maximum, twenty-three hundred dollars—in one shot. The small donors tended to give and give again, often small amounts on a monthly basis, ten or fifty or a couple of hundred dollars, like subscribers to National Public Radio. Many of those small donors surprised themselves: they ended up maxing out, too.

In the last days of October, the McCain–Palin rallies grew increasingly discordant and threatening. They were painful to watch. But ever larger crowds were showing up to see and hear Obama in unlikely places:

in St. Louis, a hundred thousand; in Orlando, at midnight, thirty-five thousand; in Denver, a hundred thousand again; in Manassas, Virginia, eighty-five thousand. At the weekend, as October became November, my anxiety began to loosen its grip. By Monday it felt as if it might really happen. And on Tuesday it did. And I'm still marvelling.

This book, whose title comes from a campaign poster I saw on a dusty desert road not far from Santa Fe, New Mexico, is not a formal history of the campaign, or an insider's revelatory account, or a reporter's diary from the campaign trail. It's simply a real-time, contemporaneous record of one person's observations, cogitations, and indignations over the course of the quadrennial cycle that ended with the election of Barack Obama as president of the United States. The first section, "The Wreckage," deals mostly with the second term of George W. Bush, without which a break with the past as emphatic as Obama's probably wouldn't have been possible. "The Marathon" concerns the long, eventful primary campaign, which was as severe a test of stamina and character as any our functionally sadistic political system has ever imposed on a set of candidates. "The Sprint" takes the story to its gladiatorial finish in the fall.

A note on dates. For the pieces that appeared in the magazine, I use the date they go to press instead of the issue cover dates, which are ten days later. Therefore the dates on both pieces and blog items reflect the moment when they were actually written.

PART ONE

THE WRECKAGE

IN MODERATION

September 10, 2004

When Barack Obama spoke at the Democratic Convention in Boston, a lot of people thought—and hoped—that they were seeing the future. Half Kansan and half Kenyan, half black and half white, yet all-American in a novel and exhilarating way that seemed to transcend the usual categories, Obama, who on November 2 will be elected to the United States Senate from Illinois, embodied and expressed a fresh synthesis of the American civic religion—one that fused not only black and white, and immigrant and native-born, but also self-reliance and social solidarity. "He represents the future of the party," Stephanie Cutter, the communications director for John Kerry's campaign, said by way of explaining why Obama had been chosen to deliver the keynote speech. And it is not hard to imagine circumstances under which, a decade or two hence, he might represent the future of the country as well.

There was a slight echo of this at Madison Square Garden last week, where the Republicans devoted most of their convention's prime speaking slots to a parade of politicians—Senator John McCain, of Arizona; Rudolph Giuliani, the former mayor of New York; Arnold Schwarzenegger, the spanking-new governor of California; Governor

George Pataki, of New York—who are generally regarded, by the debased standards of post-Rockefeller, post-Eisenhower, post-Lincoln Republicanism, as moderates. An inattentive viewer could be forgiven for thinking that this is how the party sees its own future face. At a glittery donors' luncheon last week, Fred Thompson, the actor-lawyer-former senator, called McCain and Giuliani "the ticket." Whether Bush wins or loses, somebody else will be the Republican presidential candidate in 2008, and these gentlemen evidently believe, or at least hope, that it might be one of them. "RUDY EYING '08 RUN?" a headline in Wednesday's *Daily News* asked. You bet he is. (The day after his speech, he had breakfast with the Iowa delegation.) They're all running for president, even Schwarzenegger, whose speech was devoted largely to glorifying the arc of his own rise from scrawny kid stuck in stuffy social-democratic Austria to global cinematic and American political star. There can be only one climax to Arnold's screenplay, and the fact that it would require a constitutional amendment is just another plot point.

Giuliani is gambling that well-watered memories of his 9/11 Churchillian moment plus an ultra-militant stance on terror and foreign policy can overcome his record of what looks to Republicans (if not to New Yorkers) like social liberalism. Schwarzenegger may figure that his action-hero manly-man gigantism could similarly wash away his pro-choice, non-anti-gay sins. The moderates are indeed popular—with voters, especially independent voters. That's why they are able to win general elections in their own states. Their kind of appeal might even propel one of them onto the bottom half of a national Republican ticket someday. But to get elected president you have to win the nomination of a major party, and for these men that means the Republicans.

"There are probably more Americans who have seen UFOs than undecided voters who have read party platforms," Charlie Cook, the inside-dopester political analyst of *National Journal*, wrote last week. "Such documents are for partisans and ideologues." Platforms are unreliable guides to what a prospective administration will actually do once in power, and it's true that practically nobody reads them. But they are useful as indications of what the activist base of a party can and cannot stomach. The platform for 2004 again calls for the total recriminalization of abortion—no exceptions mentioned, not even for the life of the mother—and it omits any suggestion that people of good will may honestly disagree, which had been included in at least one recent platform. On the question of gay marriage, the platform goes further even than President Bush, who has merely endorsed a constitutional amendment banning it. In the only simulacrum of a platform fight this year, conservatives inserted language opposing recognition of "other living arrangements as equivalent to marriage," adding, just to drive the point home, that "legal recognition and the accompanying benefits afforded couples should be preserved for that unique and special union of one man and one woman which has historically been called marriage." In other words: no civil unions, no hospital visitation rights or medical benefits, no adoptions, no entry for gays into the heart of the American family.

In a Republican Party that is far more integrated with religious conservatism than it was in the days of Ronald Reagan, a Giuliani or a Schwarzenegger will have to spend the next four years taking social-issue flip-flopping to Olympic levels in order to have any hope of evading the veto of the hard right. McCain—who in 2008 will be three years older than Reagan was in 1980—faces a different problem. Though wobbly on gays, he is solidly anti-abortion and firmly in favor of the Iraq war. But it's hard to see how he can ever win back the trust of the hard core. McCain's fellow Republicans are no less aware than his now sulky Democratic admirers that whenever he actually thinks through an issue, such as tax cuts or campaign finance reform, he generally ends up with an opinion that qualifies him for the label Rush Limbaugh stuck on him in an op-ed piece in last Friday's *Wall Street Journal*: liberal. Nor does he much care for what might be called the Christianists. The feeling is mutual. In their view, he just won't do.

Moderate politicians were used at this Republican Convention the way people of color were used at the last one: as props. McCain, Giuliani,

Schwarzenegger, and the rest were allowed to show themselves. They were allowed to praise Bush and (if they wished, as Giuliani did and McCain didn't) to attack Kerry, and they were allowed to recommend civility (as McCain did feelingly and at length and Giuliani did hypocritically and in brief). But none of them said a word about the social and environmental issues that mark them as moderates. If 2000 was minstrelsy, this was mime.

The moderate mute show was part of a two-act convention play. Act II, which built upon the backstory established in the public mind by the ongoing "independent" campaign of lies about Kerry's military service, was a concerted effort to make Kerry out to be an enemy of American national security and a friend of Islamist terrorism. The attacks on Kerry by the nominally Democratic, cartoonishly bitter Senator Zell Miller and by Vice President Cheney were based largely on mendacious distortions of things Kerry has said or votes he has cast in the Senate; in some cases they were based on simple falsehoods, such as Miller's claim that Kerry "has made it clear that he would use military force only if approved by the United Nations." (What Kerry did say, in his acceptance speech, was this: "I will never give any nation or international institution a veto over our national security.") It would be tempting to call Miller's falsehoods intentional, but it's unclear that he had any idea of what he was talking about. In post-speech interviews, he seemed to be unaware that many of the offenses for which he damned Kerry (such as calling the American occupation of Iraq an occupation and opposing the F-14 fighter) had also been committed by Bush and Cheney. Cheney's distortions were a little less blatant, but, being better informed, he had less excuse for them.

What was missing at the Republican Convention was any genuine defense of Bush's record, domestic or (more surprisingly) foreign. Bush was praised for his "leadership" and his "steadfastness," but leadership to what purpose, and steadfastness with what result, was hardly mentioned. There were plentiful denunciations of "the terrorists," but the masses of verbiage devoted to questions of national security were mostly given over to the wholesale conflation of the struggle against terror with the war in Iraq, plus assurances that the president was strong and unwavering in his determination. It's an old dodge: if you can't measure output, measure input.

Kerry's convention was all about Kerry and matters military, and so was Bush's. Kerry's was "positive," Bush's "negative." By persistently ignoring Bush's record, the Kerry camp probably made a political mistake. By ruthlessly distorting Kerry's, the Bush camp certainly made a moral mistake. Unfortunately for Kerry, moral mistakes, unlike political ones, don't generally lose elections.

BLUES

November 5, 2004

Here in the bluest borough of the bluest city of the bluest state in all our red-white-and-blue American Union, it has not been a happy week. A cocktail of emotions was being felt in these parts after last week's presidential election, and the most potent ingredient was sadness. We've got the blues, and we've got 'em bad.

The grief that so many felt at Senator Kerry's defeat was quite unexpected, and profound enough that, for the moment at least, it held off bitterness and recrimination. On both sides, this was a campaign that vast numbers of people threw their hearts into. There was a huge volunteer outpouring for Kerry, from Bruce Springsteen and George Soros on high to the hundreds of thousands, maybe millions, who manned phone banks and travelled to "swing states" and wrote the first political checks of their lives. To be sure, something along these lines had happened before, in the campaigns of Adlai Stevenson, Eugene McCarthy, Robert Kennedy, and George McGovern on the Democratic side, and of Barry Goldwater on the Republican. But this time the scale was larger and the yearning was greater, because in contrast to the campaigns of 1952 and 1964 and 1968 and 1972, all of which had the quixotic quality of gallant but doomed struggles, the chance of victory in 2004 seemed real, especially as Election Day approached. And this time the stakes felt higher—higher than in any election for at least three decades and maybe longer.

During the campaign it was routinely remarked that the Democrats' fervor was rooted much more in anti-Bush than in pro-Kerry sentiments. That was certainly true at the beginning, when many primary voters calculated that a decorated war hero, even one from liberal Massachusetts, would be more "electable" than a volatile Vermont doctor. It was far less true at the end. Grave and formal, steady and decent, more emotionally accessible as Election Day approached, John Kerry wore well. He earned the respect of his supporters and had begun to earn their affection. (Perhaps that will protect him from the kind of scapegoating to which Al Gore was so relentlessly subjected.) All Kerry needed to become thoroughly presidential was the presidency. His supporters risked heartbreak, and they found it.

Along with the sadness, there is puzzlement. Incumbents, especially in time of war, have a built-in advantage. But this incumbent had led the country into a war, the war in Iraq, that half the public had come to see as a mistake, and had led the country down what more than half the public saw, in pollster's shorthand, as "the wrong track." The election's outcome defies logic, and perhaps that is the point. The early analyses credited Bush's victory to religious conservatives, particularly those in the evangelical movement. In voting for Bush, as eighty percent of them did, many of these formerly nonvoting white evangelicals are remaining true to their unworldliness. In voting for a party that wants to tax work rather than wealth, that scorns thrift, that sees the natural world not as a common inheritance but as an object of exploitation, and that equates economic inequality with economic vitality, they have voted against their own material (and, some might imagine, spiritual) well-being. The moral values that stirred them seem not to encompass botched wars or economic injustices or environmental depredations; rather, moral values are about sexual behavior and its various manifestations and outcomes, about family structures, and about a particularly demonstrative brand of religious piety. What was important to these voters, it appears, was not Bush's public record but what they conceived to be his private soul. He is a good Christian, so his policy failures are forgivable. He is a saved sinner, so the dissipations of his early and middle years are not tokens of a weak character but testaments to the transformative power of his faith. He relies on God for guidance, so his intellectual laziness is not a danger.

What people on what might be called the cultural blue side, which includes many who voted for Bush, find deeply unsettling about him is not his religious faith—he is hardly the first devout president—but the way he speaks of making decisions with his gut, which, he has often suggested, takes its direction from God. In his second term, given the validation he received on Election Day, he is likely to be more confident—in himself, in his "instincts," and in Almighty Gut. He will be less inclined than ever to listen to his earthly father, or to his earthly father's earthly surrogates, such as Colin Powell.

Along with the sadness and the puzzlement, there is apprehension. Here in the big coastal cities, we have reason to fear for the immediate safety of our lives and our families—more reason, it must be said, than have the residents of the "heartland," to which the per-capita bulk of "homeland security" resources, along with extra electoral votes, are distributed. It was deep-blue New York (which went three to one for Kerry) and deep-blue Washington, D.C. (nine to one Kerry), that were, and presumably remain, Al Qaeda's targets of choice. In the heartland, it is claimed, some view the coastal cities as faintly un-American. The terrorists do not agree. They see us as the very essence—the heart, if you like—of America. And, difficult as it may be for some rural gun owners to appreciate, many of us sincerely believe that President Bush's policies have put us in greater peril than we would be facing under a Kerry (or a Gore) administration. There is apprehension that the well-documented failure to devote adequate resources to the protection of our cities, seaports, and airports will not be remedied. There is apprehension that the colossal incompetence and bad judgment—accompanied by ideological hubris, diplomatic arrogance, and an eagerness to ignore or suppress inconvenient evidence—that have tied up our military might in the knots of Iraq will, having been rewarded at the polls, continue. There is apprehension that the anti-Bush sentiments that are manifest throughout much of the world will now transmute into fully fledged anti-Americanism. The governments of our estranged European allies, led by reality-based statesmen, will do their best to accommodate the practical fact of a second Bush term. But these are, after all, democratic countries, and their publics may not be so patient or so sensible.

And there is apprehension about where this administration will try to take our society. In his victory statement on Wednesday Bush spoke of "a new opportunity to reach out to the whole nation." By Thursday, at his postelection press conference, this had been modified to "I'll reach out to everyone who shares our goals." One of those goals is to revamp the tax system in ways that would shift the burden further downward, including the permanent abolition of the inheritance tax. Another is to privatize part of Social Security, which by definition would mean a reduction in guaranteed benefits for future retirees. Achieving the first of these goals would impose the pitiless culture of winners and losers on the beginning of life; achieving the second would impose it on life's end. Together they would constitute a fundamental revocation of an American social contract that was hammered out seventy years ago during the New Deal.

In Thursday's *Times*, a front-page news analysis argued that "it is impossible to read President Bush's reelection with larger Republican majorities in both houses of Congress as anything other than the clearest confirmation yet that this is a center-right country—divided yes, but with an undisputed majority united behind his leadership." That is certainly true in institutional terms. But it is not true in terms of people, of actual human beings. Though the Republicans won nineteen of the thirty-four Senate seats that were up for grabs last Tuesday, for a gain of four, the number of voters who cast their ballots for Republican Senate candidates was 37.9 million, while 41.3 million voted for

Democrats—almost exactly Bush's popular-vote margin over Kerry. When the new Congress convenes in January, its fifty-five Republicans will be there on account of the votes of 57.6 million people, while the forty-four Democrats and one independent will be there on account of the votes of 59.6 million people. As for the House, it is much harder to aggregate vote totals meaningfully, because so many seats are uncontested. But the Republicans' gain of four seats was due entirely to Tom DeLay's precedent-breaking re-gerrymandering of the Texas district lines.

The red-blue split has not changed since 2000. This is not a center-right country. It is a center-right country and a center-left country, but the center has not held. The winner-take-all aspects of our system have converged into a perfect storm that has given virtually all the political power to the right; conservative Republicans will now control the presidency, the House of Representatives, and the Senate so firmly that the Supreme Court, which is also in conservative hands, has abruptly become the most moderate of the four centers of federal power. The system of checks and balances has broken down, but the country remains divided—right down the nonexistent, powerless middle.

UNSOCIAL SECURITY

January 14, 2005

The administration's campaign to do something about, or to, Social Security will get its prime-time launch next month in the State of the Union extravaganza, but President Bush is already busy softening up the battlefield. Last week, he granted his first newspaper interview since the election, to the *Wall Street Journal*, the parish bulletin of the nonevangelical wing of his political base. The first question was about his agenda for Social Security, and whether he would just be laying out general principles and leaving the details to Congress. "No, not necessarily so," he said, adding:

> That's part of—that's part of the advice my new National Economic Council head will be giving me as to whether or not we need to—here is the plan, or here is an idea for a plan, or why don't you just fix it. I suspect given my nature, I'll want to be—the White House will be very much involved with—I have an obligation to lead on this issue—I think this will be an administrative-driven idea—to take it on. And therefore, that that be the case, I have the responsibility to provide the political cover necessary for members, I have the responsibility to make the case if there is a problem, and I have the responsibility to lay out

potential solutions. Now, to the specificity of which, we'll find out—
you'll find out with time.

Even a professional actuary might have trouble parsing that one. But
the initial thrust of the Bush approach—as laid out in his own comments, in speeches and memos by various assistants, and in material put
out by groups such as the Alliance for Worker Retirement Security—is
clear enough. It has two big themes. First, Social Security is in crisis,
running out of money, about to go bankrupt unless something dras-
tic is done. Second, privatization—eliminating part of Social Security
and replacing it with a system of individual private investment accounts
financed from a portion of workers' payroll taxes—is somehow the key
to avoiding the catastrophe, and is also a fine thing in its own right.

"This is one of my charges, is to explain to Congress as clearly as
I can: the crisis is now," Bush proclaimed at an "economic summit"
a month ago. He does indeed have some 'splaining to do. This year,
the Social Security system—the payroll tax, which brings money in,
and the pension program, which sends money out—will bring in about
$180 billion more than it sends out. It will go on bringing in more than
it sends out until 2028, at which point it will begin to draw on the $3.5
trillion surplus it will by then have accumulated. The surplus runs out
in 2042, right around the time George W. Bush turns ninety-six. After
that, even if nothing has changed, the system's income will continue to
cover seventy-three percent of its outgo.

That's using the Social Security Administration's economic and
demographic assumptions, which are habitually pessimistic. Using the
assumptions of the nonpartisan Congressional Budget Office, the surplus runs out in 2052. And if one uses the economic growth assumptions that Bush's own budget office uses when it calculates the effects of
his own tax cuts, the surplus runs out in—er, maybe never.

The "crisis," therefore, is not "now." It's as bogus as the Alliance for
Worker Retirement Security—which, in reality, is an "astroturf," or
fake-grassroots, front for the National Association of Manufacturers.

There is no Social Security crisis, and there is not likely to be one. At some point over the next couple of decades, of course, some adjustments will have to be made. There are many reasonable possibilities: a modest rise in the retirement age, to reflect increases in health and longevity; a rise in the cap on wages subject to the payroll tax, which now cuts out at ninety thousand dollars a year; adding a bit to the progressivity of the benefits. One can even imagine a national decision to devote a larger proportion of national resources to the care of the old, given that a larger proportion of the population will be old—preferably to be paid for by taxing something we'd like to see less of (like fossil-fuel consumption) instead of something we'd like to see more of (like jobs).

Administration spokesmen have been suggesting that privatization will solve Social Security's future financing problems. They're fibbing, though. The much-hyped "crisis" looks suspiciously like the Social Security equivalent of W.M.D.s. This time, though, we have better intelligence. "White House officials privately concede," the *Times* reported last week, "that the centerpiece of Mr. Bush's approach to Social Security—letting people invest some of their payroll taxes in private accounts—would do nothing in itself to eliminate the long-term gap." The comptroller general of the United States, David M. Walker, agrees. "The creation of private accounts for Social Security," he said in a speech last month, "will not deal with the solvency and sustainability of the Social Security fund." The solvency and sustainability of Social Security, when and if it requires shoring up, will have to be dealt with the old-fashioned way: by increasing revenue and/or reducing guaranteed benefits.

The cynical, or maybe just the political, interpretation of the rush to privatization is that private accounts would, as David Brooks, the *Times'* freshman columnist, wrote the other day, "create Republicans. People who have them will start thinking like investors." (They won't actually *be* investors, not in any meaningful sense—they'll still be workers for hire. But, come election time, they'll take their cue from the Dow, not from wage scales or income gaps or the unemployment rate.) The really cynical explanation is that privatization is a nice, clean way to transfer gigantic sums to Wall Street brokerage houses.

A third explanation—and, who knows, maybe a more accurate one—is that the true impetus to privatization is ideological. To say that is not to say, "How awful!" It's actually a compliment. Ideology is less depraved than crude self-interest, even when it gets you to the same place. And one person's ideology is another person's "values." The values behind Social Security privatization are not terrible. It is good to save. It is good to be self-reliant. It is good to plan ahead. It is good to be the little pig who builds his house of brick rather than straw.

But it's not as if these values were not being taught in hundreds of other ways in our lives. And there are other values, too—values that are suggested by the words "social" and "security." Yes, self-reliance is good; but solidarity is good, too. Looking after yourself is good, but making a firm social decision to banish indigence among the old is also good. Market discipline is good, but it is also good for there to be places where the tyranny of winning and losing does not dominate. Individual choice is good. But making the well-being of the old dependent on the luck or skill of their stock picks or mutual-fund choices is not so good. The idea behind Social Security is not just that old folks should be entitled to comfort regardless of their personal merits. It is that none of us, of any age, should be obliged to live in a society where minimal dignity and the minimal decencies are denied to any of our fellow citizens at the end of life. "Thou shalt not covet thy neighbor's house"—that's a good admonition to keep in mind when making social policy. But so is "Honor thy father and thy mother, that thy days may be long upon the land which the Lord thy God giveth thee."

LANDMARKS

February 4, 2005

Last week, midway between Iraq's surprisingly successful election day and President Bush's State of the Union address—in which he asserted, not unreasonably, that the election proved that "the Iraqi people value their own liberty"—excerpts from a purported newspaper clipping began rocketing around cyberspace, from Web sites to inboxes to chat rooms and back around again. At first glance, the item looked like a bit of Internet apocrypha, but a visit to the microfilm reader proved it to be genuine.

U.S. ENCOURAGED BY VIETNAM VOTE

Officials Cite 83% Turnout Despite Vietcong Terror

By Peter Grose

Special *to* The New York Times

Washington, Sept. 3—United States officials were surprised and heartened today at the size of turnout in South Vietnam's presidential election despite a Vietcong terrorist campaign to disrupt the voting.

> According to reports from Saigon, 83 per cent of the
> 5.85 million registered voters cast their ballots yesterday. Many
> of them risked reprisals threatened by the Vietcong. . . .
>
> A successful election has long been seen as the keystone in
> President Johnson's policy of encouraging the growth of consti-
> tutional processes in South Vietnam.

Most of those who passed around this scrap of 1967 historical flotsam probably meant it as no more than a prudent caution against irrational exuberance. ("A flawed analogy, but resonant all the same," was one correspondent's accompanying note.) For others, no doubt, it was a petulant denial that something good might actually have happened in Iraq on George W. Bush's watch. Either way, it wouldn't be the first time that "landmark events in the history of liberty," to borrow a trope from Bush's speech, have been greeted sourly in certain quarters back home.

"We must not be euphoric," a senior American official grumped in the autumn of 1989, as Europe was exploding with joy at the fall of the Berlin Wall. "We have to be a little reserved about formulating major policy shifts until we have an opportunity to see what happens," he muttered. "I'm as enthusiastic as anyone else, but behind what's left of the Wall, there are still three hundred and eighty thousand Soviet troops in East Germany," he groused. The senior official, who has since ascended to even more senior officialdom, was Secretary of Defense Dick Cheney. Three years earlier, as a congressman, Cheney had been similarly churlish—and similarly blind to the power of the democratic spirit—when he voted against a resolution calling for the South African regime to release Nelson Mandela from prison and negotiate with the African National Congress, on the ground that Mandela and his organization were terrorists who would establish a Communist dictatorship.

Cheney was wrong about the durability of the Soviet bloc and wrong about the villainy of Nelson Mandela, and it may yet turn out that the clipping-clippers are wrong about the possibility of something like democracy in Iraq. No one knows. There are plenty of Vietnam echoes in America's Iraq adventure, especially in the corrosive effects on domestic comity, the use of false or distorted intelligence to create a sense of immediate threat, and the arrogance, combined with ignorance of local realities, of many senior strategists. But the differences are large, beginning with the nature of the enemy. The Vietnamese Communists possessed a legitimacy derived from thirty years of anticolonial struggle—against France, then Japan, then France again, and, finally, willy-nilly, the United States. Iraq's insurgency has support in the Sunni minority, but it is no national liberation movement. And for all the cruelty of the Iraq war's "collateral damage," it has produced no equivalents of Vietnam's carpet bombings, free-fire zones, or strategic hamlets. (Nor, it must be said, did Vietnam produce an equivalent of Abu Ghraib; but then Vietnam was a war in which both sides held prisoners.)

Iraq is not Vietnam, and Iraq's election was not like Vietnam's in 1967. The latter was a winner-take-all presidential and vice presidential "contest," staged on American orders. The predetermined winners were the military strongmen already in power, Generals Nguyen Van Thieu and Nguyen Cao Ky. The exercise was as meaningless as one of those plebiscites by which the cowed citizens of banana republics ratify whichever colonel or corporal has lately mounted a coup. The Iraq election was the real thing. Voters had a choice of a hundred and eleven party lists, ranging from Communists to theocrats to secularists. (The murderous "security situation" made personal campaigning next to impossible, but this was less important than one might think; there were some seventy-seven hundred candidates on the national lists, far too many for voters to keep track of, so the election was about political, religious, and ethnic identity, not about personalities.) Moreover, the voting was the first stage of a process that, if it goes as planned, will provide fairly strong incentives for consensus and disincentives for civil war. Once the votes are counted—a laborious process—the result will be an extremely diverse two-hundred-and-seventy-five-member assembly, which will choose a transitional government and write a constitution.

Since the draft constitution can be vetoed by two-thirds of the voters in any three of Iraq's eighteen provinces—a provision which, though originally designed to protect the Kurds, could prove equally efficacious in protecting the Sunnis—the assembly will have every reason to design a mechanism that accommodates the interests of minorities.

Critics of the Bush administration can take comfort in the fact that the apparent success of the Iraqi election can be celebrated without having to celebrate the supposed wisdom of the administration. Like the Homeland Security Department and the 9/11 Commission, the Iraqi election was something Bush & Co. resisted and were finally maneuvered into accepting. It wasn't their idea; it was an Iraqi idea—specifically, the idea of Grand Ayatollah Ali al-Sistani, Shiism's most prominent cleric. In a way, it was a by-product of the same American ignorance and bungling that produced the unchallenged post-Saddam looting and the myriad mistakes of the Coalition Provisional Authority. But this time—for the first time—the bungling seems to have yielded something positive.

Iraq is still a very, very long way from democracy. And even if it gets there, the costs of the journey—the more than ten thousand (so far) American wounded and dead, the tens of thousands of Iraqi men, women, and children killed, the hundreds of billions of dollars diverted from other purposes, the lies, the distraction from and gratuitous extension of the "war on terror," the moral and political catastrophe of systematic torture, the draining of good will toward and sympathy for America—will not necessarily justify themselves. But, for the moment at least, one can marvel at the power of the democratic idea. It survived American slavery; it survived Stalinist co-optation (the "German Democratic Republic," and so on); it survived Cold War horrors like America's support of Spanish Falangism and Central American death squads. Perhaps it can even survive the fervent embrace of George W. Bush.

MATTERS OF LIFE

March 25, 2005

Last week, Theresa Marie Schindler Schiavo, known to cable news viewers and talk radio listeners as Terri, was as ubiquitous as Elián González and Laci Peterson once were. Yet she was also hidden, obscured behind layers of political and religious posturing, legal maneuvering, emotional projection, and media exploitation that swaddled her like strips of linen around a mummy.

Terri Schiavo was born on December 3, 1963, near Philadelphia, the first of three children of Robert and Mary Schindler. As a teenager, she was obese—at eighteen, she weighed two hundred and fifty pounds—but with diligence she lost a hundred pounds, and by the time she married Michael Schiavo, in 1984, she was an attractive and vivacious young woman. By the end of the decade, she had moved with her husband to Florida, was undergoing fertility treatments, and had slimmed down further, to a hundred and ten pounds. On February 25, 1990, Terri suffered cardiac arrest, leading to severe brain damage. The cause was a drastically reduced level of potassium in her bloodstream, a condition frequently associated with bulimia. Her death that day was forestalled by heroic measures, including a tracheotomy and ventilation. But when, after a few weeks, she emerged from a coma, it was only to enter a "persistent vegetative state," with no evidence or hope of improvement—a diagnosis that, in the fifteen years since, has been confirmed, with something close to unanimity, by many neurologists on many occasions on behalf of many courts. The principal internal organs of Terri's body, including her brain stem, which controls such involuntary actions as heartbeat, digestion, respiration, and the bodily sleep cycle, continued to function as long as liquid nourishment was provided through a tube threaded into her stomach through a hole in her abdomen. The exception was her cerebral cortex, which is the seat of language, of the processing of sense impressions, of thought, of awareness of one's surroundings and one's inner state—in short, of consciousness. Her EKG flatlined. The body lived; the mind died. "At this point," the Florida Supreme Court wrote six months ago, "much of her cerebral cortex is simply gone and has been replaced by cerebral spinal fluid. Medicine cannot cure this condition. Unless an act of God, a true miracle, were to recreate her brain, Theresa will always remain in an unconscious, reflexive state."

Terri Schiavo's life, as distinct from the life of her unsentient organs, ended fifteen years ago. But that did not prevent her from becoming the star of an unusually morbid kind of reality TV show. The show was made possible by two factors. The first was a bitter struggle between Terri's husband, Michael Schiavo, who wanted to allow her body to die in accordance with what he said, and what an unbroken series of court decisions has affirmed, was her own expressed wish, and her parents and siblings, who wanted to keep her body alive at all costs. The second factor was a set of video snippets, provided by the Schindler family and broadcast incessantly by the three cable news networks—CNN, Fox News, and MSNBC—which are themselves entangled in a desperate struggle for dominance. Sometimes the snippets are identified by the year of their taping (2001 and 2002); sometimes they are not. Sometimes they are accompanied by inflammatory captions (FIGHTING FOR HER LIFE); sometimes the captions are merely dramatic (SCHIAVO SAGA). They show Terri's blinking eyes seeming to follow a balloon waved in front of her; or her mouth agape in a rictus that could be interpreted as a smile; or her face turned toward her mother's, with her head thrown back, Pietà-like. As neurologists who have examined her have explained, the snippets are profoundly misleading. A few seconds of maximum suggestiveness culled from many hours of tape, they are more in the nature of special effects than of a documentary record. Without them, there would have been no show—and, most likely, no televised vigils outside her hospice, no cries of "murder" from Tom DeLay, the egregious House majority leader; no midnight special sessions of the House and Senate; no calling Dr. Frist for a snap video diagnosis; no visuals of President Bush returning from Texas to land on the White House south lawn, striding dramatically across the grass as if it were the deck of an aircraft carrier.

To read through the documents generated by the years of legal wrangling over Terri Schiavo is to be impressed by the thoroughness and conscientiousness with which the courts, especially the Florida courts, approached her case. On legal, substantive, and constitutional grounds, they seemed to have reason and justice on their side. Yet it was a cold sort of reason and justice. On a human level, it was hard to see what concrete harm there could be in indulging her family's desire to keep her body alive, its care presumably underwritten by the hospice and the family's supporters.

Meanwhile, the language of the debate over her fate, pitting a "right to die" against a "right to life," turned rancid in its abstraction. Terri Schiavo, the person, had no further use for a right to die, because Terri Schiavo, the person, had long since exercised that right. Did it really matter if she had told her husband, when she was young and healthy, that she would not wish to live "that way"? Her body notwithstanding, she was not living "that way," or any other way. By the same token, she had no use for a right to life, because her ability to benefit from such a right had long ago been rendered as moot as the legal pleadings on her alleged behalf would soon become.

As the week progressed, it was harder and harder to deny that the fervor of Terri's Christianist "supporters" was motivated by dogmas unrelated to her or her rights. If she truly had a "right to life," if removing her feeding tube was truly tantamount to murder, then neither the disapproval nor the approval of her family (or anyone else) could make the slightest moral difference. If her parents had agreed with her husband that the tube should be removed, would their acquiescence have somehow transubstantiated murder into mercy? And, with or without their acquiescence, if Michael Schiavo had spent the last ten years adhering strictly to the orthodox code of family values—if he had remained faithfully celibate, if he had not taken a mistress and had children with her—then might not some of those now accusing him of murder be demanding that his biblically ordained husbandly authority be respected?

Terri Schiavo has become a metaphor in the religio-cultural struggle over abortion. This—along with the advantages of demonizing the judiciary in preparation for the coming battle over Supreme Court nominees—explains the eagerness of Republican politicians to embrace her parents' cause. Her lack of awareness actually increased her metaphoric usefulness. Like a sixty-four-cell blastocyst, she was without consciousness. Unlike the blastocyst, she was without potential. If letting her body die is murder, goes the logic, then thwarting the development of the blastocyst can surely be nothing less.

Last weekend, as Good Friday gave way to Holy Saturday and Holy Saturday to Easter Sunday, Florida's made-for-TV passion play neared its climax. The death of Terri Schiavo's body will only enhance her symbolic value, elevating her to her destined place as another martyr in this dismal age of martyrs.

WITHOUT DELAY

April 15, 2005

A current Washington joke, in the mordant style that used to be a Moscow specialty, has it that Republicans and Democrats have finally found something they can agree on: Tom DeLay must stay as the majority leader of the House of Representatives.

The DeLay Must Stay movement, like all popular fronts and uneasy alliances, brings together participants of varying motives. Republican members want to continue being led by the Texas bug exterminator turned hard-right Christianist crusader because they agree with him on the great political and religious issues of the day; because he is nice to them, feeding them pizza when they have to work late and finding places for the smokers among them to indulge without having to shiver on the Capitol steps; because they are terrified of him, on account of his well-deserved reputation for vengefulness; because he saved them from losing House seats in the 2004 election by persuading Texas to adopt a precedent-breaking mid-decade gerrymander that netted their party an overall gain of three seats; because he has raised millions for their campaigns, mostly from business interests that have reaped billions and expect to reap billions more from the policies he promotes; and because, using threats and inducements, he has insured that the choicest, highest-paying, most enviable lobbying jobs on Washington's K Street corridor go overwhelmingly to Republicans in general and DeLay loyalists in particular. Democrats don't mind if DeLay stays a while, because he is so repellent. Self-righteous, humorless, resentful, scowling, perpetually angry, he has many of the irritating qualities of his former colleague Newt Gingrich without any of the latter's childlike charms. (There are no DeLay equivalents of Gingrich's boyish enthusiasms for dinosaurs, sci-fi fantasies, and big, shiny theories of History.) And then there are the scandals, which cling to the majority leader like flakes of dandruff.

DeLay's ethical lapses center on campaign-finance chicanery, with sidelines in petty nepotism and lavish trips to exotic locales near golf courses. The details tend to be numbingly dull—there are no Monicas or burglaries to spice them up—but the lapses themselves are real enough. Last year, three of them attracted the attention of the House ethics committee, which formally (though toothlessly) "admonished" him, making him one of only three representatives, and the only repeat offender, to be disciplined in the past three years. DeLay has since had the three most unreliable Republicans removed and replaced with stooges, and the ethics committee has devolved from torpid to moribund. But various newspapers (not just bastions of the coastal "liberal media" like the *Times* and the *Washington Post* but also red-state gazettes like the *American Press*, of Lake Charles, Louisiana) have continued to make inquiries, as has the (Democratic) district attorney for Austin, Texas, Ronnie Earle, who has already indicted three of DeLay's closest associates and eight of their corporate donors. So far, only one serving Republican congressman—Christopher Shays, of Connecticut—has openly called upon DeLay to give up his leadership post. But cracks are beginning to appear in the outer wall. "DELAY MUST GO" was the title last week of an editorial in the staunchly Republican *Richmond Times-Dispatch*. The editorialists of the *Wall Street Journal*, who last year dismissed ethics criticisms of DeLay as "amusing," now write sternly, "Mr. DeLay, who rode to power in 1994 on a wave of revulsion at the everyday ways of big government, has become the living exemplar of some of its worst habits." The headline on that one was "SMELLS LIKE BELTWAY."

What is most odiferous about DeLay, however, is not his Tammany-like antics but his Torquemada-like ones. The current fuss reached the boiling point on March 31, when, after the body of Terri Schiavo was allowed to expire, DeLay—in a prepared statement, not an off-the-cuff remark—warned ominously, "The time will come for the men responsible for this to answer for their behavior, but not today." The anodyne interpretation of this is that DeLay was talking about the hereafter, where various members of the Florida and federal judiciaries, having died of presumably natural causes, will stand before their Maker, who will proceed to drop-kick them into the fiery pit. Some observers, noting the recent spate of actual, attempted, and threatened assassinations of judges, perceived a touch of this-worldly incitement; Senator Frank Lautenberg, of New Jersey, suggested that DeLay might have violated a statute outlawing such threats against federal judges.

Meanwhile, as new ethics allegations surfaced, DeLay huddled with colleagues from the other body for a strategy session. According to the Associated Press:

> His private remarks to Senate Republicans were in keeping with the response frequently offered on his behalf by House Republicans: Blame the Democrats and occasionally the news media for the scrutiny he faces. House Republicans intend to follow the script later in the week, hoping to showcase passage of bankruptcy legislation and estate tax repeal as a counterpoint to Democratic charges that they are merely power-hungry.

The hope, evidently, was to deflect charges of being merely power-hungry by inviting charges of being—on behalf of wealthy contributors—merely money-hungry. (The bankruptcy bill, which has since passed, is a gift to the banking and credit card industries; estate tax repeal, still pending in the Senate, would be an even bigger gift to the superrich.) Where DeLay is concerned, at least, the ploy hasn't worked. Gingrich, of all people, has now called upon DeLay to account for himself. ("DeLay's problem isn't with the Democrats," the former Speaker told the *CBS Evening News* last week. "DeLay's problem is with the country.")

Finally, last Wednesday, DeLay expressed regret for the style of his March 31 remarks. "I said something in an inartful way, and I shouldn't have said it that way, and I apologize for saying it that way," he said at a news conference. No apologies for the substance, though. "I believe in an independent judiciary," he said, and went on to explain what he meant: "We"—Congress—"set up the courts. We can unset the courts. We have the power of the purse." He declined to say whether the judges in the Schiavo case should be impeached, though that particular remedy for "judicial activism" is one that he has been advocating since 1997.

Earlier that day, DeLay had given an interview to the *Washington Times*, the far right's daily organ in the capital. For the most part, he was careful to avoid getting himself in more trouble. "I'm not sure I want to go there," he said in answer to a question about which bits of the government he'd like to abolish. And, to a question about Israeli settlements in the West Bank: "You're not going to get me in a fight with the President." But when asked who is to blame for "activist judges," he was jaw-droppingly candid:

> I blame Congress over the last fifty to a hundred years for not standing up and taking its responsibility given to it by the Constitution. The reason the judiciary has been able to impose a separation of church and state that's nowhere in the Constitution is that Congress didn't stop them. The reason we had judicial review is because Congress didn't stop them. The reason we had a right to privacy is because Congress didn't stop them.

So there you have it, the DeLay agenda: no separation of church and state, no judicial review, no right to privacy. Next to this, the president's effort to repeal the New Deal social contract by phasing out Social Security is the mewing of a kitten. DeLay may stay or DeLay may go. But the real danger is not DeLay himself. It's DeLay's agenda. It's his vision. It's his "values."

MUD

August 12, 2005

How did we—not just Americans but human beings in general—come to be? Opinions differ, but for most of recorded history the consensus view was that people were made out of mud. Also, that the mud was originally turned into people by a being or beings who themselves resembled people, only bigger, more powerful, and longer-lived, often immortal. The early Chinese theorized that a lonely goddess, pining for company, used yellow mud to fashion the first humans. According to the ancient Greeks, Prometheus sculpted the first man from mud, after which Athena breathed life into him. Mud is the man-making material in the creation stories of Mesopotamian city-states, African tribes, and American Indian nations.

The mud theory is still dominant in the United States, in the form of the Book of Genesis, whose version of the origin of our species, according to a recent Gallup poll, is deemed true by forty-five percent of the American public. Chapter 2, in verses 6 and 7, puts it this way:

> But there went up a mist from the earth, and watered the whole face of the ground.
>
> And the Lord God formed man of the dust of the ground, and

breathed into his nostrils the breath of life; and man became a living soul.

Mud is not mentioned by name, but you'd have to be a pretty strict biblical literalist not to infer that mud is what you get when you add water to dust.

A competing theory is that people, along with the rest of the earth's animals and plants, evolved over billions of years, beginning as extremely simple organisms and, via the accumulation of the tiny fraction of random mutations that turn out to be useful, developing into more complex ones. This view has gained many adherents since it was conceived, a century and a half ago, by Charles Darwin. It commands solid majorities in most of the developed world, and, thanks to the overwhelming evidence for its validity, has the near-unanimous support of scientists everywhere. Here in the United States, according to Gallup, it is subscribed to by about one-third of the populace—still running second to mud, but too large a market share to ignore altogether, especially in some of the battleground states.

On the one hand this, on the other hand that. George W. Bush is not normally the type to endorse shilly-shallying, but this time he went for it. At a "round table" with Texas reporters, the president was asked to comment on "what seems to be a growing debate over evolution versus intelligent design" and whether "both should be taught in public schools."

> THE PRESIDENT: I think—as I said, harking back to my days as my
>   governor—both you and Herman are doing a fine job of dragging me
>   back to the past. (*Laughter*) Then, I said that, first of all, that decision
>   should be made to local school districts, but I felt like both sides ought
>   to be properly taught.
> Q: Both sides should be properly taught?
> THE PRESIDENT: Yes, people—so people can understand what the
>   debate is about.

Q: So the answer accepts the validity of intelligent design as an alternative to evolution?

THE PRESIDENT: I think that part of education is to expose people to different schools of thought, and I'm not suggesting—you're asking me whether or not people ought to be exposed to different ideas, and the answer is yes.

Looked at one way, this colloquy is an occasion for national shame, albeit with a whiff of the risible: here is our country's leader, the champion-in-chief of educational standards, blandly equating natural science and supernatural supposition as "different schools of thought." Looked at another way, it represents progress of a sort. Twenty-five years ago, Ronald Reagan, then the Republican candidate for president, endorsed the teaching of "creationism"; five years ago, George W. Bush did the same. "Creationism" holds that dinosaurs and people coexisted, and that the fossil record is a product of Noah's flood. Next to that, "intelligent design" represents a scientific advance, or a tactical retreat, or maybe just the evolutionary process at work. I.D. recognizes that the age of the universe is measured in billions, not thousands, of years; that fossils are evidence, not divine tricks to test believers' faith; and that organisms change over time, sometimes via natural selection. This is tantamount to an admission that the Genesis story is poetry, not history; allegory, not fact.

But I.D.—whose central (and easily refuted) talking point is that certain structures of living things are too intricate to have evolved without the intervention of an "intelligent designer" (and You know who You are)—enjoys virtually no scientific support. It is not even a theory, in the scientific sense, because it is untestable and unsupportable by empirical evidence. It is a last-ditch skirmish in a misguided war against reason that cannot be won and, for religion's sake as well as science's, should not be fought. If the president's musings on it were an isolated crotchet, they would hardly be worth noting, let alone getting exercised about. But they're not. They reflect an attitude toward science that has infected every corner of his administration. From the beginning, the Bush White House has treated science as a nuisance and scientists as an interest group—one that, because it lies outside the governing conservative coalition, need not be indulged. That's why the White House—sometimes in the service of political Christianism or ideological fetishism, more often in obeisance to baser interests like the petroleum, pharmaceutical, and defense industries—has altered, suppressed, or overridden scientific findings on global warming; missile defense; H.I.V./AIDS; pollution from industrial farming and oil drilling; forest management and endangered species; environmental health, including lead and mercury poisoning in children and safety standards for drinking water; and non-abstinence methods of birth control and sexually transmitted disease prevention. It has grossly misled the public on the number of stem cell lines available for research. It has appointed unqualified ideologues to scientific advisory committees and has forced out scientists who persist in pointing out inconvenient facts. All this and more has been amply documented in reports from congressional Democrats and the Union of Concerned Scientists, in such leading scientific publications as *Nature*, *Scientific American*, *Science*, and the *Lancet*, and in a new book, *The Republican War on Science*, by the science journalist Chris Mooney.

Mooney's book is more judicious than its move-product title, which, as he acknowledges in an opening chapter, is not meant to apply to moderate Republicans past (such as Dwight D. Eisenhower) or present (such as John McCain). Anyway, a few small fissures are beginning to appear in the stone wall. Bill Frist, M.D., the Senate majority leader, has broken with the White House on stem cell research. The White House science adviser, John H. Marburger III, evidently embarrassed by his boss's evolutionary equivocations, told the *Times* that "intelligent design is not a scientific concept." And the cover story in the current *National Journal*, a well-informed and relentlessly nonpartisan Washington weekly, reports that growing numbers of Republican politicians and corporate chieftains "who once dismissed as unproven the idea that the burning of fossil fuels is causing a harmful rise in Earth's temperature have now concluded that global warming is real—and very dangerous." As a result, the magazine says, "Advocates of muscular governmental efforts to slow or reverse global warming predict that the United States will eventually take strong action—but they doubt that such action will come on Bush's watch." In this White House, science's name is mud. And, unlike those intelligent designers in the sky, all this crowd knows how to do is sling it.

DISARRAY THIS

March 17, 2006

The Democrats are in disarray. Everybody says so. In the *Times*, Adam Nagourney, the paper's chief political correspondent, indicts them for sending "scattershot messages," having no "overarching theme," and lacking "a strategy for governing." In the *Daily News*, Michael Goodwin dismisses them as "more of a collection of disparate interest groups than people united around a political philosophy." In the *Washington Post*, Shailagh Murray and Charles Babington point to "the failure of congressional leaders to deliver a clear message" and note that, after months of meetings and focus groups aimed at finding a slogan for the midterm elections, the best they could come up with was the ungrammatical—and, frankly, pathetic—"Together, America Can Do Better."

The Democrats are in disarray. Everybody says so; some even sing so. A week ago, at the Gridiron Club dinner—that's the annual white-tie event where Washington's most elite politicians and journalists kid each other and themselves in an atmosphere dank with chumminess—a Marine Corps singer impersonating a Democratic bigwig belted out this chorus: "What do we stand for? We don't know. What's our platform? We ain't sure." The designated jokester from the Democratic side was Barack Obama, the freshman senator from Illinois. "You hear this constant refrain from our critics that Democrats don't stand for any-thing," he said. "That's really unfair. We *do* stand for anything." And although most of the evening's material, inescapably, concerned Dick Cheney's shotgun, the Associated Press noted that "Democrats didn't have an easier time, as they were mocked for being in disarray over the party's message and strategy, its position on the Iraq war and even whom to field for president in 2008."

Last week's disarray display was touched off by Russ Feingold, the maverick senator from Wisconsin, who, on Monday, introduced a resolution to censure President Bush for his program of warrantless electronic surveillance. Censure is a purely symbolic form of punish-ment. Though it carries no concrete penalties, the shame of it has a cer-tain Roman gravity. The Senate has voted nine times to censure one of its own errant members—most notably, in 1954, Joseph R. McCarthy, who felt the sting so keenly that he drank himself to death three years later, aged forty-eight. Censure of a president has been occasionally proposed—in 1999, forty-four Democratic senators supported censur-ing Bill Clinton, as an alternative to impeaching him—but has been done only once, in 1834, when President Andrew Jackson incurred the displeasure of Henry Clay's Whigs in their struggle over the national bank.

The immediate consequence of Feingold's gambit was not Repub-lican dismay but, yes, Democratic disarray—or, at least, every appear-ance of it. In the *Washington Post*, Dana Milbank described a stampede through the marble halls as Democratic senators fled from taking a position. "I haven't read it" (Obama). "I really can't right now" (John Kerry). "I'm not going to comment" (Charles Schumer). "Ask her after lunch" (Hillary Clinton's spokesman). Meanwhile, the left-populist blogosphere—a reliable barometer of the Democratic equivalent of the famous Republican "base"—erupted with praise for Feingold and con-tempt for his cautious party colleagues. The adjectives used to limn the latter were pungent: "Spineless." "Sluggish." "Weak."

There is very little doubt that Bush deserves censure, not only for the warrantless wiretapping but also for the many other catastrophes his administration has generated, including the manipulation of intelligence to justify the Iraq war, the willful failure to heed warnings of what the invasion's aftermath would entail, the sanctioning of torture, and the neglect of "homeland security"—to say nothing of a set of domestic policies that sacrifice solvency, safety, the environment, and elementary fairness on the altar of enriching the rich in the name of Christian compassion. And there is scarcely less doubt that, ever since 9/11, Democratic opposition to Bush's war-related policies has been inordinately muted. (Even a figure as non-populist as Zbigniew Brzezinski protested last week that "Democratic leaders have been silent or evasive.") But none of that means that those who prefer strategies different from Feingold's are, ipso facto, spineless, sluggish, and weak.

Feingold sprang his resolution on his Democratic colleagues without a word of advance warning or consultation. His Republican colleagues welcomed it, or professed to welcome it, as a distraction from Bush's manifold, ever-mounting troubles. Feingold focussed on the wiretapping because that is the one area where the administration has admitted—indeed, boasted of—overriding a particular law. But it is also practically the only area of security policy where Bush retains some lingering public support. Feingold has "energized the base," but to what end? Apart from establishing a beachhead for his own fledgling presidential campaign, he has succeeded mainly in deflecting the anger of a good many Democrats from Bush to—well, to "the Democrats."

Everyone complains that the Democrats have no clear, unified position on Iraq, and they don't. But what this analysis ignores is the fact that they can't. Without either a federal power center or an imminent presidential election—without a president, a Speaker of the House, a Senate majority leader, or a presidential nominee—no institutional instrument or leader has the clout to impose a consensus. Democrats advocate a spectrum of more or less similar positions—an array, not a disarray—ranging from Representative John Murtha's call for rapid disengagement to the detailed "strategic redeployment" plan backed by the Center for American Progress. But the Bush administration has created a dilemma to which a satisfactory solution, no matter what new policies are adopted, has become vanishingly remote. As for the Democrats, their point is more implicit than explicit. It is that if they had had power they would not have made the same strategic, prudential, and moral errors that Bush and the Republicans have made, and that if they are entrusted with power they will not be wedded to a manifestly failing policy. Their job is to win power without either being completely cynical or talking themselves into a box that would make it impossible for them to exercise it wisely once they got it.

A poll taken last week by the American Research Group showed that a plurality of voters—forty-eight percent—actually favor Feingold's resolution, with forty-three percent opposed. Among Democratic respondents, support was seventy percent. For senators whose seats are safely Democratic, supporting the resolution is a personally cost-free choice. (The same is true of the thirty-one members of the House who have endorsed an impeachment resolution: in 2004, all won with at least fifty-seven percent of the vote. The average was seventy-five percent.) That A.R.G. poll also showed independent voters narrowly opposing censure. The midterm election will be decided in places where no Democratic candidate can prevail without overwhelming independent support. Tactical calculations like these are never pleasant. But they are not always sordid, and sometimes they are necessary.

CONSUMPTION

April 7, 2006

Perhaps you have been wondering who or what is to blame for the high cost of medical care in this land of ours—and, more broadly, for the ungainly, unjust mess that is the American health-care system. If so, wonder no more. Your government has fingered the culprit: it's "the vast majority of Americans."

The perp having been collared, the trial held, and the verdict rendered, only the sentencing phase remains. Providentially, our leaders have come up with a punishment that fits the crime. We, the guilty, are to be condemned—or invited, but in any case for the rest of our natural lives, without possibility of parole—to turn over our bodily well-being to "consumer-directed Health Savings Accounts" in conjunction with "high-deductible health policies."

This judgment was handed down last Monday, in the form of an article on the op-ed page of the *Times*. The piece was no Dowdy jestfest or Friedmanesque memo-to-the-mullahs, and not only because of the dreariness of its style and the banality of its content. Its author, Allan B. Hubbard, identified as "assistant to the president for economic policy and director of the National Economic Council," has lately emerged as the White House point man on health policy, and, in subsequent days, his op-ed proved to have been the overture to a veritable symphony of spin conducted by President Bush himself, including an Air Force One ride to Bridgeport, Connecticut, for a stagy "Panel on Health Savings Accounts."

Hubbard's article, headlined "The Health of a Nation," begins with a frank-sounding acknowledgment that "in the past five years"—that is, since the present administration took office—"private health insurance premiums have risen 73 percent," with the result that "some businesses" have dropped coverage altogether. "What is driving this unsustainable run-up in health insurance costs," Hubbard asks, "and how can we make things better?" Then comes what bloggers call the money quote:

> Health care is expensive because the vast majority of Americans con-sume it as if it were free. Health insurance policies with low deductibles insulate people from the cost of the medical care they use—so much so that they often do not even ask for prices.

Can this really be the administration's view of the health-care crisis? That its root cause is that Americans are (a) malingerers and (b) free-loaders who perversely refuse to go comparison shopping when illness strikes? That we're *over*insured? Hard as it is to believe that this is what they say, it's even harder to believe that this is what they believe.

Health care is indeed expensive, but not because people are too quick to call the doctor when they experience a scary symptom or merely an annoying one, and not because some of them may bridle at entrusting their health to the lowest bidder. Throughout the Western world, health care is expensive, first of all, because it is expensive, and is bound to get more so as populations age and medical technology advances. Indeed, it *should* get more expensive, both in absolute terms and as a proportion of national income, because what it aims to provide—healing, the relief of suffering, the staving off of death—is of such inestimable value.

American health care is the most expensive on earth, but this, too, has little to do with overindulgence in seeking medical attention.

(Overindulgence in cheeseburgers is another matter.) It has a lot to do with the waste built into what Paul Krugman calls our crazy-quilt health-care system, which has a lot to do with the fact that so much of that system is private rather than public, which in turn has a lot to do with two other factors. One is historical: during the Second World War, industry (with prodding from organized labor) got around wage controls by offering workers health benefits in place of cash, thus saddling the United States with "employer-based" private health insurance—a system now in slow-motion collapse under the competitive pressures of globalization. The other is institutional: even though there has long been popular support here for universal, government-run health care, as there is in Europe and Canada, America's fragmented political system—riddled with weak points where well-organized, well-financed minorities can thwart the unfocussed will of a majority—has been able to deliver only for seniors and, less generously, for the poor.

Medicare—a mixed system, under which the insurance function is socialized while the care itself remains in private hands—dedicates two percent of its resources to administration. By contrast, the private health insurance industry spends a fortune—more than ten percent of its income—on administrative dreadnoughts devoted largely to vetoing treatments, sloughing off sick or potentially sick clients, and scheming to stick someone else with the bill. In the United States, we spend fifteen percent of our gross domestic product on health care; the French and the Canadians spend ten percent. Yet their "health outcomes," measured by indices like longevity, are better than ours. If they spent the kind of money we do, they'd live forever.

Hubbard is an initiate of the cult of the market, which he evidently regards as the fundamental model for all human relations. For him, sick people who require care are "consumers." That word and its derivatives appear ten times in the eight hundred and fifty words of his *Times* piece. ("Patient" appears once. "Sick," "ill," and "under the weather" appear not at all.) Accordingly, the solution that he and Bush are pushing—so-called health savings accounts—puts the onus on "consumers" to fend for themselves in the medical "marketplace." It's probably unnecessary to add that this solution would solve nothing. It would be yet another gift to people in the higher tax brackets, would undermine traditional insurance by pulling young and healthy people out of risk pools, and, with a fine evenhandedness, would discourage people from going to the doctor for real and imaginary illnesses alike. This is a worthy follow-up to the administration's prescription drug program for seniors, another excrescence of market cultism. The elderly had hoped for a straightforward benefit that would have allowed them to acquire, at some affordable price, the medicines their doctors prescribed. What they got was a parody of "choice," sadistic in its complexity, which forces them or their children or caretakers to game out which of dozens of private "plans" might give them access both to the medicines they need now and the ones they might unpredictably need in the future. The solicitude their government might have bestowed on them was reserved instead for the insurance and pharmaceutical industries. The administration's message to the old and sick is the same as its message to the country after the September 11 attacks: Go shopping.

RUMMYACHE

April 26, 2006

In the ongoing South Americanization of political culture north of the border—a drawn-out historical journey whose markers include fiscal recklessness, an accelerating wealth gap between the rich and the rest, corruption masked by populist rhetoric, a frank official embrace of the techniques of "dirty war," and, by way of initiating the present era, a judicial *autogolpe* installing a dynastic *presidente*—what has been dubbed the Revolt of the Generals is one of the feebler effusions. But it is striking all the same. By last week, the junta had swelled to six members: General Anthony C. Zinni, of the Marine Corps (four stars); Lieutenant General Gregory Newbold, also of the Marines (three stars); and Major Generals John Batiste, Paul D. Eaton, John Riggs, and Charles H. Swannack, Jr., of the Army (two stars). Some reckon that Wesley Clark (Army, four stars), William E. Odom (ditto, three stars), and Bernard E. Trainor (Marines, three stars) are entitled to spots as auxiliary members. All these generals have said devastating things about the job performance of the current secretary of defense, particularly with respect to the Iraq war. Their critiques vary—some of them see the war as a series of tactical blunders, others as a strategic disaster doomed from the start—but on one point the Pentagon Six are unanimous: Please. Bring us the head of Donald Rumsfeld.

This brass band of clarion calls for Rumsfeld's resignation or dismissal has occasioned a certain amount of hand-wringing about alleged threats to the constitutional principle of civilian control of the military. But, as military coups go, this one is pretty weak tea by hemispheric standards. Instead of seizing the radio stations and the Presidential Palace, our disgruntled generals are content to overrun the op-ed pages, the bookstore signing tables, and the greenrooms of the cable TV news talk shows. Also (and this is not a small point), the generals in question, however youthful and vigorous some of them may appear, are retired. They are no longer links in the chain of command; not being subordinate, they can't be insubordinate. They are civilians. And they are every bit as entitled to express their views publicly, and to give their former civilian superiors a hard time in the process, as were Andrew Jackson in 1824, and Dwight Eisenhower in 1952—not to mention the nine other ex-generals who became president, beginning with General George Washington (ret.), in 1789.

There's nothing new, let alone unconstitutional, about the bitching of pensioned-off generals. What is unusual—unprecedented, apparently—is for so many to speak out so strongly against a prominent architect of an ongoing war and to demand his removal. But then it is also unusual (though not, alas, unprecedented) for the United States to fight a war of choice on the basis of ideological fervor and faulty or falsified intelligence. And it is not just unusual but unprecedented for the stated primary aims of such a war (in this case, to prevent Iraq from obtaining weapons of mass destruction and from aiding terrorist attacks on the American homeland) to have been achieved before a shot was fired, forcing the war's advocates to scramble for new ones.

The generals' revolt of 2006 has resonated. One reason, no doubt, is that the experience of these particular generals suggests that they know what they are talking about. Three of the six—Batiste, Eaton, and Swannack—held positions of command in Iraq; a fourth, Zinni, is steeped in the region, having served as chief of the U.S. Central Command and as President Bush's own special envoy to the Middle East. A second reason is their relative immunity to assaults of the kind that right-wing publicists and talk radio hosts routinely launch at the patriotism and integrity of Iraq war critics. One or two bemedalled warriors can be taken down that way; a dense pack is not so easily Swift-boated.

If the generals have struck a chord, a third reason, surely, is a widespread public hunger for some sort of accountability. The White House dimly understands this; hence last week's highly touted "shake-up," which saw the departure of the president's hapless press secretary and the lateral transfer of Karl Rove from deputy chief of staff for policy to just plain deputy chief of staff. These moves, though, are entirely beside the point. If Bush were serious about stanching the hemorrhage of public support for any kind of American role in Iraq, then Rumsfeld's exit—a step that has been suggested not only by generals and Democrats but also by conservative hawks like George Will, Max Boot, David Brooks, and Bill Kristol—would be the obvious beginning. The president's response has been an adamant refusal. "I'm the decider," he said last Tuesday. "And I decide what is best. And what's best is for Don Rumsfeld to remain as the secretary of defense."

His reasons for this decision are obscure, a matter for speculation—wild speculation, as he might phrase it. "We had an accountability moment," Bush said a few days before his second inaugural, "and that's called the 2004 election." Perhaps he thinks that that was the last such moment he owes the country; perhaps dumping Rumsfeld would feel too much like another one. Perhaps his attachment to Rumsfeld—whom the elder President Bush is known to dislike—has something to do with the younger's need for substitute fathers. Perhaps he is simply afraid to lose him, for reasons he understands no better than the rest of us. A couple of weeks ago, answering a question from a student after giving a speech at Johns Hopkins University's School of Advanced International Studies, Bush provided a hint of the emotional texture of his extraordinary dependence on his secretary of defense. "My question," the young woman said,

> is in regards to private military contractors. The Uniform Code of Military Justice does not apply to these contractors in Iraq. I asked your secretary of defense a couple months ago what law governs their actions.
>
> THE PRESIDENT: I was going to ask him. Go ahead. (*Laughter*) Help. (*Laughter*)
>
> Q: I was hoping your answer might be a little more specific. (*Laughter*) Mr. Rumsfeld answered that Iraq has its own domestic laws, which he assumed applied to those private military contractors. However, Iraq is clearly not currently capable of enforcing its laws. . . . Mr. President, how do you propose to bring private military contractors under a system of law?
>
> THE PRESIDENT: I appreciate that very much. I wasn't kidding. (*Laughter*) I was going to—I pick up the phone and say, Mr. Secretary, I've got an interesting question. (*Laughter*) This is what delegation—I don't mean to be dodging the question, although it's kind of convenient in this case, but never—(*laughter*). I really will—I'm going to call the secretary and say you brought up a very valid question, and what are we doing about it? That's how I work. I'm—thanks. (*Laughter*)

Thanks? No. No, thanks. (And no laughter.) He's the decider, and there's the rub.

THE "IC" FACTOR

July 28, 2006

What is the name of a certain political party in the United States—not the one which controls the executive, legislative, and judicial branches of the federal government but the other one, which doesn't? The question is a small one, to be sure: a minor irritation, a wee gnat compared to such red-clawed, sharp-toothed horrors as the health-care mess and the budget deficit, to say nothing of Iraq and Lebanon. But it has been around longer than any of them, and, annoyingly, it won't go away.

Last week, the gnat was buzzing at a high altitude. An e-mail from none other than "President George W. Bush," arriving last Monday morning in millions of inboxes, hinted strongly at where the commander in chief stands on the name issue. To wit:

The Democrat Party has a clear record when it comes to taxes.

And:

Nothing threatens our hard-won reforms and economic prosperity more than a Democrat victory this November.

And:

> The difference is clear: if you want the government in your pocket,
> vote Democrat.

An alternative view is that it's called the Democratic Party. The
Democratic Party itself takes this view, and many nonpartisan authori-
ties agree. The *American Heritage College Dictionary*, for example, defines
the noun "Democratic Party" as "One of the two major US political parties, owing its origin to a split in the Democratic-Republican
Party under Andrew Jackson in 1828." (It defines "Democrat *n*" as
"A Democratic Party member" and "Democratic *adj*" as "Of, relating
to, or characteristic of the Democratic Party," but gives no definition
for—indeed, makes no mention of—"Democrat Party *n*" or "Democrat *adj*".) Other dictionaries, and reference works generally, appear to
be unanimous on these points. The broader literate public also comes
down on the "Democratic" side, as indicated by frequency of usage. A
Google search for "Democratic Party" yields around forty million hits.
"Democrat Party" fetches fewer than two million.

There's no great mystery about the motives behind this deliberate
misnaming. "Democrat Party" is a slur, or intended to be—a handy
way to express contempt. Aesthetic judgments are subjective, of course,
but "Democrat Party" is jarring verging on ugly. It fairly screams "rat."
At a slightly higher level of sophistication, it's an attempt to deny the
enemy the positive connotations of its chosen appellation. During
the Cold War, many people bridled at obvious misnomers like "German Democratic Republic," and perhaps there are some members of
the Republican Party (which, come to think of it, has been drifting
toward monarchism of late) who genuinely regard the Democratic
Party as undemocratic. Perhaps there are some who hope to induce
it to go out of existence by refusing to call it by its name, à la term-
ing Israel "the Zionist entity." And no doubt there are plenty of others

who say "Democrat Party" just to needle the other side while signal-
ling solidarity with their own—the partisan equivalent of flashing a
gang sign.

The history of "Democrat Party" is hard to pin down with any precision, though etymologists have traced its use to as far back as the
Harding administration. According to William Safire, it got a boost in
1940 from Harold Stassen, the Republican Convention keynoter that
year, who used it to signify disapproval of such less than fully democratic Democratic machine bosses as Frank Hague of Jersey City and
Tom Pendergast of Kansas City. Senator Joseph McCarthy made it a
regular part of his arsenal of insults, which served to dampen its popularity for a while. There was another spike in 1976, when grumpy,
growly Bob Dole denounced "Democrat wars" (those were the days!)
in his vice presidential debate with Walter Mondale. Growth has been
steady for the last couple of decades, and today we find ourselves in a
golden age of anti-"ic"-ism.

In the conservative media, the phenomenon feeds more voraciously
the closer you get to the mucky, sludgy bottom. "Democrat Party"
is standard jargon on right-wing talk radio and common on winger
Web sites like NewsMax.com, which blue-pencils Associated Press dispatches to de-"ic" references to the party of F.D.R. and J.F.K. (The
resulting impression that "Democrat Party" is O.K. with the A.P. is
as phony as a North Korean travel brochure.) The respectable conservative journals of opinion sprinkle the phrase around their Web sites
but go light on it in their print editions. William F. Buckley, Jr., the
Miss Manners *cum* Dr. Johnson of modern conservatism, dealt with the
question in a 2000 column in *National Review*, the magazine he had
founded forty-five years before. "I have an aversion to 'Democrat' as an
adjective," Buckley began.

Dear Joe McCarthy used to do that, and received a rebuke from this
at-the-time 24-year-old. It has the effect of injecting politics into

language, and that should be avoided. Granted there are difficulties, as when one desires to describe a "democratic" politician, and is jolted by possible ambiguity.

But English does that to us all the time, and it's our job to get the correct meaning transmitted without contorting the language.

The job of politicians, however, is different, and among those of the Republican persuasion "Democrat Party" is now nearly universal. This is partly the work of Newt Gingrich, the nominal author of the notorious 1990 memo "Language: A Key Mechanism of Control," and his Contract with America pollster, Frank Luntz, the Johnny Appleseed of such linguistic innovations as "death tax" for estate tax and "personal accounts" for Social Security privatization. Luntz, who road-tested the adjectival use of "Democrat" with a focus group in 2001, has concluded that the only people who really dislike it are highly partisan adherents of the—how you say?—Democratic Party. "Those two letters actually do matter," Luntz said the other day. He added that he recently finished writing a book—it's entitled *Words That Work*—and has been diligently going through the galley proofs taking out the hundreds of "ic"s that his copy editor, one of those partisan Dems, had stuck in.

In days gone by, the anti-"ic" tic tended to be reined in at the presidential level. Ronald Reagan never used it in polite company, and George Bush *père* was too well brought up to use the truncated version of the out party's name more than sparingly. Not so Bush *fils*—and not just in e-mails sent to the party faithful, which he obviously never reads, let alone writes. "It's time for the leadership in the Democrat Party to start laying out ideas," he said a few weeks ago, using his own personal mouth. "The Democrat Party showed its true colors during the tax debate," he said a few months before that. "Nobody from the Democrat Party has actually stood up and called for actually getting rid of the terrorist surveillance program," he said a week before that. What he meant is anybody's guess, but his bad manners were impossible to miss. Hard as it is to believe from this distance in time, George W. Bush came to office promising to "change the tone." That he has certainly done. But, as with so much else, it hasn't worked out quite the way he promised.

LOST LOVE

September 11, 2006

After the calamity that glided down upon us out of a clear blue sky on the morning of Tuesday, September 11, 2001—five short years ago, five long years ago—a single source of solace emerged amid the dread and grief: a great upwelling of simple solidarity. Here in New York, and in similarly bereaved Washington, that solidarity took homely forms. Strangers connected as friends; volunteers appeared from everywhere; political and civic leaders of all parties and persuasions stood together, united in sorrow and defiance. In certain regions of the country, New York had been regarded (and resented) as somehow not quite part of America; that conceit, not shared by the terrorists, vanished in the fire and dust of the Twin Towers. The reconciliation was mutual. In SoHo and the Upper West Side, in the Village and the Bronx, sidewalk crowds cheered every flag-bedecked fire engine, and the Stars and Stripes sprouted from apartment windows all over town. New York, always suspect as the nation's polyglot-plutocratic portal, was now its battered, bloody shield.

The wider counterpart to our traumatized togetherness at home was an astonishing burst abroad of what can only be called pro-Americanism. Messages of solidarity and indignation came from Libya and Syria as well as from Germany and Israel; flowers and funeral wreaths piled up in front of American embassies from London to Beijing; flags flew at half-staff across Europe; in Iran, a candlelight vigil expressed sympathy. "Any remnants of neutrality thinking, of our traditional balancing act, have gone out of the window now," a Swedish political scientist told Reuters. "There has not been the faintest shadow of doubt, not a trace of hesitation of where we stand, nowhere in Sweden." *Le Monde's* front-page editorial was headlined "NOUS SOMMES TOUS AMÉRICAINS," and Italy's *Corriere della Sera* echoed, "We are all Americans. The distance from the United States no longer exists because we, our values, are also in the crosshairs of evil minds." In Brussels, the ambassadors of the nineteen members of NATO invoked, for the first time in the alliance's fifty-two-year history, Article 5 of the North Atlantic Treaty, affirming that "an armed attack against one or more of them in Europe or North America shall be considered an attack against them all" and pledging action, "including the use of armed force."

No one realistically expected that the mood of fellow-feeling and cooperation would long persist in the extraordinarily powerful form it took in the immediate wake of September 11. The normal divisions of American politics and society were bound to make themselves felt again, and whatever the United States did in response to the attacks would provoke the tensions and misunderstandings that inevitably accompany the actions of a superpower in distress, no matter how deft its diplomacy or thorough its consultations. But it was natural to hope that domestic divisions would prove less rancorous in the face of the common danger, and that international frictions could be minimized in a struggle against what almost every responsible leader in the world recognized, or claimed to recognize, as an assault on civilization itself.

What few expected was how comprehensively that initial spirit would be ruined by the policies and the behavior of our government, culminating in, though hardly limited to, the disastrous occupation of Iraq. This shouldn't have been so surprising. George W. Bush campaigned in 2000 as a "compassionate conservative," one who recognized that government was not the enemy, praised bipartisanship, proclaimed his intention to "change the tone in Washington," and advocated a foreign policy of humility and respect. None of that happened. Nine months into his presidency, an economic policy of transferring the budget surplus to the wealthy, a social policy hewing to the demands of the Christianist far right, and a foreign policy marked by contempt for international instruments (the Kyoto protocol, the anti-ballistic-missile treaty) and the abandonment of diplomatic responsibilities (the nego-tiations over North Korea's nuclear activities, the Israeli-Palestinian stalemate) had pushed Bush's job ratings lower than those of any of his predecessors at a like point in their tenures. September 11 offered him a chance for a new beginning, and at first he seemed willing to seize it. Although the war against Al Qaeda and the Taliban in Afghanistan was not as widely backed at first as is often assumed (particularly among many on the European left and some on the American), it is now almost universally supported in the Western world, with some forty countries involved and NATO troops carrying an increasing share of the military burden. But then came a reversion to form, and Iraq.

In *America Against the World: How We Are Different and Why We Are Disliked*, based on ninety-one thousand interviews conducted in fifty nations from 2002 to 2005 by the Pew Research Center, Andrew Kohut and Bruce Stokes write that while "the first hints that the world was becoming troubled by America came soon after the election of George W. Bush," and that "whatever global goodwill the United States had in the wake of the September 11 attacks appears to have quickly dissipated," after the Iraq invasion "favorable opinions had more than slipped. They had plummeted." It's grown worse since May, when the book was pub-lished. The most recent Pew findings show that "favorable opinions of the U.S." have gone from eighty-three percent in 2000 to fifty-six percent in 2006 in Britain, seventy-eight to thirty-seven in Germany, and sixty-two to thirty-nine in France. The majorities saying that the Iraq war has made the world more dangerous are equally impressive: sixty percent in Britain, sixty-six in Germany, and seventy-six in France.

On this point, the United States is catching up. The most recent CNN poll, taken in late August, found fifty-five percent of Americans saying that the Iraq war has made them less safe from terrorism.

Last week, the administration launched a new public relations campaign aimed at marketing the war in Iraq as the indispensable key to the struggle against terrorism. The vice president and the secretary of defense gave speeches attacking the war's opponents (a category that includes, if that same CNN poll is to be believed, sixty-one percent of the American public) as the contemporary counterparts of the appeasers of Nazism. President Bush, as one of his contributions to the P.R. campaign, granted an interview to Brian Williams, of NBC. As the two men, shirtsleeved in the sun, strolled together down a bleak New Orleans street, Williams wondered if the president shouldn't "have asked for some sort of sacrifice after 9/11." Bush's reply:

> Americans are sacrificing. I mean, we are. You know, we pay a lot of taxes. America sacrificed when they, you know, when the economy went into the tank. Americans sacrificed when, you know, air travel was disrupted. American taxpayers have paid a lot to help this nation recover. I think Americans have sacrificed.

And so we have. Not by paying "a lot of taxes," of course; we pay less of those than we did before, and the very, very richest among us pay much, much less. But we have sacrificed, God knows. "The military occupation in Iraq is consuming practically the entire defense budget and stretching the Army to its operational limits," John Lehman, secretary of the Navy in the Reagan Administration and a member of the 9/11 Commission, wrote in the *Washington Post* a couple of days after Bush's interview. "This is understood quite clearly by both our friends and our enemies, and as a result, our ability to deter enemies around the world is disintegrating." That's a sacrifice. And here's another: our country's reputation.

HEARTS AND BRAINS

October 27, 2006

The great bafflement of next week's midterm congressional elections
is that there is even a sliver of a hint of a shadow of a doubt about the
outcome. The polls are unequivocal. In a mid–October NBC/*Wall Street
Journal* survey, the public's "job approval" of the Republican Congress
stood at a wan sixteen percent, as against seventy-five percent disapprov-
ing. Another measurement normally regarded as electorally predictive,
the one pollsters call "right track/wrong track," is nearly as one-sided.
In last week's *Newsweek* survey, twenty-five percent of respondents
pronounced themselves satisfied with "the way things are going in the
United States at this time," while sixty-seven percent registered dissat-
isfaction. The *Newsweek* poll also found that, by a 55–37 margin, likely
voters generically prefer Democratic candidates for the House of Representatives to Republican ones. Those numbers are a near mirror image
of the same survey's job rating for President Bush: thirty-five percent
approve of his performance, fifty-seven percent disapprove of it.

There's a lively debate among historians over the question of
whether the record of the forty-third president, compiled with the
indispensable help of a complaisant Congress, is the worst in American
history or merely the worst of the sixteen who managed to make it

into (if not out of) a second full term. That the record is appalling is by now beyond serious dispute. It includes an unending deficit—this year, it's $260 billion—that has already added $1.5 trillion to the national debt; the subcontracting of environmental, energy, labor, and health-care policymaking to corporate interests; repeated efforts to suppress scientific truth; a set of economic and fiscal policies that have slowed growth, spurred inequality, replenished the ranks of the poor and unin-sured, and exacerbated the insecurities of the middle class; and, on Capitol Hill, a festival of bribery, some prosecutable (such as the felo-nies that have put one prominent Republican member of Congress in prison, while another awaits sentencing), some not (such as the reported two-million-dollar salary conferred upon a Republican congressman who became the pharmaceutical industry's top lobbyist immediately after shepherding into law a bill forbidding the government to negoti-ate prices for prescription drugs).

In 2002 and 2004, the ruling party avoided retribution for offenses like these by exploiting the fear of terrorism. What is different this time is that the overwhelming failure of the administration's Iraq gamble is now apparent to all. This war of choice has pointlessly drained Ameri-can military strength, undermined what had originally appeared to be success in Afghanistan, handed the Iranian mullahs a strategic victory, immunized the North Korean regime from a forceful response to its nuclear defiance, and compromised American leadership of the demo-cratic world. You can read all about it, not only in the government's own recently leaked National Intelligence Estimate, which reports that the Iraq war has intensified the danger of Islamist terrorism, but also in a shelf of books—a score or more of them, beginning two and a half years ago with Richard A. Clarke's *Against All Enemies* and continuing through Bob Woodward's *State of Denial*—that document the mendac-ity, incompetence, lawlessness, and ideological arrogance surrounding the origins and conduct of that war.

In a normal democracy, given the state of public opinion and the record of the incumbent government, it would be taken for granted that come next Tuesday the ruling party would be turned out. But, for reasons that have less to do with the wizardry of Karl Rove than with the structural biases of America's electoral machinery, Democrats enter every race carrying a bag of sand. The Senate's fifty-five Republicans represent fewer Americans than do its forty-five Democrats. On the House side, Democratic candidates have won a higher proportion of the average district vote than Republicans in four of the five biennial elections since 1994, but—thanks to a combination of gerrymandering and demographics—Republicans remain in the majority. To win back the House, Democrats need something close to a landslide. Their opponents, to judge from their behavior, seem to think they might get one.

During the past week, the foul mood of the leaders of the Republican Party and its hard-right outriders touched what one must earnestly hope was bottom. In Tennessee, where a talented, relatively conservative young Democrat, Harold Ford, Jr., is campaigning to become the first African-American senator from a Southern or border state since Reconstruction, a television ad is making a nauseating kind of political history. The ad, which appeals to a poisonous stereotype of black sexuality, is destined for a long life as a reference point in discussions of political perfidy. Its only moment of honesty—an involuntary moment, compelled by the McCain-Feingold law of 2002—is provided by a hurried off-camera voice: "The Republican National Committee is responsible for the content of this advertising." Meanwhile, Rush Limbaugh, the radio broadcaster who is the Republican Party's most prominent unofficial spokesman, unleashed an unusually ugly attack on the integrity of the actor Michael J. Fox, who has been appearing in spots for Democratic candidates who support embryonic stem cell research. (In 2004, he did the same for a Republican, Senator Arlen Specter.) Fox has Parkinson's, and it shows.

Here is what Limbaugh said of one such spot: "In this commercial, he is exaggerating the effects of the disease. He is moving all around and shaking. And it's purely an act. . . . This is really shameless of Michael J. Fox. Either he didn't take his medication or he's acting, one of the two."

(In reality, Fox's body movements are a side effect of his medication, without which he is unable to speak.) And in one of the most important of next Tuesday's contests—Virginia's, which pits the incumbent senator, George Allen, against James Webb—Allen is employing a tactic that combines prurience with philistinism.

Allen, as the now famous "Macaca" incident and its aftermath showed, is a bigot and a bully. Webb is a Democrat turned Republican—he was President Reagan's secretary of the Navy—whom the Iraq war turned back into a Democrat. He is a novelist by profession. At the end of last week, as a new poll showed Allen slipping behind, he put out a press release consisting of annotated snippets from Webb's novels, which draw on his experiences and observations as a marine in Vietnam. The snippets record callous behavior, bleak sexuality, and rough talk. (To suggest that their author advocates such things is akin to saying that *Ben-Hur* is a brief for crucifixion.) Like the novels from which they are torn, the snippets are about men at war, so it is perhaps not so surprising that they are short on what Allen's press release primly calls "positive female role models."

There is much more along these lines, from many places, almost all of it of Republican provenance. But the most depraved pronouncement of the week came from the vice president of the United States, Dick Cheney. In an interview with one of three dozen right-wing radio hosts invited to spend a day broadcasting from the White House, Cheney was asked if he didn't think it was "silly" even to debate about "dunking a terrorist in water." "I do agree," he replied. The interviewer pressed: "Would you agree a dunk in water is a no-brainer if it can save lives?" Cheney: "It's a no-brainer for me."

The "dunk in water" they were talking about is waterboarding. It has been used by the Gestapo, the North Koreans, and the Khmer Rouge. After the Second World War, a Japanese soldier was sentenced to twenty-five years' hard labor for using it on American prisoners. It is torture, and torture is not a no-brainer. It is a no-souler. The no-brainer is the choice on Election Day.

THUMP

November 10, 2006

Interviewing President Bush aboard Air Force One a few days before his second inauguration, a *Washington Post* reporter noted that American forces in Iraq had neither been welcomed as liberators nor found any of the promised weapons of mass destruction. "The postwar process hasn't gone as well as some had hoped," the reporter ventured. "Why hasn't anyone been held accountable, either through firings or demotions, for what some people see as mistakes or misjudgments?" The president's reply—as iconically Bushian as "Bring 'em on"—came to mind last Tuesday night as the big blue waves started rolling in. "Well," he said back then, "we had an accountability moment, and that's called the 2004 election."

Actually, it was more like an impunity moment. "Let me put it to you this way," Bush had said the day after John Kerry's concession. "I earned capital in the campaign—political capital—and now I intend to spend it." And spend it he did. Whatever he had left over after he blew a wad trying to turn Social Security into a bonanza for the financial services industry was squandered on an unending skein of assurances that the war in Iraq was going fine. By last week, the coffers were empty, and not even the hurried-up sentencing of Saddam Hussein to be hanged by the neck until dead could refill them. The accountability moment had arrived at last.

Americans have had enough, and their disgust with the administration and its congressional enablers turned out to be so powerful that even the battered, rusty, sound-bit, TV-spotted, Diebolded old seismograph of an American midterm election was able to register it. Thanks to the computer-aided gerrymandering that is the only truly modern feature of our electoral machinery, the number of seats that changed hands was not particularly high by historical standards. Voters—actual people—are a truer measure of the swing's magnitude. In 2000, the last time this year's thirty-three Senate seats were up for grabs, the popular-vote totals in those races, like the popular-vote totals for president, were essentially a tie. Democrats got forty-eight percent of the vote, Republicans slightly more than forty-seven percent. This time, in those same thirty-three states, Democrats got fifty-five percent of the vote, Republicans not quite forty-three percent. In raw numbers, the national Democratic plurality in the 2000 senatorial races was the same as Al Gore's: around half a million. This time, despite the inevitably smaller off-year turnout and the fact that there were Senate races in only two-thirds of the states, it was more than seven million.

This election was a crushing rebuke to Bush and his party. The rest is interpretation. Nearly everyone agreed that public anger about the Iraq catastrophe was paramount. To the surprise of much of the political class, exit polls suggested that corruption was almost as formidable a factor, especially among independents and disaffected Republicans. On the right, some commentators complained that the G.O.P.'s problem was that it hadn't been conservative enough: too much spending, too much nation-building, too much foot-dragging on abortion and the like. Others took comfort in the hypothesis that, because a number of Tuesday's new faces are Democrats of a (relatively) conservative stripe, the election was actually a victory for the ideology, if not the party, of George W. Bush. In a blog post titled "All's Well on the Conservative Front," Lawrence Kudlow, of *National Review,* pointed to the "conservative Blue Dog Dems who won a whole bunch of seats" as proof that "Republicans may have lost—but the conservative ascendancy is still alive and well."

Maybe. Or maybe those Blue Dogs won't hunt. In truth, the great majority of Capitol Hill's new Democrats will be what used to be called liberals, and in every case Tuesday's Republican losers were more conservative than the Democrats who beat them. Moreover, the fate of ballot initiatives around the country suggests that, on balance, the conservative tide may be ebbing. In six states, mostly out West, proposals to raise the minimum wage won easily. Yes, seven ballot measures banning same-sex marriage passed, albeit by smaller margins than has been the pattern; but one, in Arizona, was defeated—the first time that has happened anywhere. Missourians voted to support embryonic stem cell research. Californians and Oregonians rejected proposals to require parental notification for young women seeking abortions, and the voters of South Dakota overturned a law, passed by the state legislature and signed by the governor eight months ago, that forbade abortion, including in cases of rape or incest, except when absolutely necessary to save the mother's life. Rick Santorum, the Senate's most energetic social conservative, went down to overwhelming defeat—man on dog won't hunt, either, apparently.

A more persuasive analysis than the all's-well theory holds that Tuesday's debacle reveals the limitations of the "mobilize the base" strategy, which Karl Rove devised on behalf of his boss, and which has required the Republican Party to entrust itself entirely to a hard core of taxophobes, Christianists, and dittoheads. Rove's strategy, this analysis suggests, seemed to work only in 2000 (when Bush came in second at the ballot box) and in 2002 and 2004 (when its weaknesses were masked by fear of terrorism). Traditionally, America's two big political parties have been loose coalitions, one center-left and one center-right. Rove transformed the Republicans into something resembling a European-style parliamentary party of the right, politically disciplined and ideologically uniform. This year, in response, many on the center-right acted like Europeans, too: they voted not the man (or woman) but the party (Democratic). That sealed the fate of Rhode Island's popular senator Lincoln Chafee, among other remnants of moderate Republicanism. For the center part of the center-right, there was nowhere to go except to the center part of the center-left.

The day after the election, at a press conference in the East Room of the White House, the curtain rose on Act III of *Oedipus Bush*. On one level, the current President Bush was all crisp decisiveness as he announced the replacement of his secretary of defense, Donald Rumsfeld, with Robert Gates, a former C.I.A. director and the president of Texas A. & M. University. Below the surface, but only a little below, something altogether more unsettling was going on. Rumsfeld was one of the first President Bush's least favorite people; Gates is one of his most trusted confidants. He is also an active member of the Iraq Study Group, which is headed by another of the father's intimates, James Baker. The group's report, expected in the New Year, will offer the outlines of a different course in Iraq—an offer the president may be unable to refuse. At the Pentagon, Rumsfeld yields to Gates; in the Oval Office, adolescent rebellion gives way to sullen acquiescence.

Bush said some of the right things at his press conference, but he chose his words carelessly. He congratulated the "Democrat leaders" and promised bipartisanship—a goal he is unlikely to advance by referring to his hoped-for new partners by a name calculated solely to annoy them. Impressions are inherently subjective, of course; but he looked like a man who at that moment would much prefer to be commissioner of baseball, the job he longed for in 1993, before falling back on running for governor of Texas. It has been obvious for some time that, as president of the United States, George W. Bush is in very far over his head. He does not know how to use power wisely. He will now have a Democratic Congress to restrain him, and, perhaps, to protect him—and us—from his unfettered impulses. This may not be the Thanksgiving he was looking forward to, but the rest of us have reason to be grateful.

IT'S HIS BIPARTY

November 24, 2006

According to the "Backwards Bush" countdown clock, available on the Web and in keychain and desk-accessory form at selected novelty and toy stores around the nation, the sitting administration in Washington will, as of this writing, be in office for another seven hundred and eighty-nine days, five hours, twenty-three minutes, and 36.2 seconds. But, if present trends continue, it's going to feel like forever. On November 8, the day after the midterm election, President Bush vowed to "find common ground," "work with the new Congress in a bipartisan way," and "overcome the temptation to divide this country between red and blue." By way of launching "a new era of cooperation," he announced a personnel change: Donald Rumsfeld was out as secretary of defense, to be replaced by Robert Gates, widely viewed as a member of the reality-based community. A day later, on November 9, Bush had Nancy Pelosi, the incoming Speaker of the House, over for a nice lunch and an Oval Office photo op. "We've had a—I would call it a very constructive and very friendly conversation," the president said, graciously. "We both extended the hand of friendship," the Speaker-designate replied, graciously. "Thank you all," the president concluded. Graciously.

While they were having lunch, the White House Press Office dropped the news that the nomination of John R. Bolton "to be the Representative of the United States of America to the United Nations, with the rank and status of Ambassador Extraordinary and Plenipotentiary," had been resubmitted to the Senate. The new era of cooperation may or may not be definitively dead, but at the moment it appears to have been not so much an era as a news cycle.

The first time that John R. Bolton's name was sent up to Capitol Hill, in March of last year, the nomination got nowhere, even though the Senate was in Republican hands. The administration waited till Congress adjourned and then gave him a recess appointment, which will expire in January. Bolton is by all accounts a clever and energetic fellow, but cleverness is not competence, and energy can amplify vice as readily as virtue. At the U.N., Bolton has earned a reputation—in the not very diplomatic words of sixty-four former American ambassadors and diplomats who recently signed a letter opposing him—for "egotistical intolerance," "arrogant actions," and a "hard-core, go-it-alone posture" that "has alienated the bulk of the diplomatic community and cost the United States its leadership role." ("With so much at stake, our country cannot afford to permit John Bolton to continue his destructive course during the next two years," the diplomats wrote.) "He has succeeded in putting almost everyone's backs up, even among some of America's closest allies," last week's issue of the *Economist* quotes a "senior Western diplomat" as saying. To put it another way, the man's resemblance to Yosemite Sam does not end with the mustache.

There is little chance that the lame-duck Senate will confirm Bolton and no chance that the new one will. So the administration is toying with the idea of giving him another recess appointment (which would enable him to keep the job without drawing the salary) or naming him to a deputy position without filling the top spot (which would enable him to stay on as "acting" ambassador without the extraordinary and plenipotentiary title). Nor is the renomination of Bolton the only personnel-related sign that Bush's commitment to comity may have already peaked. On November 14, the president renominated Kenneth Y. Tomlinson, a former editor in chief of *Reader's Digest* and a close friend of Karl Rove, to be chairman of the Broadcasting Board of Governors, which supervises the Voice of America and other government radio and television operations aimed at overseas audiences. Never mind that last summer the State Department's inspector general found that, among other antics, Tomlinson used his office to support a "horse racing operation" (he owns thoroughbreds), or that a year ago he had to resign from the board of the Corporation for Public Broadcasting after *that* agency's inspector general caught him violating rules meant to protect public broadcasting from political meddling. On November 15, the president renominated four of his hardest-right candidates for the federal courts of appeals: a Defense Department lawyer who has been denounced by a score of retired generals and admirals for his role as an architect of the administration's infamous interrogation regime; a former Interior Department attorney and mining and ranching lobbyist who sees the Clean Water Act as "regulatory excess"; a district court judge whose decisions have been reversed or vacated more than a hundred and fifty times, an astounding record that includes two reversals from the Supreme Court—one of them in a unanimous opinion written by Justice Clarence Thomas—in voting rights cases; and a former aide to Senator Trent Lott who is the first federal appeals court nominee in a quarter of a century to be unanimously rated "not qualified" by the American Bar Association.

Finally (or maybe not so finally), on November 16, Bush appointed one Eric Keroack to be the new chief of "population affairs" at the Department of Health and Human Services. In this post, Dr. Keroack, a gynecologist, will oversee what is called Title X, a Nixon-era program that distributes contraceptives to poor or uninsured women. Until recently, he was the medical director of a Christianist pregnancy-counselling organization that regards the distribution of contraceptives as "demeaning to women." One of his odder theories makes him a sort of family-friendly version of General Jack D. Ripper. In Keroack's case, the precious bodily fluid of concern is the hormone oxytocin, a.k.a. "God's Super Glue." Apparently, oxytocin is released during certain enjoyable activities, including hugging, massage, and, of course, sex. It is also, according to Keroack, the fluid that keeps married couples bound to each other. Therefore, if a young woman squanders her supply on too much fooling around, she can forget about ever becoming a committed wife. Keroack's appointment, unlike the others, does not, alas, require Senate confirmation.

Perhaps what we are seeing is one last White House attempt to reenergize the legendary "base," after which the new era of cooperation will resume. Or perhaps the president has simply reverted to type. Last week, he found himself in Vietnam, where the United States once fought a big, bloody, disastrous war of choice. In Hanoi, which under its nominally Communist rulers is more vibrantly capitalist than Ho Chi Minh City ever was when it was called Saigon, he was asked if the American experience in Vietnam offered any guidance about Iraq. "One lesson is that we tend to want there to be instant success in the world, and the task in Iraq is going to take a while," he replied, and added, "We'll succeed unless we quit." What did he mean? That the peaceable, bustling, unthreatening (if unfree) Vietnam of today represents an American success, made possible by the fact that we didn't quit until fifty-eight thousand Americans and three million Vietnamese were dead? Or that it represents an American failure, which would have been averted by another decade of war, another fifty-eight thousand, another three million? Who knows? And who knows, really, what this president has been taught by this month's election? The present President Bush, after all, is a decider of decisions, not a learner of lessons. And he likes to decide that he was right all along.

DESOLATION ROWS

January 5, 2007

The hanging of Saddam Hussein was meant to be, by the depraved standards of the Iraq war, something of a feel-good moment. President Bush saw it that way, or claimed to. A statement issued in his name stressed that Saddam's execution had been made possible by "the Iraqi people's determination to create a society governed by the rule of law." The deposed dictator's dangling, the president said, "is an important milestone on Iraq's course to becoming a democracy. . . . We are reminded today of how far the Iraqi people have come since the end of Saddam Hussein's rule."

Compared to many of the other horrors that have served as milestones along the four-year journey from shock and awe through stay the course to surge and pray, what happened at 6:10 A.M. on December 30 in that dank, foul-smelling execution chamber was relatively free of bloodshed. Only one person was killed, and he was anything but an innocent civilian. Yet in many quarters—here, in Iraq, and around the world—there has been a conspicuous failure to feel good.

It did not take long for the hanging to become a metaphor for the overall disaster of which it is part. Although the deed was done in a rush, under conditions of dubious legality, and with little regard for its aftermath, initial reports suggested that it had at least been done with appropriate solemnity, and that the condemned man had gone to his death meekly, as if acknowledging, even repenting, his crimes. According to the first dispatch posted online by the *Times*, "Those in the room said that Mr. Hussein was dressed entirely in black and carrying a Koran and that he was compliant as the noose was draped around his neck." One witness was quoted as saying, "He just gave up. We were astonished. It was strange. He just gave up."

Mission accomplished, you might say. But as the details trickled out—first via officially provided videotape, silent and redacted; then via cell phone camera samizdat, jerky and noisy; finally via fuller eyewitness accounts—a truer picture emerged. The hangmen's black ski masks, the jeers, the jostling in the dark, the shouts of "God damn you," the chanted prayer cut short by the sudden *chunk-chunk* of the trapdoor and the violent interruption of the prisoner's free fall, the display of the glassy-eyed corpse—the brutal spectacle bore an irresistible resemblance to a video from some terrorist Web site. The sectarian subtext compounded the catastrophe. "Moktada! Moktada! Moktada!" guards chanted—Moktada being Moktada al-Sadr, the militant cleric whose Shiite militia is responsible for the wholesale murder and torture of Sunnis and whose support is vital to the political survival of Iraq's nominal government. Saddam's tormentors gave him an unexpected, undeserved gift. Their taunts chased away his fear and awakened his contempt. "Moktada?" he shot back. "Is this how real men behave?" A few seconds later, the trap sprang. The ex-tyrant died with a curse on his lips and a sneer on his face, a plausible candidate for warrior-martyr mythmaking.

Within the limits of its reach, Saddam's regime was as murderous and fearsome as all but a handful of the modern era's many dictatorships: not quite on the level of Hitler's or Stalin's, but far worse than the likes of Pinochet's or Ceausescu's. No trial was required to prove

Saddam's guilt; no punishment could be commensurate to his offenses. The aims of any proceedings against him were not forensic or punitive but educational and, in the highest sense, political. The best venue would have been an international court, like the one that prosecuted Slobodan Milosevic; but the Bush administration's disdain for such institutions was nearly a match for Saddam's own. A trial or trials under Iraqi auspices had, or should have had, several purposes: to bolster the legitimacy of the fledgling government; to demonstrate the impartiality of its justice system; to promote national reconciliation; to act as an inquest into the full scope and range of the dictatorship's crimes, and to draw a line under its methods; to deny impunity to the dictator himself. Only the last of these purposes was served. The others have actually been damaged, especially reconciliation. Saddam, a Sunni, had been convicted only of the deaths of a hundred and forty-eight Shiite men and boys. His trial in the genocidal killings of a hundred thousand Kurds was still in progress. His execution—which snuffed out any light he might, over time, have cast on the dark history of his rule—was timed, as if in deliberate insult, for the first day of the Sunni celebration of the Muslim holiday of Eid al-Adha; the Shiites' Eid al-Adha began a day later. And the severity and the ugliness of that execution, as well as its tincture of sectarian hatred, betrayed a sad continuity with the ways of the regime whose leader went to the gallows.

The hanging raises the same question as the war: was the problem the thing itself, or merely that the thing was botched? By Thursday, even Bush was showing signs of recognition that Saddam's execution had not been a wholly positive development. "I wish, obviously, that the proceedings had been done in a more dignified way," he told reporters. But it is legitimate to doubt—in fact, it is grotesque to suggest—that hanging (or beheading, stoning, shooting, electrocution, or lethal injection, the other methods currently in use in the countries, most of them unfree, that still practice capital punishment) can possibly be done in a "dignified way." On page 1 of last Wednesday's

Times, the lead story, in the right-hand column, concerned the Iraqi government's ordering an investigation into "the abusive behavior at the execution of Saddam Hussein." Across the page, the second lead was headlined "PANEL SEEKS END TO DEATH PENALTY FOR NEW JERSEY." It reported a legislative commission's findings that there is no good evidence that capital punishment serves any legitimate purpose and much evidence that it "is inconsistent with evolving standards of decency."

The death penalty remains lawful in thirty-eight states. Though its application has been suspended in ten of them, including, last month, Florida and California, none have abolished it in the thirty years since the Supreme Court reinstated it. Slightly more than three thousand people are locked in the death rows of the United States—a pungent number, given the tolls of 9/11 and of American forces in Iraq. And the fate of those who die strapped to our gurneys and electric chairs is crueller than Saddam Hussein's. He was hanged fifty-five days after he was sentenced, and the elapsed time between his transfer to Iraqi custody and his execution was forty minutes. In our country, the pattern is to be condemned in youth and executed in middle age. A person is sentenced, in effect, to an indefinite period of imprisonment—an average of between ten and twelve years, but often much longer—in conditions of constant anxiety and isolation, after which, at a year and date and time unknown, he is taken from his cell and burned or poisoned to death. California's first judicial killing of 2006 disposed of a man who had been on death row for twenty-three years. Seventy-six years old, legally blind from diabetes, suffering from heart disease, he made the journey to the death chamber in a wheelchair. It is an irony, and not a nice one, that this uniquely American brand of sadism is a result of the obstacles that our justice system rightly demands be overcome before an execution can take place.

Some have charged that those who objected to Saddam's hanging thereby minimized his crimes. But if Saddam's guilt were to be the measure of his punishment he would have to have been tortured to death—and even then the retribution would have been inadequate. Capital punishment's worst affront is not to the dignity and humanity of the condemned. It is to the dignity and humanity of the polity that decrees it.

WEBBCAST

January 26, 2007

For more than forty years, it has been the custom for the president's State of the Union address to be followed by a formal televised response. In 1966, the leaders of the Republican minority in Congress, the florid Senator Everett Dirksen and the stolid Representative Gerald Ford, appointed themselves to deliver the first of these, after one of Lyndon Johnson's lordly extravaganzas. The Ev and Jerry Show, though charming in a ramshackle way, was less than a monster hit, and nearly all the subsequent post-SOTU presentations have likewise been little noted nor long remembered. Senator Bob Dole, with characteristic bleak wit, evaluated his response to President Clinton's 1996 address thusly: "I gave a fireside chat the other night, and the fire went out." It was different this time. This time the fire was on, and it was the rebuttal that had something truthful to say about the state of the union.

James Webb is a writer, the highly acclaimed author of six densely textured novels of men in battle. As of last Tuesday evening he had been a United States senator for all of twenty days. He was an unusual choice to deliver the Democrats' reply to President Bush's address, and, as it turned out, a canny one. Normally, the replier speeds through a miniature of the traditional SOTU laundry list, administering quick shoulder massages to as many interest groups as possible. Webb, pugnacious of temperament, chose instead to use his nine minutes to speak of "two areas where our respective parties have largely stood in contradiction." The first was the ballooning of economic inequality at home. The second was Iraq, where, he said,

> this country has patiently endured a mismanaged war for nearly four years. Many, including myself, warned even before the war began that it was unnecessary, that it would take our energy and attention away from the larger war against terrorism, and that invading and occupying Iraq would leave us strategically vulnerable in the most violent and turbulent corner of the world.

Webb was able to speak bluntly ("The president took us into this war recklessly") not only because he writes that way but also on account of a Kevlar résumé. In addition to having served—in the Reagan administration, no less—as secretary of the Navy, he is a decorated Marine combat veteran of the Vietnam War. So is his brother. His father flew B-29s during the Second World War. His son is a marine, too, now serving in Iraq. Mentioning that history, Webb noted that he and his kin, like many other soldiers,

> trusted the judgment of our national leaders. . . . We owed them our loyalty, as Americans, and we gave it. But they owed us sound judgment, clear thinking, concern for our welfare, a guarantee that the threat to our country was equal to the price we might be called upon to pay in defending it.

None of that, he made plain, has been forthcoming from the present administration.

As for Bush's speech, its principal merit was that it provided a pretext for Webb's. The president began with some graceful words for Nancy Pelosi, the new (and first female) Speaker of the House, and then spoiled the effect with a reflexive slur: "I congratulate the Democrat majority." ("Democratic majority" were the words on his teleprompter, but he apparently couldn't help himself.) Still, he went easy on the social-issue red meat: no stem cells this time, no abortion, no gay marriage. Instead, he served up a thin menu of, so to speak, Democrat veggies: rhetorical recognition that health care, education, and energy are problems, with a side dish of timid proposals, mostly drawn from the conservative think-tank cookbook, that the new Congress is sure to send back to the kitchen. What had been heralded in advance as a dramatic breakthrough on global warming turned out to be a half-sentence assurance that "technologies" would "help us to confront the serious challenge of global climate change." He concluded with the traditional (since Reagan) introduction of model citizens up in the gallery, including Julie Aigner-Clark, the founder (with her husband, a generous donor to Republican campaigns) of the Baby Einstein Company. The president did not explain how Aigner-Clark, whose business sells "developmental" videos for infants, which the American Academy of Pediatrics has dismissed as at best valueless, exemplifies what he called "the heroic kindness, courage, and self-sacrifice of the American people." Maybe it was just another Bush SOTU puzzler, like last year's warning against "human-animal hybrids." (To be fair, America remains proudly centaur-free.)

Between the veggies and Baby Einstein fell the shadow: Iraq. The president pointed to his "new strategy," begged Congress and the country "to give it a chance to work," and added, "Whatever you voted for, you did not vote for failure."

True, but not true enough. Last November, the voters didn't endorse failure—they simply acknowledged it. And they certainly didn't vote for escalation, which is what Bush is giving them. With this address, in conjunction with his January 10 "new way forward" speech, the president has taken full ownership of the Iraq war. Four years ago, many were complicit to one degree or another in the decision to invade, including a bipartisan majority in Congress and the governments of

Britain and other members of the "coalition." That is no longer so. The generals on the scene, who resisted Bush's "surge," have been removed. The Senate is on the point of passing a resolution of disapproval. The coalition is crumbling, and its British component is likely to ratchet itself down once Tony Blair leaves office. Senator John McCain, who a month ago passionately warned against a surge of fewer than thirty thousand troops, now supports a surge of twenty thousand—largely because, he says, the new American commander in Iraq, David Petraeus, thinks it has a chance of working. But Petraeus conceded, in testimony last Tuesday before the Senate Armed Services Committee, that the new troop levels fall short of his own previous estimate of what would be necessary. Soldiers follow orders, and General Petraeus has his.

In a Saturday radio talk before the State of the Union address, the president said, "Those who refuse to give this plan a chance to work have an obligation to offer an alternative that has a better chance for success." The day after the address, Vice President Cheney—in an instantly notorious CNN interview in which he dismissed talk of blunders as "hogwash"—said, "The critics have not suggested a policy." *That* is hogwash. The Senate Foreign Relations Committee is in its fourth week of hearing such suggestions. The Iraq Study Group has a plan. Senator Joseph Biden and Leslie Gelb have a plan. The Center for American Progress has a plan. But what all their plans have in common is that they recognize that what remains is the search for the least bad of a bad bunch of options. Implicitly, they recognize that Bush's policy—and, therefore, Bush—is a failure. And so, rather than looking for a policy that might be within our means and might mitigate the disaster, Bush is betting all his chips—all our chips—on the only choice that allows him the fantasy that in the end people will say: Bush was right. He is sending twenty thousand because twenty thousand is all he has. Next to nothing in the way of ground forces remains for other contingencies. His presidency and his "legacy" are in ruins anyway, so he imagines he has nothing to lose. If only that were true of the rest of us.

TOO MANY CHIEFS

February 9, 2007

According to some of the calendars and appointment books float-
ing around this office, Monday, February 19, is Presidents'
Day. Others say it's President's Day. Still others opt for Presidents Day.
Which is it? The bouncing apostrophe bespeaks a certain uncertainty.
President's Day suggests that only one holder of the nation's supreme
magistracy is being commemorated—presumably the first. Presidents'
Day hints at more than one, most likely the Sage of Mount Vernon
plus Abraham Lincoln, generally agreed to be the greatest of them all.
And Presidents Day, apostropheless, implies a promiscuous celebration
of all forty-two—Jefferson but also Pierce, F.D.R. but also Buchanan,
Truman but also Harding. To say nothing of the incumbent, of whom,
perhaps, the less said the better.

So which is it? Trick question. The answer, strictly speaking, is none
of the above. Ever since 1968, when, in one of the last gasps of Great
Society reformism, holidays were rejiggered to create more three-day
weekends, federal law has decreed the third Monday in February to
be Washington's Birthday. And Presidents'/'s/s Day? According to
Prologue, the magazine of the National Archives, it was a local department store promotion that went national when retailers discovered that,

mysteriously, generic presidents clear more inventory than particular ones, even the Father of His Country. Now everybody thinks it's official, but it's not. (Note to Fox News: could be a War on Washington's Birthday angle here, similar to the War on Christmas.)

Just to add to the presidential confusion, Washington's Birthday is not Washington's birthday. George Washington was born either on February 11, 1731 (according to the old-style Julian calendar, still in use at the time), or on February 22, 1732 (according to the Gregorian calendar, adopted in 1752 throughout the British Empire). Under no circumstances, therefore, can Washington's birthday fall on Washington's Birthday, a.k.a. Presidents Day, which, being the third Monday of the month, can occur only between the fifteenth and the twenty-first. Lincoln's birthday, February 12, doesn't make it through the Presidents Day window, either. Nor do the natal days of our other two February presidents, William Henry Harrison (born on the sixth) and Ronald Reagan (the ninth). A fine mess!

Here is the question thus raised: at this chastening juncture in our republic's history, wouldn't everyone welcome a moratorium on presidential glorification? Isn't the United States a little too president-ridden, much as post-medieval Spain was a little too priest-ridden? Our capital city groans under the weight of obelisks, equestrian statues, and grandiose temples fit for the gods but devoted to the winners of presidential elections. "Presidential historians" populate the greenrooms of our cable news networks. Presidential suites sit atop Vegas hotels. Presidential libraries gobble up ever-growing swathes of urban and, as the unhappy faculty of Southern Methodist University recently learned, campus real estate. Time to throttle down.

A good place to start, after securing the retailers' and calendar-makers' agreement to call Washington's Birthday by its true name (if not its true date), would be with the most sacred object our society mass-produces: money. At the moment, of the seven denominations of banknotes in general circulation, no fewer than five have presidents on them, ranging chronologically from Washington (who would have frowned on the honor, as smacking of monarchy) to Grant (who would have appreciated the irony, given that he was habitually broke and presided over an administration rife with financial scandals). The two others are the ten-spot (Alexander Hamilton, who might have been president if he hadn't been a duellist) and the hundred (Benjamin Franklin). On the coins, it's pretty much presidents all the way, except for Susan B. Anthony and Sacagawea, who are on dollar coins that barely circulate and are obvious affirmative-action benchwarmers, destined for the hook once a female president or two comes along, or even sooner. Beginning this year, the Mint plans to roll out new circulating dollar coins, four different ones a year, for as many years as it takes. Who will be on them? Why, presidents, of course—all of them, in the order they served, scoundrels and heroes alike. Someday, like a bad penny, a George W. Bush dollar will turn up. Heads you lose.

As it happens, a federal district court has ordered the Treasury to redesign our paper money to make it friendlier to blind people. Why not take the opportunity to go further than changing sizes or adding texture? Franklin shows the way. Yes, he was a politician, but he was equally or more famous as a scientist, a diplomat, a newspaperman, an aphorist, a satirist, and a boulevardier. Let's keep Washington on the single, and then let's start printing bills with pictures of the other sorts of people that make us proud to be Americans. With rotating portraits, we can have a musicians' fin (Foster, Gershwin, Ellington), a scribblers' sawbuck (Twain, Melville, Dickinson), a performing-arts twenty (Marian Anderson, Keaton, Balanchine), a secular saints' fifty (Douglass, Jane Addams, King), and a scientists' C-note (Franklin, Edison, Einstein). As a three-fer (president, saint, writer), Lincoln could have the two-dollar note all to himself. A three-spot could be introduced, with Whitman ("What you give me I cheerfully accept, / A little sustenance, a hut and garden, a little money, as I rendezvous with my poems"). As with presidents, a decent interval would be required. The Dylan fiver will have to be deferred until another decade of the sixties rolls around.

One can dream. Meanwhile, if you think you're sick of presidents, wait till you see the parade of presidents-in-waiting. Wait? You don't have to wait. Decision 2008 is already upon us, full-bore. A generation or two ago, political scientists used to complain that American campaigns dragged on for eight or nine months, in contrast to the three to six weeks that is normal elsewhere. Those were the days. As of last week, ten Republicans and nine Democrats, all of them plausible enough to claim a place in televised debates, have either filed formal exploratory committees or declared their candidacies outright, and another half-dozen or so are on the verge. The first such debate is ten weeks from now—even though the first primary is nearly a year away, the conventions don't convene for a year and a half, and the election itself is twenty-one long months down the road. Unsurprisingly, as the *Washington Post* reported last week, 2008 is fated to be "the nation's first billion-dollar presidential campaign." No doubt "the issues" will get a full airing, but, more than ever, it's going to be all about the Benjamins, and not just who gets his picture on them.

THE DARKSIDER

June 29, 2007

t took thirty years for *Frost/Nixon* to reach Broadway. Assuming that civilization survives and the Great White Way remains above water, we can expect *Cheney/Bush* to mount the boards sometime in the late twenty-thirties or early twenty-forties. The playwright and the actors, whoever they are, will have plenty to work with. The story of the scowling, scheming, domineering, silently sinister vice president and the spoiled, petted prince who becomes his plaything is irresistible—set in a pristine White House, played against an ominous, unseen background of violence and catastrophe, like distant thunder, and packed with drama, palace intrigue, and black comedy.

A thick sheaf of new material has lately been added to the Cheney folder. For four days last week, the front page of the *Washington Post* was dominated by a remarkable series of articles slugged "ANGLER: THE CHENEY VICE PRESIDENCY." ("Angler," Cheney's metaphorically apt Secret Service code name, refers to one of his two favorite outdoor pastimes, the one less hazardous to elderly lawyers.) The series, by Barton Gellman and Jo Becker, occupied sixteen broadsheet pages and topped out at twenty thousand words. The headline over last Monday's installment encapsulates the burden of the whole: "The Unseen Path to Cruelty."

Some of the *Post*'s findings have been foreshadowed elsewhere, notably in Jane Mayer's dispatches in the *New Yorker*. But many of the details and incidents that Gellman and Becker document are as new as they are appalling. More important, the pattern that emerges from the accumulated weight of the reporting is, as the lawyers say, dispositive.

Given the ontological authority that the *Post* shares only with the *New York Times*, it is now, so to speak, official: for the past six years, Dick Cheney, the occupant of what John Adams called "the most insignificant office that ever the invention of man contrived," has been the most influential public official in the country, not necessarily excluding President Bush, and his influence has been entirely malign. He is pathologically (but purposefully) secretive; treacherous toward colleagues; coldly manipulative of the callow, lazy, and ignorant president he serves; contemptuous of public opinion; and dismissive not only of international law (a fairly standard attitude for conservatives of his stripe) but also of the very idea that the Constitution and laws of the United States, including laws signed by his nominal superior, can be construed to limit the power of the executive to take any action that can plausibly be classified as part of an endless, endlessly expandable "war on terror."

More than anyone else, including his mentor and departed co-conspirator, Donald Rumsfeld, Cheney has been the intellectual author and bureaucratic facilitator of the crimes and misdemeanors that have inflicted unprecedented disgrace on our country's moral and political standing: the casual trashing of habeas corpus and the Geneva Conventions; the claim of authority to seize suspects, including American citizens, and imprison them indefinitely and incommunicado, with no right to due process of law; the outright encouragement of "cruel," "inhuman," and "degrading" treatment of prisoners; the use of undoubted torture, including waterboarding (Cheney: "a no-brainer for me"), which for a century the United States had prosecuted as a war crime; and, of course, the bloody, nightmarish Iraq war itself, launched under false pretenses, conducted with stupefying incompetence, and escalated long after public support for it had evaporated, at the cost of scores of thousands of lives, nearly half a trillion dollars, and the crippling of America's armed forces, which no longer overawe and will take years to rebuild.

The stakes are lower in domestic affairs—if only because fewer lives are directly threatened—but here, too, Cheney's influence has been invariably baleful. With an avalanche of examples, Gellman and Becker show how Cheney successfully pushed tax cuts for the very rich that went beyond what even the president, wanly clinging to the shards of "compassionate conservatism," and his economic advisers wanted. They show how Cheney's stealthy domination of regulatory and environmental policy, driven by "unwavering ideological positions" and always exerted "for the benefit of business," has resulted in the deterioration of air and water quality, the degradation and commercial exploitation of national parks and forests, the collapse of wild salmon fisheries, and the curt abandonment of Bush's 2000 campaign pledge to do something about greenhouse gases. They also reveal that it was Cheney who forced Christine Todd Whitman to resign as the Environmental Protection Agency's administrator, by dictating a rule that excused refurbished power plants and oil refineries from installing modern pollution controls. "I just couldn't sign it," she told them. Turns out she wasn't so anxious to spend more time with her family after all.

Cheney, Gellman and Becker report, drew up and vetted a list of five appellate judges from which Bush drew his Supreme Court appointments. After naming John Roberts to the Court and then to the chief justice's chair, the president, for once, rebelled: without getting permission from down the hall, he nominated his old retainer Harriet Miers for the second opening. ("Didn't have the nerve to tell me himself," Cheney muttered to an associate, according to the *Post*.) But when Cheney's right-wing allies upended Miers, Bush obediently went back to Cheney's list and picked Samuel Alito. The result is a Court majority that, last Thursday, ruled that conscious racial integration is the moral equivalent of conscious racial segregation.

That unfortunate day among the quail wasn't the only time the vice president has seemed more Elmer Fudd than Ernst Blofeld; last week, Cheney provoked widespread hilarity by pleading executive privilege (in order to deny one set of documents to the Senate Judiciary Committee) while simultaneously maintaining that his office is not part of the executive branch (in order to deny another set to the Information Security Oversight Office of the National Archives). On Cheney's organization chart, it seems, the location of the Office of the Vice President is undisclosed. So are the powers that, in a kind of rolling, slow-motion coup d'état, he has gathered unto himself. The laughter will fade quickly; the current administration, regrettably, will not. However more politically moribund it may become, its writ still has a year and a half to go. A few weeks ago, on an aircraft carrier in the Persian Gulf, the vice president issued threats of war with Iran. A "senior American diplomat" told the *Times* that Cheney's speech had not been circulated broadly in the government before it was delivered, adding, "He kind of runs by his own rules." But, too often, his rules rule. The awful climax of *Cheney/Bush* may be yet to come.

PART TWO

THE MARATHON

SPARRING PARTNERS

August 10, 2007

What might be called the Long Campaign has created a demand for news of political conflict, and that demand is being duly supplied. At this preposterously early date in the 2004 election cycle, the candidates for the Democratic presidential nomination had participated in exactly one "debate," as, for lack of a better word, these overpopulated, overmoderated, your-time-is-up Q & A panels are called. Two cycles ago it was zero debates. This time around, it's—already!—eight.

The political arena is ideally a marketplace of ideas, but in our country, more often than not, it's all marketplace and no ideas. Caveat emptor, Democrats. The market pressures in this particular souk almost all push in one direction: making political mountains out of policy molehills.

A case in point is the quarrel, nominally about foreign policy, that the two leading Democratic hopefuls have been carrying on for the past few weeks. It began during the YouTube/CNN extravaganza. A video questioner, citing Anwar Sadat's visit to Israel, asked, "In the spirit of that type of bold leadership, would you be willing to meet separately, without precondition, during the first year of your administration, in

Washington or anywhere else, with the leaders of Iran, Syria, Venezuela, Cuba, and North Korea, in order to bridge the gap that divides our countries?"

Senator Barack Obama, called upon to answer first, said, "I would. And the reason is this: that the notion that somehow not talking to countries is punishment to them, which has been the guiding diplomatic principle of this administration, is ridiculous." After noting that Cold War presidents regularly spoke to Soviet leaders, evil empire and all, he went on, "One of the first things that I would do in terms of moving a diplomatic effort in the region forward is to send a signal that we need to talk to Iran and Syria, because they're going to have responsibilities if Iraq collapses."

Senator Hillary Clinton, who was next up, spotted a chink in Obama's armor and went for it:

> Well, I will not promise to meet with the leaders of these countries during my first year. I *will* promise a very vigorous diplomatic effort. Because I think it is not that you promise a meeting at that high a level before you know what the intentions are. . . . I will use a lot of high-level presidential envoys to test the waters, to feel the way. But certainly we're not going to just have our president meet with Fidel Castro and Hugo Chávez and, you know, the presidents of North Korea, Iran, and Syria until we know better what the way forward would be.

The commentariat, from David Brooks, of the *Times*, to the *Nation*'s David Corn, scored this exchange as a stumble for Obama, a palpable hit for Clinton. Over the next few days, things got huffier. Obama's remarks were "irresponsible and, frankly, naïve," Clinton said. Obama, aiming at Clinton's greatest vulnerability with the Democratic base, shot back, "I think what is irresponsible and naïve is to have authorized a war without asking how we were going to get out." A day later, he swung a left hook: "I don't want Bush-Cheney lite." Clinton's parry: "This is getting kind of silly. I've been called a lot of things in my life, but I've never been called George Bush or Dick Cheney. . . . I don't want to see the power and prestige of the United States president put at risk by rushing into meetings with the likes of Chávez, and Castro, and Ahmadinejad."

It was left to another Clinton, former president Bill, to try to calm things down a bit. "I don't want to get in the middle of that whole spat Hillary and Senator Obama had, but there's more than one way to practice diplomacy," he told a gathering of the Democratic Leadership Council. The point, he added, is that they had "a vigorous agreement on the big question, which is 'Should we have more diplomacy?' The answer is yes. Then you can parse their answers to the specific questions and decide who you think is right."

Very well, then, let's parse. Obama didn't commit to meeting with the quintet of villains; he expressed a willingness to do so, which is not the same thing. What he advocated was "send[ing] a signal that we need to talk to Iran and Syria," a signal Clinton has been sending, too. "Without precondition" does not mean without preparation. Nor is it inconsistent with waiting until one has a better idea of the probable outcome. It simply means being ready to sit down and negotiate even if no concessions have been made in advance. On the other hand, although Clinton voted to authorize force against Iraq, it's crystal clear that she would not have gone to war there had she been president. And "Bush-Cheney lite"? Them's fightin' words, and most unfair ones.

In truth, each candidate is exaggerating, even distorting, what the other is saying. Their squabble is mutually advantageous to the extent that it advances their respective (to use the buzzword of the moment) "narratives." Hers: the steady, experienced, disciplined, battle-tested veteran, aggressive and cautious in equal measure. His: the inspiring new face, unfettered by past mistakes and unafraid to defy "the conventional wisdom" and "Washington." She's showing she can deliver a punch; he's showing his jaw's not made of glass. She's pointing to his gaffe (and it was a gaffe, if only because it opened him to attack); he's proving that by holding his ground he can turn a sow's ear into, if not a silk purse, at least a nylon backpack.

Clinton—Bill, that is—is right. Substantively, there's much less disagreement here than meets the eye. The same is true of the subsidiary spats that followed. When Obama, in a speech on terrorism at the Wilson Center in Washington, said, "If we have actionable intelligence about high-value terrorist targets [in Pakistan] and President Musharraf won't act, we will," he came under attack not only from Hillary Clinton but also from Senators Joseph Biden and Christopher Dodd. It turned out, though, that their objection was not to what he said—which they agree with—but to the undiplomatic indiscretion of saying it out loud. Similarly, when Obama said he would not use nuclear weapons to attack terrorists, Senator Clinton tut-tutted him, saying, "I don't believe that any president should make any blanket statements with respect to the use or non-use of nuclear weapons. But I think we'll leave it at that, because I don't know the circumstances in which he was responding." Yet no one imagines that President Hillary Clinton would order a nuclear attack on a terrorist training camp in the wilds of Waziristan, even if bin Laden himself were in residence.

The circumstances, by the way, were these: A Capitol Hill reporter for the Associated Press, spotting Obama emerging from a breakfast with constituents, asked him a question. He answered, "I think it would be a profound mistake for us to use nuclear weapons in any circumstance"—he paused—"involving civilians." He paused again. "Let me scratch that," he added. "There's been no discussion of nuclear weapons. That's not on the table."

Let me scratch that, indeed. The sentence you are reading has been tweaked a half-dozen times. But in an age of omnipresent microphones, instant transcripts, cell phone videos, and merciless cable TV hosts, politicians have no such luxury. When they open their mouths, the first draft is the final. Off the cuff is engraved in granite. Between the two parties there are twenty-nine more debates and forums scheduled, all before the first primary. Start parsing.

●

GHOSTBUSTERS

September 21, 2007

A spectre is haunting the leading candidate for the Democratic presidential nomination. It was with her last week when she outlined her health-care proposal, and it was no wispy phantom. It was an apparition solid enough to attract the notice of political reporters inured to paranormal phenomena by long months on the campaign trail.

> DES MOINES, Sept. 17—Senator Hillary Rodham Clinton unveiled a plan on Monday to guarantee health insurance to all Americans, but in a way carefully designed to avoid the political flaws in her failed proposal of 1993-94.

That's how the *Times* led its Tuesday story from Iowa. But whether the collapse of the most ambitious domestic policy initiative of the (Bill) Clinton administration is a horrid fiend, red of eye and gnarled of hand, or more of a winsome Friendly Ghost, like Casper, depends on one's point of view. Senator Clinton, naturally, is of the Casper school. In her Des Moines speech, she said she had "learned some valuable lessons that have shaped how I approach health-care reform today." Her opponents for the nomination, naturally, would prefer that voters see her experience as something more apt to be repeated than learned from. "The cost of failure fourteen years ago isn't anybody's scars or political fortune," John Edwards said. "It's the millions of Americans who have now gone without health care for more than fourteen years." And Barack Obama said, "The real key to passing any health-care reform is the ability to bring people together in an open, transparent process that builds a broad consensus for change."

What this kind of (still relatively civilized) political jousting should not be allowed to obscure is that—within the Democratic Party, at least—a broad consensus for change has already emerged. Clinton's proposal comes nearly eight months after Edwards's and four months after Obama's, but all three are remarkably similar, and those of Edwards and Clinton nearly identical. She and her staff used the extra time to advantage: her program is the most expertly packaged and tidiest of the three, and manages to sound at once nonthreatening and far-reaching. If you like the health plan you've already got—and, gee, who doesn't?—you keep it. If you don't like it, or if you're uninsured, you can choose from the same menu of private plans offered to members of Congress. Or you can opt for a new public plan modelled on Medicare. You can't be blackballed or socked with unaffordable premiums on account of having a "preexisting condition." You can buy a gold-plated executive policy if you wish, but you'll have to pay the difference yourself, with post-tax dollars. Whatever you choose, you have to take it upon yourself to choose *something*—the "individual mandate" that policy wonks talk about. It's like having to get car insurance. Clinton estimates the cost of all this at a hundred and ten billion dollars a year—a third of the annual bill for Medicare. The bulk of it would come from letting the Bush tax cuts on incomes over a quarter of a million dollars expire on schedule.

There's a lot more detail, of course. And by the time the Clinton plan—or the Edwards plan or the Obama plan—got fed through the congressional wood chipper, it would probably make Rube Goldberg's craziest invention look like the Lever of Archimedes. But it would do two important things. First, it would end the disgrace of America's being the only advanced capitalist democracy on earth that does not guarantee health care to its citizens. Second, with any luck, it would create a slow-motion showdown between private and public health insurance. Given that private insurers spend around fifteen percent of their budgets on administration—much of it devoted to keeping the sick off the rolls and, failing that, figuring out ways to avoid paying their medical bills—while Medicare spends two percent, it ought to be an interesting and instructive contest.

The Clintons blew it last time, but they weren't the first to break their picks against the unyielding granite of the American political system. Every Democratic president since Truman has been elected on a platform of national health insurance, and, in spite of public support for the idea by majorities as big as those in Europe, every one of them has failed to get it enacted. In this country, elections are just the beginning. To get to the finish line, a big reform has to run a gantlet of three independently elected "governments"—not just the presidency but also the House and the Senate, all the members of which are elected independently of one another, too. Besides all this, the committees of Congress, where most business actually gets done, provide plenty of dark corners where determined, well-financed, well-organized special interests can make short work of an obvious but amorphous majority will.

We've been here before, but this time the stars may really be coming into alignment. Our health-care system has continued to deteriorate. We spend twice as much as the French and the Germans and two and a half times as much as the Brits, yet we die sooner and our babies die in greater numbers. Thirty-eight million Americans were uninsured in 2000; now it's forty-seven million. Employer-based health insurance is increasingly expensive, stingy, and iffy. Companies, especially manufacturing companies, are beginning to realize that being deputized to pay the health-care costs of their employees and retirees puts them at a competitive disadvantage in the global economy.

Whether change comes will depend entirely on the next election. If a Democrat wins the presidency after outlining his or her intentions as specifically as the leading contenders have done, and if the Democrats substantially increase their congressional majorities, then it will happen. If they don't, it won't.

"People have access to health care in America," President Bush remarked last summer, expressing the view of many conservative Republicans. "After all, you just go to an emergency room." And, last Thursday, for what he called "philosophical" reasons, he promised to veto an expansion of the State Children's Health Insurance Program, a modest federal effort to help states cover children from poor and near-poor families. The Republicans who hope to succeed him offer conservative think-tank homilies about the glories of the market. Last week, Mitt Romney denounced Clinton's proposal—and, by extension, those of Edwards and Obama (to say nothing of the plan which he himself negotiated with the Democratic legislature when he was governor of Massachusetts, and which contains most of the same elements)—as "a European-style socialized-medicine plan." That rhetorical zombie, though, isn't as scary as it used to be. Americans already have some experience with European-style socialized-medicine plans. The two most efficient, merciful, and politically unchallengeable components of the American health-care system—Medicare and the Veterans Administration—closely resemble what the French and the British, respectively, provide to all their citizens. No need to get spooked.

BROUHAHAHA

October 5, 2007

Q: What don't we know about your spouse?

A: She has the world's best laugh.

—*Interview with Bill Clinton, Time.com, September 13, 2007*

n the great American tradition of Washington's teeth, Lincoln's Adam's apple, T.R.'s pince-nez, Nixon's five o'clock shadow, Ike's grin, Reagan's pompadour, and—more recently, less nostalgically— Gore's sigh, Dean's scream, and W.'s smirk, the small (but, thanks to the Internet, bigger than ever) universe of people who professionally or semi-professionally obsess about presidential campaigns has been agog over Hillary Clinton's laugh.

This momentous subject began to elbow aside scarier topics like Iraq on September 23, when the junior senator from New York got herself interviewed on all five of the Sunday-morning political variety shows, a feat known as "the full Ginsburg," in honor of William Ginsburg, Monica Lewinsky's lawyer, who, on February 1, 1998, was the first to manage it. The Ginsburg may not be Clinton's favorite trophy, but she persevered. She met the press, she faced the nation, she rode down the fox. And, sure enough, whenever George or Wolf or Tim asked her something that struck her a certain way, she laughed.

The sound of Hillary's laughter, accompanied by urgent analyses thereof, has since been echoing from the tar pits of the Internet to the lofty peaks of the major mainstream media. It began with surprising amiability, on none other than *Fox News Sunday*, just after that program's contribution to the Ginsburg. Chatting with the interviewer, Chris Wallace, about the way Clinton had burst out laughing at the opening question (which was about why she has "a hyper-partisan view of politics"), Wallace's colleague Brit Hume remarked that her laugh "is always disarming, always engaging, and always attractive."

By midafternoon, the Republican National Committee had rushed out a corrective to Hume's lapse into graciousness: an electronic "research briefing" titled "Hillary: No Laughing Matter." It was studded with subheads like "When Asked Whether Her Plan Is a Step Toward Socialized Medicine, Hillary Giggles Uncontrollably" and festooned with video clips of the former First Lady engaged in giggle-related activities. From then on, the commentary alternated between judgments of the quality of the candidate's laughter and assessments of its hidden meaning.

Media Matters, the indefatigable Web site that chronicles conservative broadcasting, kept track. Sean Hannity played an audio clip seven times and described the candidate's laughter as "frightening." Bill O'Reilly trotted out a Fox News "body-language expert" to pronounce the laughter "evil." Dick Morris, the onetime Clinton adviser turned full-time Clinton trasher, described it as "loud, inappropriate, and mirthless." Further down the evolutionary scale, the right-wing blogs bloomed like a staph infection. "Shrillary's" laugh is "chilling." It's "fakey fake fake fake." It's a "hideous hyena mating call." It's "a signal to launch her flying monkeys."

The respectables joined in, too, in their mannerly way. In the *Times*, Frank Rich wrote, "Now Mrs. Clinton is erupting in a laugh with all the spontaneity of an alarm clock buzzer." His op-ed partner Maureen Dowd wrote that Clinton's "big belly laughs" were a way of making the transition "from nag to wag." Meanwhile, in the news section, a story explored the question "What's Behind the Laugh?" And Politico, a new online political newspaper, identified the problem as "a laugh that sounded like it was programmed by computer."

How a given laugh sounds is, of course, a matter of personal taste. More than two dozen videos of Hillary laughing are available on YouTube, some of them edited so as to make her appear ridiculous or hysterical, and after repeated viewings one observer—this observer, actually—has concluded that she is, in fact, laughing. That is to say, she is responding in a more or less normal fashion to a comment or situation that she perceives as absurd or humorous. (As Jon Stewart, the well-known humor expert, noted in the course of his own riff on the Clinton laugh situation, being called hyper-partisan by Fox News is, to borrow his word, "funny.") Hillary's laugh is unusually uninhibited for a politician—especially, perhaps, for a female politician. It is indeed a belly laugh, if not a "big belly" laugh, and it compares favorably with the incumbent presidential laugh, a series of rapid "heh-hehs," at once threatening and insipid, accompanied by an exaggerated, arrhythmic bouncing of head and shoulders in opposite directions.

The just published *Journals: 1952–2000* of the late Arthur M. Schlesinger, Jr., may shed some light on the question of whether Hillary Clinton is the sort of person who is capable of genuine laughter and, by extension, of the humanness that laughter is taken to signify. With reservations, Schlesinger liked the Clintons. But you don't have to take his word for it; you can take Jacqueline Kennedy Onassis's. Schlesinger's entry for February 4, 1993:

> Last night we dined at the [McGeorge] Bundys'. Jackie was also there. I asked her about Hillary Clinton. She could not have been more enthusiastic—so intelligent, so pretty, so cozy, what a good sense of humor. This last item surprised me. I was ready to concede the first

two adjectives and even the third, but I supposed her to be somewhat on the stern and humorless side.

In later entries, Schlesinger writes of Hillary's "charm and humor" and her "infectious joie de vivre." But it must be said that she doesn't always laugh, even when something's funny. In 1998, at the height of the Full Monica, Schlesinger, then eighty-one years old, is seated next to the First Lady at a formal White House dinner celebrating the National Humanities Medals, one of which he has just been awarded. They're having a jolly, dishy time—she's "very easy to talk to"—when Arthur gets a little too expansive:

> I made the point that the liberals had stood by Clinton while the DLC [Democratic Leadership Council] people had deserted him and described the miserable [Senator Joseph I.] Lieberman as a "sanctimonious prick." Hillary said, "Well, he is certainly sanctimonious," but showed no eagerness to pursue this line of thought.

Speaking of which, or whom, if people want to find fault with Senator Clinton, there are juicier bones to pick than her funny bone. A week or so ago, for example, she was the only Democrat in the presidential race to support a Lieberman-sponsored resolution putting the Senate on record as urging the Bush administration to designate Iran's Islamic Revolutionary Guard Corps a foreign terrorist organization. Her fellow-candidate senators—Joseph Biden, Christopher Dodd, and Barack Obama—opposed it, not because they doubt that the Guard dabbles in terrorism but because they don't trust the administration not to treat the resolution as a green light for another war. A few days later, Clinton did a course correction, signing on to a bill, sponsored by James Webb, of Virginia, that would bar funding for military action against Iran without explicit congressional authorization. Complain about her triangulation if you wish, but our unhappy country needs all the laughs it can get.

DYNASTIC VOYAGE

October 19, 2007

Shortly after Hillary Rodham Clinton declared her candidacy for president last winter, Roger Cohen, writing in the *International Herald Tribune*, declared that "a delicate problem confronts her that few people are talking about: almost two decades of dynastic domination of American politics." Well, they're talking about it now. "Forty percent of Americans have never lived when there wasn't a Bush or a Clinton in the White House," a recent Associated Press story, by Nancy Benac, begins. "Talk of Bush–Clinton fatigue is increasingly cropping up in the national political debate," Benac goes on. "If Hillary Clinton were to be elected and reelected, the nation could go twenty-eight years in a row with the same two families governing the country. Add the elder Bush's terms as vice president, and that would be thirty-six years straight with a Bush or Clinton in the White House." And a cover story in the *Economist* a couple of weeks ago, while noting that a woman president "would undoubtedly be a good thing for the country," adds, ominously, "But there is a downside: dynasty."

Ruling families are not supposed to be a big part of the picture in our democratic republic, whose very Constitution states firmly, "No Title of Nobility shall be granted by the United States." Even so, we've dabbled in dynasties from the beginning, when the Lee family, of Virginia, got to work spawning two signers of the Declaration of Independence, three governors, two senators, nine members of Congress, and four Confederate generals, including Robert E. (The Lees' Washington, Randolph, and Harrison in-laws won some elections, too.) The New Jersey Frelinghuysens are well into their third century of political droit du seigneur, from Frederick (born 1753), a delegate to the Continental Congress and later a United States senator, through Rodney (born 1946), a current member of the House of Representatives.

If anything, the dynastic dynamic has picked up speed in the past half century or so. It reached a perfect storm in 1962, when Massachusetts voters filled the Senate seat vacated by John F. Kennedy, grandson of Congressman and Mayor John F. Fitzgerald and son of Ambassador Joseph P. Kennedy, when he was elected president—the very seat that, in 1952, J.F.K. had wrested from Senator Henry Cabot Lodge, Jr., who was a great-great-great-grandson of Senator George Cabot, a grandson of the Senate titan Henry Cabot Lodge, and a son of George Cabot Lodge, who, though himself a poet, married a Frelinghuysen. (Are you following this?) The 1962 Democratic nominee for senator was, of course, Edward Moore Kennedy, then thirty years old. His Republican opponent was—wait for it—another George Cabot Lodge, this one a son of Henry Cabot Lodge, Jr., and a great-great-great-great-grandson of, etc. Nor was that all. There was a third-party "peace" candidate, too, a professor of European history at Harvard: H. Stuart Hughes, grandson of Charles Evans Hughes, governor of New York, chief justice of the United States, and 1916 Republican presidential nominee. During a primary debate, Kennedy's opponent for the Democratic nomination told him that if his name were just Edward Moore his candidacy would be a joke. A real zinger, but it might have been even zingier if its deliverer, Eddie McCormack, had not been the nephew of John W. McCormack, Speaker of the United States House of Representatives.

Teddy won. But even if one of the others had prevailed the result would have illustrated the point, which is that a country with such a plenitude of political patriarchies—not only Kennedys, Lodges, Hugheses, and McCormacks but also Bayhs, Browns, Cuomos, Daleys, Dodds, Longs, La Follettes, Romneys, Tafts, and Udalls (to say nothing of Bushes and Clintons)—cannot claim immunity from the apparently universal temptation to tug the forelock. On Capitol Hill, at the moment, there are five senators whose dads were senators before them; in the House, the legacy cases begin, but do not end, with the Speaker, Nancy Pelosi, whose father was a congressman (and mayor of Baltimore).

At the presidential level, the Bushes 41 and 43 were preceded by the Adamses 2 and 6, the Harrisons 9 and 23, and, of course, the Roosevelts 26 and 32. The younger members of the first three pairs on this list—sons in the first two cases, a grandson in the third—all had the dubious distinction of winning the presidency while being defeated at the polls, which suggests a certain thinning of the blood. The Roosevelts were more distantly related; Theodore was Franklin's fifth cousin, as (once removed) was his wife, Eleanor—a spiritual and political auntie of Hillary Clinton. Which brings us to the women, who, in this country and elsewhere, have generally come to power as a result of family ties.

In most cases, the tie has been broken by death. In South Asia, which seems to lead the world in female national leaders, violent death is invariably a factor. In Sri Lanka and Bangladesh, a total of four female heads of state have come to power in the wake of male relatives' assassination; in India, Prime Minister Indira Gandhi, Jawaharlal Nehru's daughter, was herself assassinated, as was her son and successor, Rajiv. (Her daughter-in-law, Sonia, now heads the ruling Congress Party.) Burma's imprisoned opposition leader, Aung San Suu Kyi, is the daughter of the assassinated independence leader Aung San. And the father of Benazir Bhutto, Pakistan's two-time and perhaps future prime minister, was a prime minister whose life ended at the gallows; her return to Karachi last week was marked by a suicide-bomber attack that claimed more than a hundred lives.

In the United States, the widow-of and daughter-of pattern has been gentler. Of the two hundred and forty-four women who have served in the House and the Senate, forty-six succeeded their husbands and twelve their fathers. The wife-of, as distinct from widow-of, method of conferring power has been a relatively minor theme, found mostly in the nether parts of the country—one thinks of Governors Ma Ferguson, of Texas, and, especially, Lurleen Wallace, of Alabama, through whom George ruled when term limits forced him out of the state house.

Senator Clinton is different, obviously. She is indisputably a wife-of, but it was she, not he, whom *Life* selected as an icon of their generation when she graduated from college. It was she, not he, who, as a young lawyer, got the coveted job with the House Watergate investigation. She would have gone far, maybe even this far, without him. However much she benefits from the dynasty factor, though, the *Economist* is right: there's a downside. The downside's name is Bush. If, as the voters in 2000 wished, Al Gore, son of Senator Albert Gore, Sr., had been granted the White House, things might be a bit easier—not just for Hillary Clinton but also for her main Democratic rival, Senator Barack Obama. George W. Bush has been as poor an advertisement for "inexperience" as for dynasticism. It's not fair, of course. Bush's failure to learn much of anything for the past six years suggests a deficit of character, not of experience; his unwillingness to employ his father's skills and advice on behalf of the nation shows a disrespectful disregard for a dynast's biggest advantage. He has given both freshness and family a bad name.

GOING AFTER HILLARY

November 2, 2007

I t took until the final minutes of last week's debate among the Democratic presidential contenders for the flying saucers to make their appearance. Though the special effects were subtle, there was a surprise cameo by an important movie star. The magic moment came when Tim Russert, who, along with Brian Williams, was manning ground control for MSNBC, asked one of the contenders what he termed "a serious question."

Q: The godmother of your daughter, Shirley MacLaine, writes in her new book that you sighted a U.F.O. over her home in Washington state, that you found the encounter extremely moving, that it was a "triangular craft, silent and hovering," that you "felt a connection to your heart and heard directions in your mind." Now, did you see a U.F.O.?

A: I did. And the rest of the account—I didn't—it was an unidentified flying object, O.K.? It's, like—it's unidentified.

Congressman Dennis Kucinich—for it was he—is indeed the candidate whom it is easiest to imagine walking up the gangplank of the glowing mother ship in the final scene of *Close Encounters of the Third Kind*.

Many viewers may not have been aware of the identity of his daughter's godmother, or of the corollary of that fact: that Warren Beatty, a player in Democratic Party politics for forty years, is Kucinich's daughter's goduncle—and, therefore, Kucinich's godcousin, or something. There is more than one dynast in the Democratic field.

And more than one space cadet. The other, Mike Gravel, was missing this time, having been triaged out on the ground that his campaign has consisted almost entirely of showing up for TV debates, to which his passport, now expired, was his service as a senator, which ended a quarter century ago. Of the remaining seven, six—Hillary Clinton, Barack Obama, and John Edwards, plus Governor Bill Richardson and the two senatorial lions, Joseph Biden and Christopher Dodd—are plausible presidential figures. Kucinich, though implausible, at least represents something outside himself—the Pacifica Radio wing of the party—and he does not always finish last in the polls.

The earth has already circled the sun once since this campaign began and will circle it again before it's over. But last week's debate kicked the proceedings into warp speed: with a mere two months until the Iowa caucus, we have reached the primary's equivalent of the general-election campaign's post–Labor Day 2008 sprint.

By the time the lights came up in Philadelphia last week, the evening's theme had become settled wisdom among MSNBC's color commentators. "The target tonight: Hillary Clinton. Obama and Edwards are expected to come out swinging" (Tucker Carlson). Obama "has got to attack, and he has got to explain why Hillary Clinton cannot win the presidency" (Howard Fineman). "Will Barack Obama hit the champ or hit the tank? Tonight's the night!" (Chris Matthews). Obama himself had helped write this script, giving a pre-debate interview to the *Times*, in which, according to the reporters' distillation of a nearly hour-long conversation, he promised to "start confronting" Clinton and "go on the offensive." But those were the reporters' words, not Obama's. His words, which could be found in an excerpted transcript on the *Times* Web site, were calmer. "I think she is an admirable person, I think she's a capable senator, I think there's overlap between some of her ideas and mine," he said. "The case I'm making is not that she's a terrible person or would be a terrible President. The case I'm making is that I would be better at those things that the country needs right now."

Not exactly a prescription for a "steel-cage match," for which, as David Axelrod, Obama's chief strategist, correctly told the *Washington Post*, "there's a tremendous bloodlust out there in the political community." And a steel-cage match it wasn't. The nastiest questioning of Clinton came from Russert, not from Edwards or Obama, who (Edwards especially) were frequently sharp with her but never uncivil. At bottom, the differences among them on questions of substance are small; in domestic matters they are almost invisible. Even on foreign policy, they are not the stuff of slashing, indignant attack. This is not 1968, when the bitter enmity between Democrats who supported the Vietnam War and Democrats who opposed it sundered friendships and lamed the party for a generation. Unlike Vietnam, Iraq is a Republican war. All the Democrats are against it. Obama is more than within his rights to highlight Clinton's vote to authorize it, but, for reasons both temperamental and tactical, he does so in measured tones. Millions of rank-and-file Democrats were snookered into supporting this war, or at least the threat of it. Like Clinton, they were for it before they were against it, and they may not appreciate having their noses rubbed too vigorously in what was their mistake as well as hers. Anyhow, Democratic voters want a Democratic victory more than they want any particular candidate. Compared with her primary rivals, Clinton provokes ambivalent, sometimes negative, reactions; but if Clinton it must be, few of her rivals' supporters will want to be complicit in lessening her chances of winning next November.

On two of the matters about which Clinton was harried in last week's debate—her White House records and New York State's current controversy over driver's licenses for undocumented workers, a.k.a. illegal aliens—her opponents saw a tactical opening and lunged for it. Fair enough. Still, her sins in these matters are as minor as their penumbras are large. The torpor of ex-presidential paper processing is mostly due to rules changes dictated by the present administration, which have slowed the Reagan Library's response time to Freedom of Information Act requests, for example, from a year and a half to six and a half years. But the kerfuffle is a reminder of the former First Lady's long-ago stubbornness about releasing her (perfectly harmless) Rose Law Firm records, thus stoking the (perfectly bogus) Whitewater "scandal." More broadly, it conjures up the baggage which would accompany the return of the Clinton marital drama to the White House stage. If she had been prepared for the driver's-license question, as she should have been, she might have pointed out that seven states now issue licenses regardless of immigration status, that doing so actually improves security with respect to terrorism (because applicants must produce a passport or other proof of identity as well as proof of residence in the state), and that the New York proposal has been amended to allow the undocumented to obtain a driver's certificate that cannot be used for federal identification purposes, as in boarding airplanes. Instead, she waffled. She was right to argue that the states have been left to cope with the detritus of President Bush's failed immigration reform. But driver's licenses for the undocumented is a perilous issue for Democrats, tailor-made for nativist demagoguery.

Meanwhile, back in outer space, Congressman Kucinich struggled to legitimatize his close encounter. "Jimmy Carter saw a U.F.O.," he protested. A true fact, but one unlikely to impress the gang at Fox News, where John Gibson rushed out an Internet column titled "Dennis Kucinich's U.F.O. Comments Prove He's Nuts." Maybe, but he and Carter aren't the only saucer spotters. Ronald Reagan saw two.

HUCKABEE?

November 23, 2007

Huckabee. Funny, improbable name; funny, improbable candidate. How funny? Well, have a look at the first Huckabee for President campaign commercial, aired last week in Iowa and now ubiquitous on the Web. In it, the former governor of Arkansas trades straight-faced non sequiturs with Chuck Norris, the B-list action star. (Norris: "Mike Huckabee wants to put the I.R.S. out of business." Huckabee: "When Chuck Norris does a pushup, he isn't lifting himself up, he's pushing the earth down.") It's an unusually entertaining spot—or, rather, meta-spot, the subtext of which is its own absurdity and, by extension, that of the whole genre.

How improbable? Well, up until the tail end of the summer, polls had Huckabee's support for the Republican nomination hovering between zero and three percent, usually closer to zero. In October, he broke into a trot, in November into a Gallup. In a poll released on Thanksgiving eve by Reuters/Zogby, he is in third place, at eleven percent, nosing past not only John McCain but also Mitt Romney and narrowing the gap with the fading Fred Thompson to four points. In Iowa, where actual voting will occur on January 3, he has surged into what is essentially a tie with Romney for first place.

Huckabee, who at fifty-one is the youngest Republican running, spent half of his adult life as a Southern Baptist minister. Most of his support, so far, comes from the evangelical Christian right. Yet to those who are not in that category his affect is curiously unthreatening. "I'm a conservative, but I'm not mad at anybody," he likes to say. His manner and appearance are reassuringly ordinary. When he smiles or laughs, which is often, his dimpled face looks interestingly like that of Wallace, of Wallace & Gromit.

On a recent day that Huckabee spent in Seattle, where he went to scare up a little cash (he has raised and spent a tiny fraction of his opponents'), his unexpectedness was fully on view. A luncheon speech to a roomful of like-minded supporters—such people do exist even in the land of Microsoft—was remarkable for what it wasn't. The snobbery of cultural elites, the "homosexual agenda," the alleged desire of Democrats to surrender to Islamofascists—these went unmentioned, as did abortion, gay marriage, and the liberal media. Nor did he have anything unpleasant to say about any of the other candidates of either party, unless you count an otherwise respectful reference to Hillary Clinton as "the presumptive Democrat nominee." ("We get along cordially," he said, referring to the Clintons. "They've campaigned against me and raised money for every opponent I ever had, and that's O.K., because I've campaigned against them just as fervently.")

Huckabee speaks calmly, in stories, parables, and extended metaphors. The foreign-policy section of his talk (what there was of it) was a leisurely account of how his children laugh at him when he tells them that his grade-school class used to "duck and cover" in fear of a Soviet nuclear attack. "Somehow, in our naïveté," he said, "we thought that if the world is coming to an end the crosshairs of the first nuclear missile would be aimed at the Brookwood Elementary School, in Hope, Arkansas." The section's conclusion—and the speech's only hint at how the speaker might deal with what he called "a very dangerous world"—was a single sentence: "I want to be the president that helps to make it so that your grandchildren laugh at you when you tell them you used to have to put your toothpaste in a plastic bag and take your shoes off to get on an airplane to go somewhere in this country."

Like another governor from Hope who once ran for president, Candidate Huckabee reserves his real passion for matters domestic. On education, he talked not about standardized tests or back-to-basics but about something like their polar opposite. "We have to change and reform the education system so that we're capturing both the left and the right sides of the kid's brain," he said. "There ought to be a new focus not just in math and science—which there needs to be—but also a balanced focus on music and art and right-side-of-the-brain activities. Otherwise, we end up with an education system that's like a data download—a great database but no processor." On health, he skipped the usual denunciations of socialized medicine and noted, as Republicans seldom do, that "we spend so much more per capita than any other country on earth"—far more than second-place Switzerland. "The current system says, 'We won't pay a hundred and fifty dollars for the visit to the podiatrist, we'll wait until there's a thirty-thousand-dollar amputation and we'll cover that.'" Huckabee, who has Type 2 diabetes (but lost a hundred pounds and now runs marathons), knows what he's talking about.

In the question period, the candidate declined several invitations to serve up red meat. Asked about immigration, he hurried through the assurances required by the current perfervid mood among Republicans—seal the border, no amnesty—to add, "People who come to this country would rather come here legally if they had the choice. Nobody wants to break the law because it's fun to break the law. . . . When it takes seven to twelve years to get a permit to come so you can pick lettuce, you'll decide, 'In seven years my family will have starved. I think what I'll do is, I'll just pay somebody a couple of thousand bucks to haul me across the border, and maybe I'll never get caught.'" If there was demagoguery in any of this, it was the demagoguery of policy vagueness and simplistic hope, not the demagoguery of anger and fear. At least Huckabee's stories of people in need don't have the patronizing, self-congratulatory sound of "compassionate conservatism." (Anyhow, Huckabee calls it "conservativism.")

Such signals have begun to excite the suspicions of the economic-royalist wing of the G.O.P. In a conversation after the speech, mention was made of the Club for Growth. Only then did Huckabee have something impolite to say. The Club for Growth is the secular church of supply-side fundamentalism; it promotes tax cuts and nothing but tax cuts, especially for the rich. It has spent months attacking Huckabee as a tax-and-spend liberal, because, in office, he presided over a mixture of tax hikes and tax cuts. "The Club for Greed, I call them," he said. "They hate that. Oh, they hate it. And I enjoy giggin' them about it, because I think they're a despicable political hit organization that takes people's money and anonymously attacks candidates, with no integrity to say, 'This person here is attacking this public official.' And when you do it in hiding, from the trees, I just think it's cowardly."

None of this is to say that Huckabee's policy positions are much better than those of his Republican rivals; in some cases, they're worse. He wants to replace the federal tax code with a gigantic, horribly regressive sales tax; he cannot name a single time he has ever disagreed with the National Rifle Association; he wants to amend the Constitution to ban gay marriage and abortion. In practice, however, the sales tax and the amendments would go nowhere, and he couldn't do much about abortion except appoint Scalia-like justices to the Supreme Court—which his rivals have promised to do, too. God knows what his foreign policy would look like, but no one else does.

To all appearances, Huckabee's gentle rhetoric is a reflection of temperament, not a stylistic tactic. Arkansans caution that he is capable of churlishness. But his history suggests that he prefers consensus to confrontation, that he regards government as a tool for social betterment, and that he has little taste for war, cultural or otherwise. He seems to regard liberalism not as a moral evil, a mental disease, or a character flaw—merely as a political point of view he mostly disagrees with. That may not seem like much, but it makes a nice change. If talk radio hears about it, though, it might be enough to keep him from the top of the ticket.

ROUND ONE

December 28, 2007

Out in Iowa, with the bell at last ringing and the combatants charging out of their corners, the Republican card has come down to the Maulin' Mormon versus the Battlin' Baptist. Would the Framers be pleased? Doesn't seem likely, somehow. The deists, freethinkers, and assorted Protestants (plus two Catholics) who drafted the Constitution sternly forbade theological sucker punches—"No religious Test shall ever be required as a Qualification to any Office or public Trust under the United States" was how they put it—but today's Republicans make their own rules. Marquess of Queensberry? Not for the new Grand Old Party. (Meanwhile, those groovy Democrats are reprising *The Mod Squad*, with the white guy, the black guy, and the blonde scrambling to see who gets to make the collar.)

The tale of the tape suggests that Mike Huckabee has to be given the edge, religion-wise. He trained at Ouachita Baptist University and turned pro early, pastoring his own church at twenty-four. A mere nine years later, he was president of the Arkansas Baptist State Convention—half a million strong, a fifth of the state's population at the time. He may not be a heavyweight these days (he shed a hundred and ten pounds as governor), but if he no longer has the belly he certainly has the fire.

The fire, yes—but, affable fellow that he is, minus the brimstone. Huckabee's sensational rise has been made possible by his success, so far, at speaking in tongues that evangelicals and nonevangelicals understand differently. "I always tell the story of a lady who asked me, was I a narrow-minded Baptist who thinks only Baptists go to Heaven?" he likes to say. "And I told her, 'No, ma'am, I'm more narrow than that. I don't think all the Baptists are going to make it, either.'" Does he mean "Let's not take this eternal damnation stuff so darn seriously"? Or is it "Everybody roasts in Hell except selected evangelicals"? And then there was his instantly famous sound bite at the November 28 YouTube debate, when he was asked where history's most revered victim of the death penalty would stand on that issue. "Jesus," Huckabee replied with a rueful smile, "was too smart to ever run for public office." This was a clever sally, allowing moderates to infer that he, Huckabee, realizes that capital punishment is morally dubious but (like his gubernatorial predecessor Bill Clinton) supports it for prudential political reasons, while assuring his co-religionists that he, Huckabee, is a humble sinner, albeit one on easy terms with the Lord—who will forgive His flock the minor sin of clamoring for the modern equivalent of crucifixion.

Lately, though, Huckabee has been getting his signals mixed, like a man putting letters to his wife and his mistress in the wrong envelopes. A few weeks ago at Liberty University (founder: the late J. Falwell), a student asked him what accounted for his rocketing poll numbers. "There's only one explanation for it, and it's not a human one," he said. "It's the same power that helped a little boy with two fish and five loaves feed a crowd of five thousand people—and that's the only way that our campaign could be doing what it's doing." To an evangelical ear, that might sound like simple wonderment. But to many other people it sounded like the ravings of someone who thinks God is his precinct captain.

In Mitt Romney's case, it's the religion itself that may have a glass jaw. When Mitt's father, George Romney, a liberal Republican governor of Michigan, ran for president, in 1968, his Mormonism was just

another biographical detail. That was before the party's firm embrace of "faith" as a mandatory political talking point. It's no longer clear that the dogmas of whatever sect a candidate happens to be affiliated with can be dismissed as irrelevant to the policies he or she might pursue in office.

And the dogmas of Mitt Romney's sect are breathtaking. They include these: that in 1827 a young man named Joseph Smith dug up a set of golden plates covered with indecipherable writing; that, with the help of a pair of magic spectacles, he "translated" the plates from an otherwise unknown language (Reformed Egyptian) into an Olde English that reads like an unfunny parody of the King James Bible; that the Garden of Eden is in Missouri; that American Indians descend from Hebrew immigrants; that Jesus reappeared in pre-Columbian America and converted so many people that the result was a series of archeologically unconfirmable wars in which millions died; that while polygamy had divine approval for most of the nineteenth century, God changed his mind in 1890, just in time for Utah to be allowed into the Union; and that God waited until 1978 to reveal that it was O.K. for blacks to be fully paid-up members of the Church of Jesus Christ of Latter-Day Saints.

One might ask, What of it? Plenty of religions have curious doctrines. (Several, for example, hold that on Sundays millions of people drink blood and eat flesh.) The Framers knew this was dangerous territory, which was one reason they tried to rule it out of political bounds. And Romney himself warned, in a speech, titled "Faith in America," that he delivered on December 6, "There are some who would have a presidential candidate describe and explain his church's distinctive doctrines. To do so would enable the very religious test the founders prohibited."

The weasel word here is "distinctive." Romney had no problem describing his church's not-so-distinctive doctrines. "There is one fundamental question," he continued, as if he were speaking on tax cuts, "about which I often am asked. What do I believe about Jesus Christ? I

believe that Jesus Christ is the Son of God and the Savior of mankind."
(But please don't ask about Jesus's post-Resurrection travel schedule.)
The candidate went on to patronize rival religions, administering quick
head pats to Catholicism ("I love the profound ceremony of the Catholic Mass"), evangelicalism (for the "approachability" of its version of
God), Pentecostalism ("tenderness of spirit"), Lutheranism ("confident
independence"), Judaism ("ancient traditions"), and Islam ("frequent
prayer"—a bit feeble, that).

Missing from this litany, of course, was something to the effect of
"I appreciate the deep commitment to reason of the agnostics and atheists." Indeed, the only "religion" that Romney had anything rude to
say about was "the religion of secularism." He pointed scornfully at the
"empty" cathedrals of Europe as evidence of "societies just too busy or
too 'enlightened' to venture inside and kneel in prayer," adding a little
later that "any person who has knelt in prayer to the Almighty" has "a
friend and ally in me." Take that, NATO. On your knees.

Secularism is not a religion. And it is not true that "freedom requires
religion just as religion requires freedom," as Romney maintained.
What freedom, including religious freedom, requires is, precisely,
secularism—which is to say, state neutrality in matters of religion. (Nor
does religion require freedom, as the European past and the Middle
Eastern present demonstrate; religions, plural, do, however.) "Americans do not respect believers of convenience," Romney thundered in
his "faith" speech. "Americans tire of those who would jettison their
beliefs, even to gain the world." These were strange observations, coming as they did from a man whose campaign has consisted largely of
jettisoning the beliefs he found convenient as a Massachusetts politician
but finds highly inconvenient now that he stands to gain the Republican
nomination for president. But then those were merely *political* beliefs.

Touch gloves, Mitt and Mike. And perhaps, if God interests Himself
in the minutiae of earthly politics, He'll arrange a double knockout.

A HUNDRED YEARS' WAR?

Manchester, NH, January 4, 2008

John McCain—who, solely because of the grievous blow to Romney, seems to have been almost as big a winner in Iowa last night as Huckabee or Obama—flew here yesterday for an early evening "town meeting." He was accompanied by his own personal Chuck Norris, Joseph I. Lieberman.

The setting was the nearby town of Derry, which looks like a Lionel Train layout, in a building called the Adams Memorial Opera House, which is not an opera house. It's a cozy little auditorium with a curvy balcony that embraced the packed room like a pair of comforting arms. The stage was reserved for an overflow of supporters; McCain and his improbably blonde wife, Cindy (whom Lieberman Yiddishly referred to as "Sidney"), mounted a platform in the middle of the orchestra. It was political theatre in the round.

I hadn't seen McCain campaigning up close since New Hampshire in 2000. There's a lot less electricity now. Eight years on, the candidate is visibly past his prime, and he seemed tired. About every third sentence began with "By the way." But there are still some sparks, and he took some shots, not by name but unmistakably, at his old nemesis George W. Bush.

McCain was strong on global warming and wasn't afraid to call it by that name. McCain said he would "restore trust in government"—not a promise one ordinarily feels compelled to make when a president of one's party has been in power for two terms. Deploring the choice of Vladimir Putin over General David Petraeus as *Time*'s man of the year, McCain said, "By the way, I looked into [Putin's] eyes—and I saw three letters: K, G, and B." McCain decried the ballooning deficits under the Republicans—though the point was rather enfeebled when he called for making the Bush tax cuts permanent, because letting them expire on schedule would "have the effect of a tax increase." Late in the session, when someone finally asked about immigration, McCain quipped, "This meeting is adjourned." (He went on to say that he knows people want the borders sealed and that he would seal them, but that immigrants, legal and illegal, "are God's children.")

The most interesting exchange came at the very end, and it was about Iraq. The money quote—the bit that could come back to haunt McCain—went like this:

Q: President Bush has talked about our staying in Iraq for fifty years.
McCAIN: Make it a hundred.

That's the sound bite. That's the headline. Now let's look at the context, which I think is worth considering in full.

McCain pointed to a burly, white-bearded man along one wall and said, "I think Ernest Hemingway is with us tonight."

When the chuckles subsided, the Hemingway look-alike (who later identified himself to *Mother Jones*'s David Corn as Dave Tiffany, a "full-time antiwar activist") asked McCain "what you hope to accomplish in Iraq and how long it's going to take." Here's my rough transcript of what followed:

McCAIN: The fact is, it's a classic counterinsurgency. And you have to get areas under a secure environment, and that secure environment then allows the economic, political, and social process to move forward. In case you missed it, New Year's Eve, people were out in the streets in Baghdad by the thousands for the first time in years. That's because we provided them with a safe and secure environment. Is it totally safe? No. I talked earlier about the suicide bombs and the continued threats. But then what happens is American troops withdraw to bases. And we reach an arrangement like they have with South Korea and Japan. We still have troops in Bosnia. The fact is, it's American casualties that the American people care about. Those casualties are on the way down, rather dramatically. You've got to consider the option. If we had withdrawn six months ago, I can look you in the eye and tell you that Al Qaeda would have said, We beat the United States of America. If we'd gone along with Harry Reid and said the war is lost to Al Qaeda, then we would be fighting that battle all over the Middle East. I'm convinced of that and so is General Petraeus. . . . I can tell you that it's going to be long and hard and tough. I can tell you that the option of defeat is incredible and horrendous. And I can look you in the eye and tell you that this strategy is succeeding. And what we care about is not American presence. We care about American casualties. And those casualties will be dramatically and continue to be reduced.

TIFFANY: I do not believe that one more soldier being killed every day is success. There were three U.S. soldiers killed today. I want to know, How long are we going to be there?

McCAIN: How long do you want us to be in South Korea? How long do you want us to be in Bosnia?

TIFFANY: There's no fighting going on in South Korea. There's no fighting in Bosnia. Let's come back to Iraq.

McCAIN: I can look you in the eye and tell you that those casualties tragically continue. . . . But they are much less, and they are dramatically reduced and we will eventually eliminate them. And again, the option of setting a date for withdrawal is a date for surrender. And we will then have many more casualties and many more American sacrifices if we withdraw with setting a date for surrender. Now you and I have an

open and honest disagreement. But I can tell you that six months ago
people like you, who believe like you do, said the surge would never
succeed. It is succeeding. And I've been there and I've seen it with my
very own eyes. Do you want to follow up?

TIFFANY: President Bush has talked about our staying in Iraq for fifty
years.

McCAIN: Make it a hundred. How long—We've been in Japan for sixty
years, we've been in South Korea for fifty years or so. That'd be fine
with me as long as Americans are not being injured or harmed or
wounded or killed. That's fine with me. I hope it would be fine with
you if we maintain a presence in a very volatile part of the world where
Al Qaeda is training and recruiting and equipping and motivating
people every single day.

TIFFANY: By the way, I hope you kick Romney's butt. That man cannot
lie straight in bed.

McCAIN: I knew there was a reason I called on you.

TIFFANY: What if U.S. soldiers are being killed at the same rate, one per
day, four years from now?

McCAIN: I can't tell you what the ratio is. But I can tell you, I understand
American public opinion, sir. I understand American public opinion
will not sustain a conflict where Americans continue to be sacrificed
without showing them that we can succeed.

TIFFANY: I hear an open-ended commitment, then.

McCAIN: I have an open-ended commitment in Asia. I have an
open-ended commitment in South Korea. I have an open-ended commitment in Bosnia. I have an open-ended commitment in in Europe.

The rest was drowned out by applause. McCain said, "This kind of dia-
logue has to take place in America today, and I thank you."

You have to hand it to McCain. It's impossible to imagine any of the
other Republicans engaging in this kind of extended conversation with
a citizen. There was more real debate in this exchange than in any of
the so-called real debates.

But what the context shows, I think, is that yanking that sound bite out of context isn't really all that unfair. McCain wants to stay in Iraq until no more Americans are getting killed, no matter how long it takes and how many Americans get killed achieving that goal—that is, the goal of not getting any more Americans killed. And once that goal is achieved, we'll stay.

He'll see your fifty years and raise you fifty. But the cards are blank.

JUST DESERETS

January 25, 2008

n a thoughtful column on the Web site of the *Deseret News*, the L.D.S. Church–owned Salt Lake City daily, Joel Campbell, the paper's "Mormon Media Observer," takes me to task for making sport of some of the tenets of the Latter-Day Saints:

> In a lengthy New York *Times Magazine* opinion [piece], Noah Feldman tried to explain "What is it about Mormonism?" . . .
>
> Hendrik Hertzberg, who wrote a recent column in *The New Yorker* magazine mocking L.D.S. beliefs, should have read Feldman's analysis before he sat down at the computer and wrote: "And the dogmas of Mitt Romney's sect are breathtaking." Certainly, "breathtaking" has a lot to do with one's experience. Sure, the unfamiliar may seem unusual, but those with open minds don't dismiss it out of hand but rather seek to understand it.
>
> Compare Hertzberg's take to Feldman's writing. "Still, even among those who respect Mormons personally, it is still common to hear Mormonism's tenets dismissed as ridiculous," Feldman wrote. "This attitude is logically indefensible insofar as Mormonism is being compared with other world religions.

"There is nothing inherently less plausible about God's revealing himself to an upstate New York farmer in the early years of the Republic than to the pharaoh's changeling grandson in ancient Egypt. But what is driving the tendency to discount Joseph Smith's revelations is not that they seem less reasonable than those of Moses; it is that the book containing them is so new. When it comes to prophecy, antiquity breeds authenticity. Events in the distant past, we tend to think, occurred in a sacred, mythic time."

So we come full circle to religious tolerance. It's not about making judgments about each others' faith or even lack thereof. It's respecting all faiths and beliefs in the context of a tolerant and civil nation. The news media has a responsibility to set this tone of respect.

Actually, I don't disagree with the thrust of Noah Feldman's take (which I did sit down and read before I wrote my piece). There is indeed nothing *inherently* less plausible about the alleged provenance of the Mormon prophet's golden plates in upstate New York than about the alleged provenance of the Hebrew prophet's stone tablets in Sinai. And it is certainly true that both tales, whatever value they may have as folkloric parables, are factually "ridiculous," to use Feldman's word. But I'm not sure it's "authenticity," exactly, that antiquity breeds. As Feldman also implies, it's a patina of myth.

The Ten Commandments were handed down—or written, or transcribed, or forged, or whatever—two and a half thousand years ago, when the earth was assumed to be flat, the sky was assumed to be a dome hung with lights, philosophical debates concerned which gods should be propitiated by animal and which by human sacrifice, and only a few priests and scribes knew how to read. By 1827, when Joseph Smith supposedly dug up the golden plates in upstate New York, Charles Darwin was in medical school, railroads were being built in Europe and America, books and newspapers were being produced by the million, and the telegraph was about to be invented. As factual claims, the stories in the Book of Exodus and the stories in the Book of Mormon may indeed be equally silly. But the former is an artifact of the age of stone and magic, while the latter is an artifact of the age of steam and science. Contextually, if not inherently, Mormonism wins the ridiculousness sweepstakes hands down.

For reasons of civil peace, people's religious beliefs should indeed be tolerated. So should their political beliefs. That's why I insist that the state must be secular and the society open. But when particular religious doctrines intrude themselves into the political realm, I fail to see why they should not be subject to the normal rough and tumble of intellectual debate and scrutiny, which includes argument, disagreement, analysis, and, yes, ridicule—none of which are incompatible with tolerance. Treating them as undiscussible is condescension, not respect.

In that spirit, let's take a ramble through Mitt Romney's "Faith in America" address—a political speech, not a sermon:

> Given our grand tradition of religious tolerance and liberty, some wonder whether there are any questions regarding an aspiring candidate's religion that are appropriate. I believe there are.

For example?

> There is one fundamental question about which I often am asked. What do I believe about Jesus Christ?

You think that's an appropriate question to ask a candidate for public office? Really?

> I believe that Jesus Christ is the Son of God and the Savior of mankind.

Good for you. But that's really none of my business, is it? Why are you telling me this in a political speech? Are you planning to do something about it once you're president?

There are some who would have a presidential candidate describe and explain his church's distinctive doctrines. To do so would enable the very religious test the founders prohibited in the Constitution.

Wait a minute. You just told me that you "believe that Jesus Christ is the Son of God and the Savior of mankind." Isn't that a—oh, I see. You don't think that's a *distinctive* doctrine. Well, it's plenty distinctive from my point of view. It's distinct from what *I* believe—to say nothing of millions of Jews, Hindus, Buddhists, atheists, agnostics, and nominal but unobservant Christians. (By the way, asking a candidate to explain his church's doctrines is not prohibited by the Constitution. What's prohibited is making him ineligible to hold office on account of religion.)

But in recent years, the notion of the separation of church and state has been taken by some well beyond its original meaning. They seek to remove from the public domain any acknowledgment of God. Religion is seen as merely a private affair with no place in public life. It is as if they are intent on establishing a new religion in America—the religion of secularism. They are wrong.

No, you are wrong. Secularism is not a religion, any more than freedom of association is an association. Secularism is a political condition that permits a variety of religions and beliefs about religion to coexist peacefully. And the existence of God (or the divinity of Jesus) is not a fact to be acknowledged, it's a belief to be protected, along with contrary beliefs or nonbeliefs.

Any believer in religious freedom, any person who has knelt in prayer to the Almighty, has a friend and ally in me.

Are these the same things? Are you saying that a "believer in religious freedom" is synonymous with a "person who has knelt in prayer to the Almighty"? Does a person have to be both to count you as a friend and ally? Or is one enough? Do you have friends and allies who kneel in prayer to the Almighty but don't believe in religious freedom? Who would you rather be allied with, Richard Dawkins or Osama bin Laden? Just what *are* you saying, Governor?

What *I'm* saying is this: If Romney had said that his religious doctrines are between him and his God or him and his church, and that he doesn't plan to be guided by them in his performance of public office, I'd have been happy to leave it at that. Live and let live. But if he goes around giving campaign speeches about who is and is not the Son of God and the Savior of mankind, he opens a door that the rest of us should feel perfectly free to walk through.

SECOND THOSE EMOTIONS

January 11, 2008

By the eve of the New Hampshire primary last week, the candidates for president, especially the ones with a realistic shot at their party's nomination, were tired—very, very tired. They had been campaigning hard for a year or more, flat out for months, nearly around the clock for weeks. The election itself, incredibly, was still ten months away. There had been no break after the Iowa caucuses. How could there be, with only four full days left until the New Hampshire voting? The schedule—the anarchic product of hundreds of uncoordinated, self-interested maneuvers by state legislatures, party committees, and campaign high commands, combining the worst features of languid lengthening and frenetic foreshortening—is insane. And brutal. What keeps the candidates going (besides a sincere desire to "give back") is the adrenaline in their veins, the addicting intensity of the experience, and the glitter of the prize.

Extreme fatigue and undiluted adrenaline make a powerful cocktail. The wonder is that none of these people have yet been carted off to the funny farm. Last week, small cracks began to appear in the façade of mastery that all candidates strive to maintain. Even Senator Barack Obama, the youngest and fittest of the bunch, was starting to show the strain. In Rochester, on Monday evening, the (then, briefly) Democratic front-runner addressed an overflow crowd packed into one of the intimate, theatre-like meeting halls that New Hampshire towns specialize in preserving. He was getting into the heart of his stump speech, surfing waves of applause. "In less than twenty-four hours, you can do what the cynics said could not be done," he orated. "We can come together, Democrats, Independents, and, yes, some Republicans, and proclaim that we are one nation, we are one people, and the time has changed for—" He stopped abruptly and mused, as if breaking the fourth wall, "That's the second time I've done this today." Then, switching immediately back into character, he picked up where he had left off: "The time for change has come!"

A somewhat more widely publicized moment of human ordinariness had occurred that morning, in Portsmouth, where Senator Hillary Clinton, attended by a scrum of cameramen and reporters, was sitting at a coffee shop table with a group of "undecided voters," mostly middle-aged and female. One of them asked her how she manages it—how she keeps "upbeat" and "wonderful"—and added, "Who does your hair?"

"Well, luckily, on special days I do have help," Clinton said. Then her eyes welled up, and she took a deep breath.

> It's not easy. It's not easy. And I couldn't do it if I just didn't, you know, passionately believe it was the right thing to do. You know, I have so many opportunities from this country. I just don't want to see us fall backwards. You know, this is very personal for me. It's not just political. It's not just public. I see what's happening. We have to reverse it.

By this point her voice had softened, taking on a never-before-heard quality of slightly mournful tenderness:

> Some of us just put ourselves out there and do this against some pretty difficult odds. And we do it, each one of us, because we care about our

country. But some of us are right and some of us are wrong. Some of us are ready and some of us are not. Some of us know what we will do on Day One and some of us haven't really thought that through enough. . . . So, as tired as I am—and I am—and as difficult as it is to kind of keep up what I try to do on the road, like occasionally exercise and try to eat right, it's tough when the easiest food is pizza. I just believe so strongly in who we are as a nation.

The media frenzy that followed had to be seen to be believed—and it was seen, everywhere in New Hampshire, and everywhere else in the country, where a television set was tuned to cable news. A common first instinct was to treat the episode as a ploy, a calculated effort to "humanize" the candidate—an interpretation that depended heavily on its having been somehow staged or faked. But the authenticity of Clinton's emotion was apparent to anyone who took the time to study the many replays with an open mind, a category that did not include the hardest-hearted hard core of conservative commentators. On Fox News, William Kristol, the editor of the *Weekly Standard* and the *Times'* newest op-ed columnist, said flatly, "She pretended to cry." Even Brit Hume was taken aback. "You think she pretended?" "Yes," Kristol replied. Hume: "I don't."

Most of the (male) press quickly came around to Hume's view, but even then the general assumption was that the incident would further damage Clinton's chances. (She was well behind in New Hampshire polls, though this had been true for less than two days.) Among grizzled veterans, the memory of 1972 was still vivid: if Senator Edmund Muskie, of neighboring Maine, had crumpled his ticket to the nomination by appearing outside the *Manchester Union Leader* building with wet cheeks (whether from tears or snow was never determined), how could Hillary survive? Much has changed since then, of course. Men, even the most macho of them, are permitted to shed a tear. The ranks of post-1972 male political weepers and misters include Richard Nixon, Bob Dole, Jimmy Carter, Ronald Reagan, Michael Dukakis,

Gary Hart, both Bushes, and the other Clinton; Mitt Romney, a leading Republican contender this year, cried three times last month alone.
(The cross-party hugfest at halftime of the back-to-back Republican
and Democratic debates on ABC was another indicator of emotional
climate change.) But things were assumed to be different for women.
Tom Lutz, in *Crying*, his erudite 1999 study of "The Natural and Cultural History of Tears," suggests a parallel with poll-driven political
centrism: "The men who cry prove that they are not too manly; the
women who maintain stoic control of their emotions prove that they
are not too 'feminine.'" And: "Hillary Clinton has been routinely condemned by some of her critics for being too masculine, too hard and
cold, but one can imagine the criticism that would rain down on her if
she were to cry on camera." If Hillary didn't quite cry, she came close.
And, sure enough, the criticism rained down. But so did the votes.

And what, one might ask, about "the issues"? The Democratic contest this year is both more substantive and more superficial than the
Republican. The Web sites of Clinton, Obama, and John Edwards
fairly groan with detailed, often far-reaching proposals for "change"—
that magic word!—in health care, the environment, foreign policy,
and more. But, because these proposals resemble nothing so much as
one another, the attention of the press and the public tends to gravitate
toward dramas of personality. The results out of Iowa and New Hampshire guarantee a spirited fight at least through the twenty-two-state
"Tsunami Tuesday" primaries next month. We will likely see many
more tears before it's all over. But in politics, as in life, fate is fickle.
Just a few months ago, why was Hillary Clinton being dissed and dismissed? For laughing.

THE SPAT

February 1, 2008

During the four or five weeks leading up to February 5—"Tsunami Tuesday," when voters in states with half the nation's population participate in a not quite national primary—the emotional texture of the Democratic side of the presidential campaign changed profoundly. For most of Year One of this insanely elongated process, the Democratic Party had been a peaceable kingdom. Its voters were proud of and pleased with the array of choices before them: proud of its diversity, pleased with its unity. A confident woman in middle age; a graceful young African-American of mixed parentage; a handsome Southerner from a white working-class family; and a Mexico City–raised, three-quarters Hispanic governor-diplomat with (for a touch of mayonnaise) a blandly "American" name—these were the Democrats' leading contenders, supplemented by a more conventional pair of distinguished senators from the East Coast. After years of talk about "looking like America," here was the real thing. On questions of policy, the views of the candidates were as reassuringly similar as their backgrounds were exhilaratingly different. Such disagreements as they had, none of them fundamental or bitter, were subsumed in their revulsion at the moral and strategic failures of the Bush administration. As for Democratic voters, it was hard to find one who wouldn't tell you something like: "I'm supporting so-and-so in the primary, but I'll be fine with any of them—just so we get a Democrat in the White House."

But as Iowa gave way to New Hampshire and then South Carolina, and the contest careered toward its ultimate form of a zero-sum game between Hillary Clinton and Barack Obama, the mood darkened. Anger and depression, the pop-psych books tell us, are two sides of the same coin: depression is anger suppressed, anger is depression liberated. Is it possible to strobe between the two? It must be, because, as the Clinton-Obama race turned nasty, a rapid alternation was noticeable among the sort of obsessive Democrats who follow every twist and turn. This was true of people all across the deep-blue universe: passionate Obama supporters; tentative Obama supporters; Obama-Clinton fence-sitters (including the fans of John Edwards, now bereft); and tentative Clinton supporters. (Passionate Clinton supporters, notwithstanding their candidate's shrinking but still sizable lead in national polls, seem to be a little rarer.)

The anger was mostly directed at Senator Clinton, her husband, and her campaign, for a series of what have come to be known, redundantly, as "negative attacks." The most egregious, because so coldly premeditated, was a radio spot that took as its hook a snippet of audio from an Obama interview in which he said, "The Republicans were the party of ideas for a pretty long chunk of time there over the last ten, fifteen years." A smooth-voiced announcer then adds:

> Really? Aren't those the ideas that got us into the economic mess we're in today? Ideas like special tax breaks for Wall Street? Running up a nine-trillion-dollar debt? Refusing to raise the minimum wage or deal with the housing crisis? Are those the ideas Barack Obama's talking about?

Uh, no. Those are *not* the ideas Barack Obama's talking about. But the spot's disingenuous questions were plainly intended to deceive the unwary into assuming that Wall Street tax breaks and the like are the very ideas Obama has been advocating. With equal honesty, the spot could have said, "Denying global warming? Torturing prisoners? Appointing right-wing ideologues to the federal courts? Are those the ideas Barack Obama's talking about?" But that might have taxed the credulity of even the unwary.

Actually, Obama was not talking about any particular ideas. He was talking about the conservative movement's success in *marketing* its policy ideas and presenting itself as an intellectual powerhouse. He can be faulted for getting the timeline wrong in a way that dismissed the Clinton years—the Republicans' "party of ideas" claim is at least thirty years old—but his basic point has long been a commonplace among Democrats. It is why liberals have spent the past decade and more trying to build a counterweight to the conservative infrastructure of think tanks and policy journals.

Obama has turned out to have a kind of political magic unseen since the Kennedy brothers of the nineteen-sixties. He has something of Jack's futuristic, ironic cool, something of Bobby's earnest, inspiring heat. His endorsement, last week, by President Kennedy's surviving brother and surviving child closed the circuit. Senator Clinton's answer to this is "I have more experience." And it's true. Her mastery of policy is deep and subtle; her sense of how the White House wields power is probably unequalled. But experience is a problematic argument, especially when voters are hungry for a new beginning.

Anyway, an argument is no match for an aura. So the Clinton campaign evidently concluded that it had no choice but to "go negative," and Bill Clinton was assigned, or assigned himself, the task. Some of his attempts to sully his wife's opponent—calling Obama's consistent opposition to the Iraq war "the biggest fairy tale I've ever seen" and dismissing his South Carolina victory as a racial one, like Jesse Jackson's twenty years ago—have been untruthful or unworthy or both. Whether or not these and similar attacks "worked" (the evidence is mixed), they certainly succeeded in diminishing both the former president and his wife. "The Clintons" used to be a Republican trope, calculated to make one or the other half of the couple look like a puppet or a victim or a co-conspirator; now it is simply descriptive. Bill Clinton's talents are immense, and so are those of Hillary Clinton. But the events of the past few weeks have suggested that the peculiar dynamics of the Clinton marriage, which distorted the workings of the first Clinton White House in areas ranging from its failed health-care initiative to its inability to quash the Whitewater hoax, would be carried over into a second.

For some Democrats, a final straw has been the Clinton campaign's sudden interest in changing the rules. In Nevada, where the state's Democratic Party had provided special caucus sites for casino workers, Clinton allies tried to get them shut down after a union representing many of those workers endorsed Obama. The Democratic National Committee warned the party's affiliates in Michigan and Florida that if they moved their primaries ahead of Tsunami Tuesday they would lose their convention delegates. They did so anyway, and now Clinton—whose name, unlike Obama's or Edwards's, was on the Michigan ballot and who carried Florida, where no one campaigned—is demanding that the two states' delegates be accredited. Those delegates, added to the bulk of the unelected "superdelegates," could conceivably put Clinton over the top if Obama arrives at the convention with a slight edge in delegates chosen by voters—a scenario that would bear an ugly resemblance to Florida, the popular vote, and the Supreme Court, circa 2000.

Last Thursday night's televised debate between the two remaining Democrats—a civilized and substantive conversation—has eased the tension. But politics ain't beanbag. One of the arguments made on behalf of the Clintons is that they know how to win. They do what is necessary. They fight hard. They've shown they can survive the worst the Republican attack machine can throw at them, next to which the relatively mild roughing-up they're giving Obama is downright Gandhian. But there are hard-nosed arguments for Obama, too. Nothing would energize the dispirited, disoriented Republicans like running against Hillary Clinton. And a late-entry challenge from Mayor Michael Bloomberg and his billions would be far less likely if Obama became the Democratic nominee.

Obama's Democratic critics worry that his soaring rhetoric of reconciliation is naïve. But, as Mark Schmitt has argued in the *American Prospect*, Obama's national-unity pitch should be viewed as a tactic as well as an ideal. It might lengthen his coattails, helping Democratic candidates for the House and the Senate in marginally red districts and states. It would not protect him from attack, of course, but it would enable him to fire back from the high ground. And, as a new president elected with a not quite filibuster-proof Senate, he would be in a better position to peel off the handful of Republican senators he would need to make meaningful legislative progress than someone who started from a defensive crouch. Hillary Clinton would make a competent, knowledgeable, and responsible president. Barack Obama just might make a transformative one.

HIGHER STANDARDS

February 15, 2008

A few days before Senator Barack Obama swept the Democratic primaries in Virginia, Maryland, and the District of Columbia, people across the country, picking up their favorite newspaper, were greeted with the following headline:

OLD FRIENDS SAY DRUGS PLAYED
BIG PART IN OBAMA'S YOUNG LIFE

In any event, that's what some readers thought they read. On second glance, they realized their mistake. The headline actually said this:

OLD FRIENDS SAY DRUGS PLAYED
BIT PART IN OBAMA'S YOUNG LIFE

Maybe, though, the mistake wasn't just the readers', especially the bleary-eyed among them who hadn't yet had their morning coffee. After all, it wasn't exactly news that "drugs" had played a part (and only a "bit part" at that) in the adolescence of the junior senator from Illinois. That particular factoid had been on the public record for more than twelve years. And if it wasn't news, what was it doing on the front page of the *New York Times*?

The big news, or bit news, about Obama and drugs had been broken by the future presidential candidate himself, in *Dreams from My Father*, published in 1995, when he was thirty-three years old. In *Dreams*, Obama treats his teenage chemical indulgences the way he treats pretty much everything else in his coming-of-age story: subtly, with impressive emotional acuity, against a richly drawn personal, cultural, and social background. Ripped from their context like the heart of an Aztec sacrifice, the facts Obama presents are these: He smoked pot during his last couple of years of high school, in Hawaii, and his first couple of years of college, at Occidental, in California. Once in a while, he treated himself to "a little blow." After his sophomore year, he transferred east, to Columbia, where he took up running (three miles a day), stopped hanging out in bars, and started keeping a journal. Also, he writes, "I quit getting high." That's about all. Substance, apparently, became more interesting to him than substance abuse.

But it's not as if the *Times'* nearly two thousand words had nothing to add to this. "Mr. Obama's account of his younger self and drugs, though, significantly differs from the recollections of others," the paper's story teases, as if promising scandal. Is a Perry Mason moment at hand? Not really:

> In more than three dozen interviews, friends, classmates and mentors from his high school and Occidental recalled Mr. Obama as being grounded, motivated and poised, someone who did not appear to be grappling with any drug problems and seemed to dabble only with marijuana.

The news here is—what, exactly? That Obama, who now appears grounded, motivated, and poised, formerly appeared grounded, motivated, and poised? That his inner uncertainties, such as they were, were more apparent to himself than to others? That he was marginally *less* of a pothead than he has made himself out to be?

If this last was the point, it at least shows that times have—to use the past participle of Obama's favorite word—changed. For a candidate to stand accused of *exaggerating* his youthful drug use is something new indeed. Yet the overall cultural trend is unmistakable. In 1987, Douglas H. Ginsburg's disclosure that (as the *Times* reported) "he had smoked marijuana a number of times after becoming a professor at the Harvard Law School" sank his Supreme Court nomination faster than you could just say no. In 1992, making an early foray into verbal hairsplitting, Bill Clinton said he had "never broken a state law," meaning that England was where he hadn't inhaled. By 2000, we were well into the age of the "experimented with marijuana" dodge, with getting zonked spun as a science project. But in 2004 the three leading Democratic hopefuls—John Kerry, Howard Dean, and John Edwards—all acknowledged without quibbling that they'd smoked pot.

As for the two other senators who currently stand a chance of being elected president, Hillary Clinton and John McCain have issued denials, though McCain seemed downright apologetic about it. Asked the question in 2000, he pointed out that he was in a North Vietnamese prison camp by the time pot became the Navy's weed of choice when the smoking lamp was lit. "Also," he added sheepishly, "remember my age: sixty-three." And the current occupier of the Oval Office? Well, George W. Bush announced in 1999 that he had been drug free since 1974.

None of this ought to matter, of course. Voters, rightly, don't much seem to care. But there is a glaring discontinuity between the lived experience of Americans and the drug policies of their government. Nearly a hundred million of us—forty percent of the adult population, including pillars of the nation's political, financial, academic, and media elites—have smoked (and, therefore, possessed) marijuana at some point, thereby committing an offense that, with a bit of bad luck, could have resulted in humiliation, the loss of benefits such as college loans and scholarships, or worse. More than forty thousand people are in jail for marijuana offenses, and some seven hundred thousand are arrested annually merely for possession. Meanwhile, the percentage of high school seniors who have used pot has remained steady, between forty and fifty percent. Nor have the prices of illicit drugs—which would rise sharply if the drug war were having any success—changed appreciably. Indeed, according to the government's *National Drug Threat Assessment* for 2008, increases in domestic pot production, combined with the continued flow from abroad, point to a future of "market saturation," which "could reduce the price of the drug significantly." Meanwhile, potency has "reached its highest recorded level."

Of all our country's ongoing wars—poverty, cancer, Iraq, Afghanistan—none is a more comprehensive disaster than the war on drugs. Unlike McCain, Obama and Clinton have at least promised to stop the feds from harassing medical marijuana patients and dispensaries in the dozen states whose laws permit marijuana to be used for medical purposes. But neither has given any indication of a willingness to rescue us from the larger disgrace of the drug war—the billions wasted, the millions harmed, the utter futility of it. On this point, hesitancy trumps hope, and expedience trumps experience.

CONDIMENT

March 7, 2008

Last Tuesday night, after Vermont, Rhode Island, Ohio, and Texas gave John S. McCain the delegates he needed to clinch his party's presidential nomination, good fellowship reigned—among Republicans, that is. "Senator McCain has run an honorable campaign, because he's an honorable man," McCain's last serious intraparty rival said. McCain returned the compliment: "I want to commend, again, my friend Governor Mike Huckabee." McCain does not always use the word "friend" in a friendly spirit; this time, though, he sounded perfectly amiable. The celestial choirs were a little more muffled the next day, in the White House Rose Garden. President Bush, offering the nominee-elect his (somewhat superfluous) endorsement, referred to McCain as "my friend" and himself as "your friend." McCain, for his part, abjured the "f" word. He did say that he looked forward to their campaigning together, "in keeping with the president's heavy schedule." In the eight minutes that remained of the ceremony, the candidate contrived to mention the president's schedule four more times, always stressing how very busy it must be.

Despite the manifold signs of a perfect Democratic storm this year, McCain is in an enviable position. He can get some sleep. He can raise some money. He can watch with interest as Hillary Clinton spends her millions trying to dismember Barack Obama and Obama spends his trying to keep his limbs attached. Meanwhile, he can continue to tack between the two ideological and stylistic identities that have got him where he is today—the rebel and the regular, the Rooseveltian (Theodore) and the Reaganite, the "maverick" and the "conservative"—without veering so far to one side that he forfeits the advantages of the other.

Over the years, McCain has performed this delicate task with some success, pairing up positions like Noah bringing animals aboard the ark. He plumped for lobbying reform but has lobbyists running his campaign. He opposed enacting Bush's tax cuts for the rich but supports extending them indefinitely. He supported a "patients' bill of rights" but refuses to treat health care as itself a right. He voted against banning same-sex marriage in the Constitution but favors banning it state by state. He once disdained the likes of the Reverend Jerry Falwell (who blamed AIDS on God's alleged hatred of a "society that tolerates homosexuals") but now embraces the likes of Pastor John Hagee (who called the Roman Catholic Church "the great whore"). He was for starting the Iraq war but against the way it was being fought; now he's for the way it's being fought but against discussing whether it should have been started. There is at least one question, however, to which two answers won't do.

"WITH MCCAIN ATOP TICKET, TALK SHIFTS TO SPOT NO. 2," the *Times* headlined the day after Spot No. 1 was definitively filled. According to the accompanying story, McCain has no vice presidential short list and no process for making one, "merely a process to find a process." Nevertheless, the paper assembled a list of its own, based, one assumes, partly on conversations with persons in the know. At the top: Governors Tim Pawlenty, of Minnesota; Charlie Crist, of Florida; Jon Huntsman, Jr., of Utah; and Mark Sanford, of South Carolina. The "mentioned as well" category included three former governors: Tom Ridge, of Pennsylvania, and two of McCain's vanquished primary opponents, Mitt Romney, of Massachusetts, and Huckabee, of Arkansas.

What shines through this list of names is the banality of the calculations behind it. All are off-the-shelf conservatives, ranging from the socially mild (Crist) to the fiscally rabid (Sanford, who labels himself "a right-wing nut"). All are white males. All, as governors or ex-governors, compensate for McCain's dearth of administrative experience. Several might help move some battleground state from purple to red. None would disturb the peace—emphatically including the peace of the Democratic Party, if it ever regains it.

This space is usually devoted to pristine moral reasoning, but, hell, it's an election year. Let's get down and dirty. If McCain really wants to have it all—to refurbish his maverick image without having to flip-flop on the panderings that have tarnished it; to galvanize the attention of the press, the nation, and the world; to make a bold play for the center without seriously alienating "the base"—then he can avail himself of a highly interesting option: Condoleezza Rice.

To deal first with the obvious: Rice may be "only" the second woman and the second African-American to be secretary of state, but she is indisputably the highest-ranking black female official ever to have served in any branch of the United States government. Her nomination to a constitutional executive office would cost McCain the votes of his party's hardened racists and incorrigible misogynists. They are surely fewer in number, though, than the people who would like to participate in breaking the glass ceiling of race or gender but, given the choice, would rather do so in a more timid way, and/or without abandoning their party. And with Rice on the ticket the Republicans could attack Clinton or Obama with far less restraint.

By choosing Rice, McCain would shackle himself anew to Bush's Iraq war. But it's hard to see how those chains could get much tighter than he has already made them. Rice would fit nicely into McCain's view of the war as worth fighting but, until Donald Rumsfeld's exit from the Pentagon, fought clumsily. And it would be fairly easy to establish a story line that would cast Rice as having been less Bush's enabler than a loyal subordinate who nevertheless pushed gently from within for a more reasonable, more diplomatic approach.

Rice is already fourth in line for the presidency, and getting bumped up three places would be a shorter leap than any of the three presidential candidates propose to make. It's true that her record in office has been one of failure, from downgrading terrorism as a priority before 9/11 to ignoring the Israel-Palestine problem until (almost certainly) too late. But this does not seem to have done much damage to her popularity. In a *Washington Post*-ABC News poll taken when opposition to the Iraq war was approaching its height, she enjoyed a "favorable-unfavorable" rating of nearly two to one. The conservative rank and file likes her. Though she once described herself as "mildly pro-choice," she is agile enough to complete the journey to mildly pro-life. And she is a preacher's daughter.

Choosing Rice would be a trick. Her failures would be buried in an avalanche of positive publicity for a personal story as yet only vaguely known to the broad public. (One of the little girls who died in the 1963 Birmingham church bombing was her playmate? We didn't know that!) But the trick would not be an entirely cynical one. Her ascension, though nowhere near as momentous a breakthrough as the election of Obama or Clinton, would be a breakthrough all the same. In this connection, a kind word for George W. Bush may be in order. By appointing first Colin Powell and then Rice to the most senior job in the Cabinet, a job of global scope, Bush changed the way millions of white Americans think about black public officials. This may turn out to be the most positive legacy of his benighted presidency.

MR. AND MS. SPOKEN

April 25, 2008

When the footage surfaced showing that Hillary Clinton, contrary to what she had been claiming in campaign speeches, had not been obliged to duck and run from sniper fire during her visit to Bosnia in 1996 but, rather, had listened smilingly as a little girl recited a poem about peace, the former First Lady, now the junior senator from New York and a candidate for president, explained, "I misspoke." When the man whom Clinton still hopes to run against in November charged that Iranian agents are "taking Al Qaeda into Iran, training them, and sending them back"—even though Shiite Iran and Sunni Al Qaeda have no use for each other—his campaign had an identical explanation: "John McCain misspoke."

Along with its various derivatives, "misspeak" has become one of the signature verbal workhorses of this interminable political season, right up there with "narrative," "Day One," and "hope." It carries the suggestion that, while the politician's perfectly functioning brain has dispatched the correct signals, the mouth has somehow received and transmitted them in altered form. "Misspeak" is a powerful word, a magical word. It is a word that is apparently thought capable, in its contemporary political usage, of isolating a palpable, possibly toxic untruth, sealing it up in an airtight bag, and disposing of it harmlessly.

Such a feat of modern hygiene is impressive in a word of such ancient origins. The *Oxford English Dictionary* finds it in Chaucer ("I me repente / If I mis spak"), but the hoary examples involve meanings that are either obsolete (to calumniate) or irrelevant to the present case (to mispronounce or speak incorrectly, a specialty of George W. "Misunderestimated" Bush). The last item in *Oxford*'s half-column entry, however, gets us where Senators Clinton and McCain want us to go:

3.b. *refl.* To fail to convey the meaning one intends by one's words.

This use of "misspeak" is of American origin. *Oxford*'s first example ("I believe he misspoke himself") is drawn from, aptly, the *Congressional Record*, 1894; its second ("The President misspoke himself") is from Richard Nixon's iconic press secretary, Ron Ziegler, in 1973, annus mirabilis of the Classical period of American misspeaking.

It is certainly true that Clinton and McCain failed to convey their intended meanings, which were, in the broadest sense, "I have put myself in harm's way for my country" and "I'm a majorly knowledgeable expert on the Middle East," respectively. But even considering their statements in a narrower, non-meta sense, you have to wonder. It is a fact, now established by videotape evidence and eyewitness testimony, that there was no sniper fire—no unusual danger of any kind—near that Bosnian tarmac. So what was Clinton thinking when, not once but several times, she said that there was? Was she lying, as many of her critics maintain? That seems improbable. More likely, she just misremembered. Her Bosnian jaunt took her into a still not completely stable area that had lately been a war zone. The military plane carrying her descended at a steep angle. For the landing, she was summoned to the armored cockpit, just in case. She was surrounded by nervous, gun-toting soldiers. She was having a radically new experience; no doubt she was nervous herself. Couldn't she have *felt* under fire, with mundane tricks of memory doing the rest?

Clinton's misspeak, or whatever it was, had no policy implications, but it fit nicely into a "narrative" left over from the scandals, real and (mostly) fake, of the Clinton administration: "travelgate," the Rose Law Firm billing records, the "secret" health-care task force, William Safire's "congenital liar" sideswipe. The trap is similar to the one sprung on Gary Hart in the 1984 campaign, when reporters seized on the "signature thing" (Hart kept changing his signature, eventually settling on a modish caps-and-small-caps slant) and the "name thing" (he had changed his name from Hartpence), because they were convinced that Hart was "Gatsbyesque." But Clinton's sniper falsehood also fit into a newer, truer story, a story of ruthlessness: her "3 A.M." ad; her suggestion that her Democratic rival, Senator Barack Obama, is, unlike her and McCain, unqualified to be president; her remark that Obama is not a Muslim "as far as I know"; her use of an interview with, of all people, Richard Mellon Scaife, who spent millions in the nineteen-nineties manufacturing smears against her and her husband, to fan the embers of the controversy over Obama's pastor; and more.

And McCain's gaffe? Well, saying "Iraq" when you mean to say "Iran," or vice versa, is a fairly common mistake. Consider this exchange from last week's Senate Foreign Relations Committee's questioning of Ryan Crocker, the American ambassador in Baghdad:

> OBAMA: Do we feel confident that the Iraqi government is directing these—this aid to these special groups? Do we feel confident about that, or do we think that they're just tacitly tolerating it? Do you have some sense of that?
>
> CROCKER: There's no question in our minds that the Iranian government, and in particular the Quds Force, is—this is a conscious, carefully worked-out policy.

It was so obvious that Obama meant "the Iranian government" when he said "the Iraqi government" that Crocker didn't bother to interrupt the flow by correcting him. (This was a genuine misspeak.) The McCain mistake was different. It's easy to say one word when you

mean to say another, nearly identical word, but it's impossible to repeatedly misspeak an entire anecdote—or, as in McCain's case, an entire
strategic reality. This wasn't the first time McCain said that Iran was
arming Al Qaeda; it was, by one count, the fifth. His spokesman put
out a press release saying that the candidate had "immediately corrected
himself," but that wasn't true, either; it was McCain's sidekick, Senator
Joseph Lieberman, the Connecticut sort-of Democrat, who corrected
him, in a whispered aside.

Unlike Clinton's, McCain's error *did* have policy implications. This
was not, as some have suggested, a "senior moment." McCain knows
perfectly well that Shiites are not Sunnis, that the enmity of the two
branches of Islam fuels Iraq's self-immolation, and that Iran's Shiite
mullahs and Iraq's Sunni terrorists are not cohorts in the same legion.
But his rhetorical conflation of them, if one assumes that it is not done
in bad faith, is of a piece with his apparent conviction that the Iraq war
is very like the Second World War, the Korean War, or Vietnam: a war
against a unified, tightly organized enemy—a war destined to end, if
ever, in a clear-cut victory (or an equally clear-cut defeat), a war with
the aim of bringing about a postwar settlement under which American
troops can be stationed indefinitely in the former battle zone as more or
less welcome guests of a stable host government. That's not misspeaking. It's misthinking—and, in both senses, it's misleading.

BITTER PATTER

April 18, 2008

Last Wednesday's two-hour televised smackdown in Philadelphia between the two remaining Democratic candidates for president, which might have been billed as the Elite Treat v. the Boilermaker Belle, turned into something worse—something akin to a federal crime. Call it the case of the Walt Disney Company v. People of the Commonwealth of Pennsylvania (and People of the United States of America, for that matter). Seldom has a large corporation so heedlessly inflicted so much civic damage in such a short space of time.

None of the other debates had been models of philosophic rigor. But, right from the start, there were clues that the sponsor of this one— ABC News, a part of the ABC network, which is owned by Disney— might establish new benchmarks of degradation. After brief opening statements from the candidates, Senators Hillary Clinton and Barack Obama, ABC immediately cut to an advertisement for a cell phone company. A commercial? Already? Were candidates for president of the United States being used as teasers?

After the break, one of ABC's moderators, Charles Gibson, asked Clinton and Obama to "pledge now" that whichever of them wins the presidential nomination take the runner-up as his or her running

mate. ABC put on the screen a solemn quote from the Constitution
(they were at the National Constitution Center, get it?)—the bit where
it says, "In every Case, after the Choice of the President, the Person
having the greatest Number of Votes of the Electors shall be the Vice
President."

It happens that this part of the Constitution was scrapped after the
election of 1800. It should no more be cited as evidence of the Framers' wisdom than should the equally defunct passage calling for "three
fifths of all other Persons"—i.e., slaves—to count toward congressional apportionment. It also happens that Gibson's question was not only
premised on nonsense but also profoundly unhelpful, because the only
answers it could elicit would be both predictable and substance-free.
And so they were.

If Gibson and his partner, George Stephanopoulos, had halted their
descent at the level of the fatuous, that would have been bad enough.
But there was worse to come. In the seven weeks since the previous
Clinton-Obama debate, the death toll of American troops in Iraq had
reached four thousand; the president had admitted that his "national
security team," including the vice president, had met regularly in the
White House to approve the torture of prisoners; house repossessions
topped fifty thousand per month and unemployment topped five percent; and the poll-measured proportion of Americans who believe
that "things have pretty seriously gotten off on the wrong track" hit
eighty-one percent, a record. Yet for most of the next hour Gibson
and Stephanopoulos limited their questioning to the following topics:
Obama's April 6 remark about "bitter" small-towners; whether each
candidate thinks the other can win; the Obama family's ex-pastor, Jeremiah A. Wright, Jr.; Clinton's tale of sniper fire in Bosnia; Obama's
failure to wear a flag lapel pin; and Obama's acquaintance with a college professor in his Chicago neighborhood who, while Obama was
in grade school, was a member of the Weather Underground. And
the problem wasn't just the questions' subject matter, or the fact that
all but the last had been thoroughly raked over already; it was their

moral and intellectual vacuity. "Number one, do you think Reverend Wright loves America as much as you do?" That was Stephanopoulos. (His follow-up: "But you do believe he's as patriotic as you are?") The idea was to force Obama either to denigrate Wright's patriotism or to equate it with his own. Obama's exasperation showed, though he slipped the trap by pointing to Wright's service in the Marines. One question—"I want to know if you believe in the American flag"—was apparently beneath the dignity of even Gibson and Stephanopoulos, so ABC hunted up a purportedly typical voter to ask it on videotape.

Still, it wasn't ABC's fault that Obama's demeanor was as listless as the assembled journalists and spinners (for both sides) judged it to be. His mind was engaged—that much is clear if one reads the transcript, in which the match is noticeably more even than it was on the screen— but his spirit was absent. His opponent, by contrast, was sharp and alert, missing no opportunity to press the lines of attack that the moderators helpfully opened up.

Obama was coming off a harrowing week that was of his own making. No one had forced him to say, of people whose "jobs have been gone now for twenty-five years," that "they get bitter, they cling to guns or religion or antipathy toward people who aren't like them or anti-immigrant sentiment or anti-trade sentiment as a way to explain their frustrations." That he said this at an off-the-record fund-raiser in San Francisco amplified the gaffe. But the context (there was one) is worth noting. Obama was arguing that his trouble with part of the "white working class" is *not* fundamentally racial:

> Here's how it is: in a lot of these communities in big industrial states like Ohio and Pennsylvania, people have been beaten down so long, and they feel so betrayed by government, and when they hear a pitch that is premised on not being cynical about government, then a part of them just doesn't buy it. And when it's delivered by—it's true that

when it's delivered by a forty-six-year-old black man named Barack
Obama, then that adds another layer of skepticism.

From 1972 onward, Republicans have successfully deployed the trope
of "elitism" against every Democratic opponent except the two winners, Jimmy Carter and Bill Clinton. But this year it has been deployed
Democrat-on-Democrat, with Hillary Clinton accusing Obama not
just of elitism but also of being condescending and demeaning. Obama
was not saying that people *acquire* religious belief on account of worldly
troubles. He was saying that when such troubles appear insurmountable
the already religious seek comfort and help from a higher power. Hillary Clinton must know this. Surely she remembers that when her husband's sex scandals threatened the survival of his presidency and their
marriage, the Clintons summoned the clergy (including, by the way,
the Reverend Jeremiah Wright).

Hillary Clinton explained her culture-war assault on Obama by saying that the "issue" in question is bound to be one "that certainly the
Republicans will be raising" (though that hardly justifies inviting them
to do so with her imprimatur). Clinton portrays herself as a seasoned
survivor of the worst that the Republican attack machine can dish out.
She has been relatively unrestrained in her battle with Obama, but he
has had one hand tied behind him in his battle with her. He cannot
mention many of her biggest general-election vulnerabilities, most of
which involve her husband's administration, the awkward role that he
might play in her own, and the potential conflicts of interest posed
by the funding of his charitable and commercial activities. Bill Clinton remains popular among Democrats, if not as popular as he used to
be. Anyway, all-out attack would undermine the unifying theme of
Obama's campaign.

Obama's argument is that he represents a new kind of politics; Clinton's is that she can practice the old kind more expertly. John McCain
will have plenty of allies and outriders eager to wield the blades

sharpened in the campaigns of George W. Bush and Karl Rove. But McCain—whose sense of honor, however selective, is real—shows few signs of wishing to take up those weapons himself. Barring a much, much bigger than expected Clinton victory in this week's Pennsylvania primary, Obama will face McCain in the fall. At least at the candidate-to-candidate level, hope and experience will square off at last. The battle might even be about ideas.

YOU DON'T NEED
A WEATHERMAN

April 22, 2008

Question: does the attempt to hang William Ayers around Barack Obama's neck amount to "McCarthyism"? Answer: yes.

McCarthyism is a term rarely heard since the Cold War ended, but, like "red-baiting," it used to get tossed around on the left entirely too loosely during the nineteen-sixties and seventies. There were those who failed to understand that it's not red-baiting to point out that a person is a Communist—*if that person really is a Communist.* McCarthyism is a little more complicated. It wasn't McCarthyism to deny a government worker who was a member of the Communist Party access to classified materials. It wasn't McCarthyism for the A.C.L.U. to bar Communists from membership. It wasn't McCarthyism to fire a person from a public school teaching job for being a Communist if that person was using his or her position to propagandize to students. Similarly, it wasn't McCarthyism to call somebody a "Communist sympathizer" if that somebody sympathized with the salient features of Communism, such as one-party rule, totalitarian repression of alternative opinions, the abolition of civil liberties, and murderous gulags. But it was, and is, McCarthyism to try to comprehensively ruin a person's life solely because that person was once a Communist (or a Fascist, or a racist, or a radical Islamist)—or even if that person is still a whatever-ist but doesn't actually *do* anything about it.

The central feature of McCarthyism, however, was accusing people of being Communists or Communist sympathizers who were not, in fact, either. And one of Senator Joseph McCarthy's favorite evidentiary techniques for carrying out this particular form of character assassination was "guilt by association."

Guilt by association is another tricky term. The Communist Party is an association, and being a member of that association does indeed makes you guilty of being a Communist. A garden club is also an association. But being in a garden club with a Communist doesn't make you a Communist. And being in a garden club with an ex-Communist doesn't even make you an ex-Communist.

Which brings us to William Ayers.

The relevant facts:

1. Ayers and his wife, Bernadine Dohrn, were prominent members of the Weather Underground nearly forty years ago, when Barack Obama was a child. They are now, respectively, a professor of education at the University of Illinois at Chicago and an associate professor of law at Northwestern. They long ago abandoned the political ideas they supported in their youth, which speaks well for them, but they never acknowledged that those ideas were mindless and vicious, which does not. They live in the same Chicago neighborhood as Obama.

2. When Obama first ran for state senator, in 1995, the incumbent he hoped to replace introduced him to Ayers and Dohrn at a social gathering in their home. Ayers later donated two hundred dollars to his campaign fund.

3. For three years, ending in 2002, Ayers and Obama were both on the board of the Woods Fund of Chicago, a local foundation that gives grants to anti-poverty and arts programs. Ayers is still on the

board, which currently has nine members, mostly bankers, lawyers, academics, and businesspeople.

4. There is absolutely no evidence that Obama ever sympathized with the politics of the Weather Underground, and there is overwhelming evidence (read his books) that he didn't and doesn't.

McCarthyism is not a charge to be levelled lightly. Even so, I conclude from these facts that attacking Obama because of his "association with" Ayers constitutes McCarthyism. Any uncertainty on this point disappears when one considers that George Stephanopoulos, who should have known better, justified making an "issue" of that association by telling Obama that it came under the heading of "the general theme of patriotism in your relationships."

OVER NOT OUT

May 9, 2008

When the polls closed in Indiana and North Carolina last Tuesday evening, a lot of Barack Obama supporters braced themselves for bad news. Their candidate had just gone through a harrowing month, divided neatly in two by his thumping in the Pennsylvania primary. He had been repeatedly gored by a pair of old bulls, his ex-president and his ex-pastor, both of them maddened by his success and aggrieved by his presumption. He had been singed in a media bonfire sparked by trivia and fanned into flame by culture-war-mongering. His remark about the bitterness of displaced workers supposedly made him an elitist; his glancing acquaintance with a sixty-something ex-Weatherman supposedly made him a friend of terrorists. On the stump, he seemed subdued, wearied by the bumpy last stage of the long, astonishing ascent he began fifteen months ago, when he set out to do battle with one of the most famous women in the world, whose arsenal included a huge war chest, backed by a fund-raising apparatus unparalleled in Democratic politics; the support of the great majority of Democratic officeholders ready to declare a preference; and, as her chief surrogate, the most successful Democratic politician of the past forty years. Although North Carolina had long been

seen as a lock for Obama, on account of its large African-American population, there were late polls that put him and Hillary Clinton within
the margin of error; Indiana seemed out of reach, according to the polls,
which in any case had a record of overestimating his strength.

Losing both states probably wouldn't have cost Obama the nomination, but it would have meant, at a minimum, a brutal, ugly,
down-to-the-wire endgame guaranteed to leave the ultimate winner
seriously, perhaps fatally, weakened. So when the returns started coming in, showing an Obama landslide in North Carolina and a shrinking Clinton lead in Indiana, Obama supporters looked at one another
in happy wonderment. As Clinton's margin in Indiana slipped below
twenty thousand, Tim Russert, of NBC, went on the air to say, bluntly,
"We now know who the Democratic nominee's going to be, and no
one's going to dispute it." Just after dawn, ABC's George Stephanopoulos decreed, "This nomination fight is over." On CBS, Bob Schi-
effer brought the networks to unanimity. "Basically," he said, "this
race is over." And the *New York Post* hit the streets with cruel tabloid
succinctness: a picture of the home-state senator over a single word—
"TOAST!"—in block letters three inches high.

When and where, it is not too soon to ask, did she go wrong? Well,
here's one answer: eight years ago, in New York. If she had chosen,
instead, to move to Illinois, where her accent is familiar and her connections deep (Chicago's her home town, after all), she could have
settled in and sought her Senate seat there, in 2004. She didn't do that,
presumably for reasons both marital (Bill's not really a Second City
kind of guy) and political (she would have had to run for president as
a first-term senator rather than as a reelected one). But Barack Obama
would still be a local or regional up-and-comer and, most likely, a Hillary supporter. Here's another: five and a half years ago, in Washington.
If she had opposed authorizing the Iraq war, the activists—grassroots
and netroots—might have mobilized for her rather than against her.
She might have cruised to the nomination, and the Democratic Party

might now be basking in the warm glow of being about to make history by electing the first woman president.

It is surely beyond galling for Hillary Clinton to find herself losing to a freshman senator who is young (forty-six, Bill Clinton's age when he got elected), whose "firstness" matches hers, who has no executive experience at any level of government and not much foreign-policy experience of the conventional kind, and whom few Americans had heard of until, at John Kerry's invitation, he stood up to deliver the keynote address at the 2004 convention. You have to feel a little sorry for the Clintons, having their restoration upended by such an unlooked-for political phenomenon. But some months ago, when it dawned on the Clintons that "winning clean" might not be a viable option, they began to explore less elevated paths. The summertime gas-tax holiday that became her hobbyhorse in Indiana and North Carolina was one of the milder examples. Its original proposer was John McCain, the presumptive Republican nominee, yet it had no support in the White House, and virtually none in the Democratic Congress. A hundred economists, including liberal stalwarts like James Galbraith, Alice Rivlin, and the Nobelist Joseph Stiglitz, denounced it, and the Clinton campaign could find none to endorse it. Obama rejected it, rightly, as a gimmick, and said that at best it might save the average motorist a total of thirty dollars. Even that was too generous; according to the economists, it would probably just transfer revenue from the government to the oil companies. It was a pseudo-populist hoax—an act of condescension far more profound than Obama's remark about bitterness. And, to judge by the results last Tuesday, it was a failure as a political ploy.

The TV pundits were both right and wrong. They were right that we now know who the nominee will be, but they were wrong about the race being over. Much will depend on how it gets to be over and, especially, on how Senator Clinton behaves. Her speech in Indiana was incoherent, part valedictory ("This has been an extraordinary experience"), part battle cry ("Full speed on to the White House!"), but more the latter than the former. She demanded that her Florida and

Michigan delegates, elected in defiance of party rules that she had agreed to follow, be fully accredited. "It would be a little strange to have a nominee chosen by forty-eight states," she said, and her husband, in an e-mail to supporters, added, "People want Hillary to stay in this race until every last voter has a say." (Never mind that in January the Clintons' chamberlain, Terry McAuliffe, had called the race "a twenty-seven-state contest" that would be "over on February 5.") Still, her speech was notably free of attacks on Obama or insinuations about his color.

The next day, however, in an instantly notorious interview with *USA Today*, Clinton was back to arguing her superior electability. "There was just an A.P. article posted that found how Senator Obama's support among working, hardworking Americans, white Americans, is weakening again, and how the whites in both states who had not completed college were supporting me," she said. "There's a pattern emerging here."

Indeed there is, and it should be painted over as soon as possible. Hillary Clinton, as her record from high school onward proves, is the very opposite of a racist. This time, she seems to have well and truly misspoken. But if she plans to drag the contest out for another month or two she will be wise to avoid this sort of demographic analysis—and, more important, to abandon the dishonorable political strategy that underlies it. If she doesn't, it won't just be Chicago that she didn't go back to. It'll be a place called hope.

AFTER PENNSYLVANIA

April 25, 2008

During the contentious runup to the Pennsylvania primary, the polling numbers (national and statewide) hardly changed. A lot of commentators concluded that Obama's Wright/Ayers/"bitter" troubles and the Clinton attacks based on them had had no effect, apart from driving Clinton's negatives up faster than his. I'm no pollster—I have only the vaguest notion of what "internals" are—but I don't believe it. I'm pretty sure that the onslaught levelled what otherwise would have been a steep upward curve for the big O.

The *Times*, in a surprisingly angry editorial (possibly reflecting the editorial board's irritation at having been ordered to endorse Clinton), had this to say about what its headline called her "Low Road to Victory":

> The Pennsylvania campaign, which produced yet another inconclusive result on Tuesday, was even meaner, more vacuous, more desperate, and more filled with pandering than the mean, vacuous, desperate, pander-filled contests that preceded it.
>
> Voters are getting tired of it; it is demeaning the political process; and it does not work. It is past time for Senator Hillary Rodham Clinton to

acknowledge that the negativity, for which she is mostly responsible, does nothing but harm to her, her opponent, her party and the 2008 election.

One may doubt that the Clinton campaign will heed exhortations of this kind. Hillary and her lieutenants, many of them, have evidently persuaded themselves that (a) it is absolutely certain that Obama would lose in November and (b) they are courageously braving the squeamish disapproval of *bien pensants* such as the *Times* (and the *New Yorker*) by destroying him before he can lure the Democratic Party to disaster. To the extent that they sincerely believe this, they are acting in a kind of twisted good faith—the kind that often marks those who have got hold of an end they see as justifying almost any means.

Their backup justification is that they are performing a service to the party and to Obama by toughening him up and giving him practice in parrying the Republican thrusts he would face as the nominee. And they are surely right that those thrusts would be nastier than the ones he has faced from the Clintons. The reasoning is that while Clinton is (to quote myself) "a seasoned survivor of the worst that the Republican attack machine can dish out," Obama isn't.

Or is she? Clinton has thrown her kitchen sink at him, but—for hardheaded as well as high-minded reasons—he has not thrown his at her. (I know—turning the other cheek got Jesus crucified. But it also got Montgomery's buses integrated. And India liberated.)

Consider this.

In the Philadelphia debate, Clinton amplified ABC's odious question about Bill Ayers by saying piously that Obama's "relationship" with Ayers

continued after 9/11 and after his reported comments, which were deeply hurtful to people in New York, and I would hope to every American, because they were published on 9/11 and he said that he was just sorry they [the Weather Underground] hadn't done more [bombing].

(I should note here that Ayers's "comments" were not among the things that New Yorkers—this New Yorker, anyway—found "deeply hurtful" that day. To the extent that we paid attention to them at all, we—I—found them contemptible, and we were—I was—grimly pleased that his long-dodged karma had, in a small way, caught up with him: his book tour was ruined.)

Hillary has her own vulnerability in this general area, and it is larger than the fact, mentioned by Obama in his riposte to her, that her husband, on his last day in office, commuted the sentences of a couple of old Weather Underground jailbirds. (After a decade and a half in stir, they had been denied parole, apparently unfairly. Good for Bill.) What Obama did *not* mention was Hillary's internship, back in the groovy summer of 1971, at the Oakland law firm of Treuhaft, Walker and Burnstein. Treuhaft (Robert Treuhaft, husband of Jessica Mitford) had left the Communist Party thirteen years earlier, but Walker (Doris Walker) was still a member, and the firm was a pillar of the Bay Area Old Left. I assume that Obama didn't mention this because doing so would have rightly pissed off a lot of Democrats, because he is running as a non-kneecapping uniter, and because there is no evidence that Clinton has or has ever had the slightest sympathy with Communism. (Of course, there is no such evidence with respect to Obama and Weather Underground-ism, either, but that didn't stop Hillary from twisting that particular knife.)

My point is that Hillary Clinton has not, in fact, survived the worst that the Republican attack machine (and its pilotless drones online and on talk radio) can dish out. We will learn what the worst really means if she is nominated. The Commie law firm will be only the beginning. Many tempting targets remain to be machine-gunned, from Bill's little-examined fund-raising and business activities during the past seven years to the prospect of his hanging around the White House in some as yet undefined role for another four or eight years to whatever leftovers from the Clinton "scandals" of the nineteen-nineties can be retrieved from the dumpster and reheated. The whole Clinton marital soap opera, obviously off limits within the Democratic fold, will offer ample material for what Obama calls "distractions." To take the most obvious example, the former president's social life since leaving the White House will become, if not "fair game," big game—and some of these right-wing dirtbags are already hiring bearers and trying on pith helmets for the safari. Is this a "there" where the Democratic Party really wants to go?

PRIEST-RIDDEN NO MORE

April 30, 2008

Yesterday, Barack Obama offered his response to the Jeremiah Wright Narcissism Tour, which culminated two days ago with a raucous appearance at the National Press Club. Obama denounced Wright, as the *Times* put it, in terms "far harsher than those he used in his speech on race in Philadelphia last month" and cut all his ties to "the man who presided at Mr. Obama's wedding and baptized his two daughters."

The reaction of the commentators has been mostly favorable (presumably excepting Fox, which I didn't watch) but also mostly of the opinion that Obama was late, perhaps too late. They may be right, tactically speaking—but not humanly speaking. And Obama was speaking very humanly indeed. He spoke without a text, from the heart and, as always, from the head. I don't mind that he decided to endure a couple of bad news cycles while he collected his thoughts and feelings.

Obama did not, by the way, throw his former pastor under the bus, as the metaphor du jour had it. Wright dashed in front of the bus all by himself and tried to pull Obama along with him, and to all appearances the pastor is enjoying the bounce as keenly as the parishioner is pained by it.

In his Philadelphia speech last month, Obama had limned some of the experience of frustration and marginalization behind the kind of collective paranoia exemplified by Wright's sermon-bites and widespread among African-Americans but by no means confined to that community. Obama was ready to understand and ultimately to forgive but not to excuse. This time, he was angry—but it was a sad anger, mixed with sorrowful determination. He was responding, this time, not only to a set of political and historical disagreements but also to a shocking personal breach. His measured performance only strengthened the conviction of many of us that his temperament is every bit as impressive, and as potentially valuable to the nation, as are his intelligence and decency.

One of the fallback positions of Obama's critics just now is that if he now believes, or claims to believe, that if Wright's opinions about AIDS and terror and the greatness of Louis Farrakhan are so objectionable, then he needs to tell us what he was doing in Wright's church to begin with. But of course he has already done that, along with describing—in print, and in greater, franker, subtler detail than any presidential candidate in our history—the American racial dilemma. As Obama suggested in his press conference yesterday, no one who has read his books could possibly imagine that he shares the outré political fantasies of his ex-pastor.

FIRST, SHOOT THE MODERATORS

May 13, 2008

S unday's *Times* mentions a notion (first reported by Bloomberg) that
is prompting some blogosphere discussion:

> In a sign of what could be an extremely unusual fall campaign, the two
> sides said Saturday that they would be open to holding joint forums or
> unmoderated debates across the country in front of voters through the
> summer. Mr. Obama, campaigning in Oregon, said that the proposal,
> floated by Mr. McCain's advisers, was "a great idea."

Great idea? The *New Republic*'s Noam Scheiber doesn't think so. He
worries that unmoderated debates would help McCain offset his financial disadvantage and "make him look much more moderate than the
Obama campaign wants him to look." Alex Massie goes further. He not
only agrees with Scheiber that McCain would be the main beneficiary
but adds that "McCain wins even if Obama rejects the idea," because
a rejection would look cowardly and hypocritical, too, given Obama's
professed wish for a more high-minded approach to politics.

Most of Scheiber's and Massie's commenters beg to differ. They think the idea would be good for both the country and Obama. I'm with the commenters on this one.

Obama's biggest advantage, even bigger than all that no-strings Internet money, is that the policies he advocates are far more appealing than McCain's. A face-to-face, man-to-man debate, unsullied by preening moderators determined to prove their toughness and boost ratings, would almost have to focus on policy. It's true that Obama has been just O.K. in most of the Democratic debates, especially compared with his performance in set speeches. But that probably reflects (a) the lack of serious ideological and policy differences on the Democratic side and (b) Obama's relative reluctance to go for broke in intra-party debates, which tend to focus on marginalia and in which one candidate's "victory" sometimes comes at the expense of his or her party's ultimate prospects. By contrast, the legitimate differences between Obama and McCain are vast. Their debates *will* be zero-sum games. Obama will no longer have any reason to hold back. On every issue, he has a case to make. McCain doesn't. Plus, McCain will be somewhat hobbled by having to defend policies he doesn't really believe in (such as extending Bush's tax cuts for the superrich), doesn't really care or know much about (such as his announced proposals for health care), or hasn't had to defend against serious opposing arguments (such as Iraq).

Granted, unstructured town hall forums have been McCain's best showcases. But it's worth noting that McCain committed his biggest blunder, the hundred years' war comment, in just such a forum.

Another reason, tactically speaking, for Obama to say yes to McCain's proposal is the dampening effect a series of buddy-movie faceoffs could have on the campaign of character assassination that is sure to be conducted by Republican surrogates and 527s.

McCain and Obama both speak of their desire to have a civil conversation. Both say they want to reach across ideological and party lines. Both say they don't regard their opponents as enemies. A series of face-to-face discussions would make it a little harder for the partisans of either candidate (I'm talking about you, Republicans) to run a parallel campaign of lies and slanders, and would ratchet up the pressure on the intended beneficiary of such a campaign to put the kibosh on it. Obama's right. It's a great idea.

MEMORY LAPSE

May 23, 2008

The precise origins of Memorial Day are a little fuzzy. According to one version, it was first celebrated in 1865, a few weeks after Lee surrendered to Grant; freed slaves and black and white Union soldiers marched to the site of a Confederate prisoner-of-war camp in Charleston, South Carolina, for some hearty hymn-singing and picnicking. Others place its beginnings in Waterloo, New York, a year later, while still others date it to 1868 and a proclamation by the commander of the Grand Army of the Republic, the Northern veterans' organization. What no one disputes is that the holiday's founding purpose was to honor the Civil War's fallen.

This year, thanks to HBO, the remembrances of the Memorial Day weekend encompassed another American civil war, happily less lethal to its combatants but far from trivial in its consequences: the election of 2000. HBO's movie *Recount* has fewer shrinks than *The Sopranos* and fewer laughs than *Curb Your Enthusiasm*, but its overall factual accuracy has been attested to by close observers of the events it portrays. It reminds us of some essential truths about the election and its aborted recount: that more Floridians went to their polling places to vote for Al Gore than for George W. Bush; that a full and fair count would have confirmed the voters' preference; that the White House was awarded to Bush, the half-million-vote loser across the nation, by a 5–4 Supreme Court diktat. The injustice of Bush v. Gore was obvious at the time; its sequel has proved it to be a tragedy.

The stock defense of Justice Antonin Scalia is a three-word sneer: "Get over it." Many people find themselves unable to take this bracing advice. The wound to the country's civic health remains fresh, though of course it is active, committed Democrats who feel it most keenly.

In the current presidential primary campaign, as in the Electoral College, the "popular vote" has no official significance. According to the party's rules, the nomination will go to whoever can garner a majority of the delegates at the convention in Denver, regardless of how many voters or caucus-goers sent them there, or didn't. (The so-called superdelegates, who make up a fifth of the convention, represent voters only in the highly attenuated sense of having earlier won public or party office.) Yet the popular vote, however juridically meaningless, carries immense moral and political weight with Democrats, for whom the 2000 travesty is a station of the cross and vote-counting a kind of sacrament. The superdelegates understand this. That's why it has been clear all along that if one of the candidates is able to claim an indisputable majority of actual flesh-and-blood Democrats it will be difficult to deny him—or her—the nomination. But what if the majority is highly disputable, and everybody has one?

"We're winning the popular vote," Hillary Clinton said last week, after prevailing in the Kentucky primary by a margin bigger than that by which she lost in Oregon. "More people have voted for me than for anyone who has ever run for the Democratic nomination." These statements must be read with the sort of close grammatical and definitional care that used to inform her husband's descriptions of his personal entanglements. They are not quite true in the normal sense, but if made under oath they would not be prosecutable for perjury, either.

In a nominating process, especially this one, the "popular vote" is an elusive phenomenon. RealClearPolitics.com, an independent Web site whose numbers political reporters and operatives tend to trust, maintains six separate tallies. At the moment, Obama leads in four of them. With or without participants in the caucus states of Iowa, Nevada, Maine, and Washington (i.e., states where voters' preferences were expressed by gathering in corners and the like, and whose numbers can be estimated but are not pinpointed), and with the totals for *both* Florida (whose primary was unsanctioned by the Democratic Party, with the consent of all the candidates, and where no one campaigned) and Michigan (also unsanctioned, and where Obama's name was not even on the ballot), Clinton's claim that more people have "voted" for her is factual. But her claim to be "ahead" depends entirely on a tally for the Michigan primary that is distinctly North Korean: Clinton, 328,309; Obama, 0. However, if the bulk of the 238,168 Michiganders who voted "uncommitted" are assumed to have been Obama supporters—a reasonable assumption—then Obama leads by every possible reckoning. And if only Florida is included, then Obama leads whether or not those four caucuses are counted.

Next week, after the three remaining primaries—Clinton is expected to sweep the largest of them, Puerto Rico's—the likelihood is that each candidate will be able to point to "metrics" showing that he or she is the people's choice. Obama will almost certainly have the better case, especially in view of opinion polls showing that his national lead among Democrats has been growing, but the reality is that the two have been almost equally strong. Obama will remain the leader in the delegate count, owing largely to a more astute strategy, and he will be the nominee. If there is a loftier lesson, it is that the nominating "system"—and not just in the Democratic Party—is an irrational mess. But that's not how Hillary Clinton sees it.

Last Wednesday, Clinton described the Democrats' long-standing reluctance to seat the Florida and Michigan delegations in their entirety, a reluctance that she shared back when she saw her nomination as inevitable, in these words: "We're seeing that right now in Zimbabwe." In a speech in Florida, she invoked the Declaration of Independence, "the

consent of the governed," the abolition of slavery, "our most fundamental values," the 1848 Seneca Falls women's-suffrage convention,
the sacrifice of soldiers, the tear gas at Selma, "equal justice under the
law," and the Voting Rights Act. Worse, she invaded the Democratic
sacristy, picked up the chalice, and flourished it like a club, saying that

> right here in Florida, you learned the hard way what happens when your
> votes aren't counted and the candidate with fewer votes is declared the
> winner. The lesson of 2000 here in Florida is crystal clear. If any votes
> aren't counted, the will of the people is not realized and our democracy
> is diminished.

Well, that depends on what the meaning of "count" is, doesn't it?
Florida's (and Michigan's) votes in January's rogue primaries were
indeed counted, and everyone understood well in advance that the
question of how they would be translated into delegates was, at best,
problematic.

In an eerie echo of the "Brooks Brothers riot" depicted in the HBO
movie, when shouting Bush operatives and Republican congressional
staffers who had been dispatched to Florida managed to shut down the
Miami-Dade County recount, CNN reported on Thursday that Clinton supporters "are planning to swarm the capital in a little over a week
to pressure Democratic Party leaders as they gather to decide the fate
of the Florida and Michigan delegations." In 2000, the candidate most
willing to deploy principles and trash them, according to the tactical
needs of the moment, was awarded the prize. In 2008, maybe not.

NO SHOVING, PLEASE

June 3, 2008

As we await the results of the last two primaries and Hillary Clinton puts her affairs in order, she and her campaign seem to be stepping up the pressure on Obama to name her as his running mate. The pressure—ranging from her own statement today that she's interested to an avalanche of supporters saying they won't vote for him unless she's on the ticket—probably means that he will have to decide quickly, one way or the other, or else risk having coverage dominated for weeks or months by nothing else.

If Hillary truly wants to be the vice presidential nominee, this pressure is a serious mistake. She would be far better off doing everything she can to take the pressure off and let Obama take his time, because if he is forced to decide soon he will have to say no. The wounds are too fresh. The feelings are too raw. It would feel like bullying—it would *be* bullying—and he cannot submit to bullying or even be seen to submit to it. She cannot be chosen in an atmosphere still dominated by anger and disappointment.

Her chances for being picked are not great anyway. The choice would muddy Obama's themes of newness, orientation to the future, generational change, and turning the page on the bitternesses of the

Clinton-Bush years. The baggage Hillary lugged through the primary campaign—especially Bill—would be transferred to Air Obama. The vetting of Bill Clinton's post-presidential activities that was left undone during the primary season, mainly because Hillary's Democratic rivals wisely avoided anything that might have cast them as Ken Starrs in the minds of Democratic voters, would happen after all. The Clinton marital soap opera would have its contract renewed. A major theme of campaign coverage, right up to the election, would be the sniping between the Obama entourage and the Clinton entourage, not to mention the triangular sniping among the Hillary Clinton entourage, the Bill Clinton entourage, and the Barack Obama entourage. It wouldn't matter if the sniping were real, imaginary, or ginned up—it would be a big story anyway.

The only way Hillary can be chosen is for the choice to be made later, as much later as possible. That way, by the time the choice is made, she'd no longer be the bitter-ender who implies that Obama can't win because hard-working white people don't like him, who compares Obama's foreign-policy inexperience unfavorably with McCain's supposed expertise, and whose husband snarls "scumbag" at critics. If the Clintons are capable of mounting a couple of months of humble graciousness—with Hillary expounding on Obama's overwhelming wonderfulness, especially to women, and Bill praising Obama's Rushmore-ready presidential qualities, especially to the lunch-pail set—then she'd be the senator from New York, the most prominent and successful woman politician in American history, the seasoned campaigner who can fill in some of Barack's blanks. At that point, putting her on the ticket, though still unlikely and maybe still unwise, would no longer be out-and-out unthinkable. And even if Obama ended up deciding on somebody else, the Clintons would have gone far to repairing their own damaged "brands" and positioning themselves as influential figures in the forthcoming Obama Era.

THE LADY DOESN'T VANISH

June 5, 2008

nteresting how different things can look from inside a bubble. Or a bunker.

On Tuesday evening, I went downtown to Baruch College, a branch of the City University at Lexington and East 24th Street, for Hillary Clinton's speech. I got there a little before 7:30. A block-long line of Hillary stalwarts stood patiently waiting to get in. As I breezed toward the press entrance (feeling the smug glow of queue-jumping privilege), I ran into some weekend friends, including Harriet Cornell, the chair of the Rockland County Legislature, Harriet's legislative colleague Connie Coker, and Enid Weishaus, who runs one of Hillary's upstate regional offices. They teased me a little about my Obamaphilia, but their overall mood (I thought) was reasonably mellow—this is a competition for a nomination, not the Battle of Armageddon. (Later, I was told that some in the waiting crowd had indulged themselves with unpleasant chants—"No Bama! McCain!" and the like—but I didn't hear any of that.)

Inside, the site fairly screamed "metaphor." The event took place in a windowless gymnasium two stories below ground level—a good place to be in case of a small nuclear explosion. There's no cell phone reception so deep underground. In the press filing center across the hall, big TV monitors were tuned to CNN, not to mean old sexist MSNBC, but there were no monitors in the gym itself. No phones, no BlackBerrys, no TVs: it made one wonder if the gathering was being deliberately shielded from the outside world, where the networks were taking note of the fact that Obama had clinched the nomination.

The gym was a set for a made-for-TV movie. On one side of the cube: a grandstand covered with video cameras on tripods and their operators. Across the cube, behind the stage, as backdrop: a raked bank of ascending benches filled with hundreds of supporters, a nice mixture of young and old of various colors. In the middle: standing room for privileged guests, mostly unphotogenic pols and contribu-tors. The supporters chanted, "We belieeeve! In Hil-a-reeee!" "Den-ver! Here we come!" "Yes, we will! Yes we will!"—this last a screen grab of the Obama campaign's "Yes we can!" (Clinton slogans tend toward the derivative. Bill's endlessly repeated 1996 "Bridge to the Twenty-first Century" was a lift from Bob Dole's far more eloquent acceptance-speech plea to "Let me be the bridge to an America that only the unknowing call myth," i.e., to "a time of tranquillity, faith and confidence in action," i.e., to the past.) A Hillary honcho I spoke with—I didn't catch her name—told me what to expect. "She's not conceding tonight," she said. "That'll come later. Tonight is about making her people feel good. It's about us, not her."

At 9:28, out came Terry McAuliffe, grinning like a Halloween pumpkin, soon followed by Chelsea, Bill, and Hillary herself, whom McAuliffe proclaimed not only the popular-vote winner but also "the next president of the United States!"

Then Hillary gave her speech.

The next day, I would learn how badly the speech went over with pretty much everybody I know. My nephew, a person not much given to rage, was enraged. Bloggers whom I respect have been merciless—e.g., Jim Fallows ("This is a new low"), Andrew Sullivan ("classless, grace-less, shameless, relentless"), Matt Yglesias ("utterly unconscionable"),

Jonathan Chait ("incredible," and not in a good way), and Ezra Klein (full text of his post: "I think Clinton may be willing to offer Obama the vice presidency"). At the *Guardian*, Michael Tomasky called it "the most abrasive, self-absorbed, selfish, delusional, emasculating and extortionate political speech I've heard in a long time." And various friends of both sexes have used words derived from digestive difficulties: disgusting, sickening, nauseating.

On reflection, I still think these reactions are overwrought, but I don't necessarily dispute the substance behind them. I'm persuaded that the speech was a bad show. Oddly, however, from inside the room— from inside the bunker—it didn't seem so bad. In fact, in light of the honcho's preview, it seemed rather good.

The tribute to the victor was less perfunctory and more graceful than I was expecting:

> I want to start tonight by congratulating Senator Obama and his supporters on the extraordinary race that they have run. Senator Obama has inspired so many Americans to care about politics and empowered so many more to get involved. And our party and our democracy is stronger and more vibrant as a result. So we are grateful. And it has been an honor to contest these primaries with him, just as it is an honor to call him my friend. And, tonight, I would like all of us to take a moment to recognize him and his supporters for all they have accomplished.

I guess I didn't notice at the time that these words could as easily be said by a winner of a loser as the reverse.

The rest of the speech, so I thought at the time, was indeed more about comforting her supporters than about continuing the fight. A recognition of the reality that she has lost was implicit in such lines as "In the end, while this primary was long, I am so proud we stayed the course together" and "I will carry your stories and your dreams with me every day for the rest of my life." In the section of the speech in which she asked herself (with what I believe was self-deprecating humor) "What does Hillary want?," she set out a series of policy goals: ending the Iraq war, health care, jobs, clean energy, restoring America's world leadership. To my ears, at least, she seemed to be saying that these goals (which, of course, Obama shares) transcend her candidacy and will outlive it. Nothing wrong with that.

The joker in that particular deck, though, was her statement that she wants those who voted for her "to be respected, to be heard, and no longer to be invisible." This curious plea, weirdly echoing Jesse Jackson, Aretha Franklin, and Ralph Ellison, was not inherently offensive, even if its premise was, shall we say, questionable. Nor, on its face, did it seem unreasonable for her to say, as she did,

> Where do we go from here? And given how far we've come and where
> we need to go as a party, it's a question I don't take lightly. This has
> been a long campaign, and I will be making no decisions tonight.

I didn't think it was necessary for Hillary to "concede" Tuesday night, and I didn't expect her to. But in saying that it "has been" a long campaign, she was clearly saying that this campaign—for her, at least—is over.

I'm sure that this speech looked confrontational and intransigent on television in ways that it just didn't in the hall, inside the bubble. In the hall, you don't see the speaker in closeup. You see her in the distance, in the midst of a crowd. The effect is communal, not egotistic. There are no replays of selected highlights, no panels of experts. You're left with a mood, and the mood was calm.

So I felt a certain relief, as did other Obama supporters in the room with whom I spoke. And as the crowd drifted out, I had the clear impression that many in it were letting go of some of their anger, allowing it to soften into disappointment, and beginning to reconcile themselves to reality.

To be sure, I began to have second thoughts almost immediately.

There was one part of the speech that I found dishonest and dangerous as soon as it flew out of her mouth. It began with this claim:

> Nearly eighteen million of you cast your votes for our campaign, carrying the popular vote with more votes than any primary candidate in history.

Then this, a minute later:

> In all of the states, you voted because you wanted a leader who will stand up for the deepest values of our party, a party that believes everyone should have a fair shot at the American dream, a party that cherishes every child, values every family, and counts every single vote.

And this, another minute later:

> A record thirty-five million people voted in this primary.

Shall we do the math, as the saying goes?

If, as Hillary said in her speech, thirty-five million people voted and eighteen million of them voted for her, then seventeen million voted for someone else.

In other words, Hillary got a million more votes than Obama! Think of it—that's nearly double Gore's half-million-vote lead over Bush in 2000! And in an electorate only a third the size! The equivalent of a three-million-vote general-election majority!

Wait a minute! Since four percent of Democrats—1.4 million people—voted for one of the non-Obama non-Hillaries, Clinton actually beat Obama by 2.4 million votes! Round it up to two and a half million! The general-election equivalent of seven and a half million! A landslide! And that's without "counting every vote"!

They stole the election! Just like 2000! A stab in the back!

Er, not quite.

According to RealClearPolitics.com's count (updated with the 17,036 votes Obama netted yesterday in Montana and South Dakota), Obama tops Clinton by 41,622 in the sanctioned primaries, which now retrospectively include Florida. If you add in the four caucus states of Iowa, Nevada, Maine, and Washington, Obama leads by 151,844. If you add Michigan, where Clinton got 328,309 votes and Obama (unsurprisingly, as he wasn't on the ballot) got zero, then Clinton leads by either 176,465 (if the four caucus states are included) or 286,687 (if they're not). If in addition to Hillary's votes in Michigan you count the 238,168 votes cast there for "uncommitted" as being Obama's, Clinton leads by 48,519. Finally, if you include everything—all primaries, all caucuses, and both kinds of Michiganders—Obama comes out on top by 61,703 votes. In no case does either candidate's margin top one percent.

In summary, neither candidate has "won" the popular vote. Or both have. Everyone is entitled to their own opinion about which of the six counts, three won by Clinton and three by Obama, is the most legit. (My opinion is that it's the last one, which Obama just barely wins, by two-tenths of a percent.) But no one, as the saying goes, is entitled to their own facts. And the facts cannot support the bald, repeated assertion by Clinton and her campaign that she "won" the popular vote. Yet an awful lot of people believe that she did. An old friend of mine I ran into last night, a journalist who has been covering presidential campaigns since the nineteen-sixties, told me that he had simply assumed she was telling the truth.

Sorry for all the numbers, but, as regular readers know, I firmly believe that the popular vote is a relevant moral category, even when, as is uniquely the case with our presidential contests among elections that can be described as free, the popular vote is a juridical irrelevancy. In the general election, the popular vote is somewhat problematic owing to the bifurcation between battleground states, where turnout is high, and spectator states, where it's low, and differences in voter eligibility, such as whether or not ex-offenders are deprived of the franchise. In the nomination stage, the popular vote is even blurrier, because you also have differences between early states and late states, caucus states and primary states, open primaries and closed ones. Under these circumstances, a primary-season popular-vote outcome as close as this one must be judged a tie. And, morally as well as juridically, a tie goes to the winner—i.e., the one with the most delegates. I.e., Obama.

Clinton's request for voters to go to her Web site, to "share your thoughts with me and help in any way that you can" as she decides what to do next, sounded to some people like a setup to provoke some sort of online groundswell begging her to stay in the race. I didn't think so, and it now seems clear that it was really one last attempt to raise money from the faithful. "Any way that you can," indeed.

A few of us stuck around the filing center long enough to watch Obama's speech. It wasn't one of his best performances, I thought, especially at the beginning. But his words about Clinton turned out to be a thousand times more generous than hers about him. And it was wonderfully audacious of him to go to St. Paul and pack a cheering, overflow crowd into the very arena where, three months from now, Republican conventioneers will nod through interminable denunciations of trial lawyers and the Far Left.

As I walked to the subway, I felt goofily happy. Barack Obama is going to be the Democratic candidate for president of the United States. It's like a dream.

PART THREE

THE SPRINT

EXHILLARATION

June 13, 2008

The presidential flight of Hillary Rodham Clinton, which had been aloft for nearly a year, began its descent stage on January 3, 2008, somewhere over Iowa. Five months later to the day, she piloted it to a smooth touchdown, though not without experiencing some turbulence during the final approach. First, there was her non-concession speech, delivered on the final Tuesday of the primary season; then, after a few days of cogitation, consultation, and commiseration, there was her Saturday speech. Tuesday's speech was anything but full of grace, and, on the whole, was poorly received. Saturday's was greeted rapturously, often by the same commentators. "The way to continue our fight now, to accomplish the goals for which we stand," Clinton said, "is to take our energy, our passion, our strength, and do all we can to help elect Barack Obama the next president of the United States." And she said, echoing the signature chant of the Obama campaign, "Today, I am standing with Senator Obama to say: Yes, we can!" She could scarcely have been more emphatic.

With that, the most astounding primary season in American history came to an end. It was astounding not because of the policy differences separating the competing sides (these were trivial compared with

their vast reaches of agreement), or because of the turmoil of the times
and the bitterness of the clash (compared with the two campaigns of
the Vietnam War era, 1968 and 1972, all was calm and collegial), but
because of who the candidates were—more precisely, because of *what*
they were. The first woman and the first man of color to have a serious chance of victory contended for the right to represent America's
party of progressive change in the contest for the most powerful office
on earth, and they fought each other very nearly to a draw. This conspicuous, astonishing fact was not much discussed by the candidates
themselves; for them, the point was to transcend "identity politics," lest
they be trapped in its stereotypes. Only when compelled by the antics
of the retiring minister of his church did Obama directly confront the
questions of race and identity, doing so in a speech of such power and
nuance that it saved his campaign. Clinton—whose "identity," after all,
comprises more than half the electorate and extends, by definition, into
every family on earth—treated her gender as a grace note, a significant
but ultimately secondary feature, like Jimmy Carter's Southernness or
Bob Dole's war wound. Only in the final appearance of her exhaust-
ing campaign did Hillary Clinton speak at length about, in her words,
"what it means to be a woman running for president."

Much of what she said was phrased in such a way as to apply to
Obama as well as to herself. "I am a woman and, like millions of women,
I know there are still barriers and biases out there, often unconscious,
and I want to build an America that respects and embraces the potential
of every last one of us," she declared. "There are no acceptable limits,
and there are no acceptable prejudices in the twenty-first century in
our country." And, speaking of herself, Obama, and the supporters of
both: "We will make history together."

In the emotional climax of her speech, she said, "Although we
weren't able to shatter that highest, hardest glass ceiling this time,
thanks to you it's got about eighteen million cracks in it—and the light
is shining through like never before, filling us all with the hope and the
sure knowledge that the path will be a little easier next time." Some

people interpreted this to imply that it was her gender that denied her the prize. Only she knows whether she meant it that way, or whether that's what she believes. In such a close race, of course, almost any factor can be viewed as decisive. But it's hard to find anyone who will dispute that if she had not voted to authorize the Iraq war, or if her delegate-hunting strategy had been as astute as her principal opponent's, or if that opponent had been a slightly more ordinary politician, or, perhaps, if her campaign messages had been more coherent and less negative, then she would have breezed to the nomination and made history all by herself.

Competitions among grievances do not ennoble, and both Clinton and Obama strove to avoid one; but it does not belittle the oppressions of gender to suggest that in America the oppressions of race have cut deeper. Clinton's supporters would sometimes note that the Constitution did not extend the vote to women until a half century after it extended it to men of color. But there is no gender equivalent of the nightmare of disenfranchisement, lynching, apartheid, and peonage that followed Reconstruction, to say nothing of "the bondsman's two hundred and fifty years of unrequited toil" that preceded it. Nor has any feminist leader shared the fate of Medgar Evers, Martin Luther King, Jr., and Malcolm X. Clinton spoke on Saturday of "women in their eighties and nineties, born before women could vote." But Barack Obama is only in his forties, and he was born before the Voting Rights Act redeemed the broken promise of the Fifteenth Amendment.

Clinton was right to say that from now on it will be "unremarkable to think that a woman can be the president of the United States"—and that, in large measure, is her doing. But the Speaker of the House is a woman; and there are, at the moment, sixteen women in the Senate and eight in the nation's governors' offices, the pools from which presidential candidates are usually drawn. There are two African-American governors, only one of whom was elected to that office. There is one African-American senator—and seven months from now that one may have a different job.

Clinton's defeat has left many of her supporters, especially among older women, not just disappointed but angry. Their anger is directed partly, sometimes mainly, at "the media," especially at a handful of commentators on the cable news networks, particularly MSNBC. (Fox News is hopeless; you might as well get angry at mildew.) One such commentator, in a fairly representative remark, described Clinton as "looking like everyone's first wife standing outside a probate court." Ugly, yes, and arguably misogynistic, but not much uglier (and probably less politically damaging) than the ridicule once heaped upon Michael Dukakis for looking wimpy in a tank and Al Gore for being stiff, or sighing, or wearing "earth tones" at the supposed urging of a feminist adviser—insults rooted, like the probate-court crack, in male stupidity. And the likelihood is that this sort of thing pushed more women into the Clinton column than men away from it.

Barack Obama—reared by a single mother, married to a strong-willed woman, father of two daughters—has an unblemished record of support for the goals of the mainstream women's movement. Yet, according to a *Wall Street Journal*/NBC poll taken over the weekend Clinton withdrew, in a hypothetical matchup with John McCain—whose record with respect to those goals ranges from indifference to hostility—she would win among white suburban women and Obama would lose. The anger of many such women is real, even if Obama is merely a momentary target of opportunity for it, even if it has little or nothing to do with anything he has done or said and everything to do with their own life experience. Fairly or unfairly, it's up to him to demonstrate anew that he respects their experience and understands their anger. And it's up to them to respond.

FLIP-FLOP FLAP

July 11, 2008

One of the World Wide Web's most distinguished organs of fake news, the Borowitz Report, leads its current issue with this flash:

> The liberal blogosphere was aflame today with new accusations that Sen. Barack Obama (D-Ill) is trying to win the 2008 presidential election.

Except that sometimes it's hard to tell fake from real. These sentiments, for example, are from actual blogs:

> If Obama believes the BS he said about the FISA Capitulation bill, then he is not fit to be President.

> He is turning on every major issue and I am not going to vote for him. From here on out, the netroots should refuse to donate to any Democratic nominee, including Barack Obama.

Obama, it turns out, is a politician. In this respect, he resembles the forty-three presidents he hopes to succeed, from the Father of His

Country to the wayward son, Alpha George to Omega George. Winning a presidential election doesn't require being all things to all of
the people all of the time, but it does require being some things to most
of the people some of the time. It doesn't require saying one thing and
also saying its opposite, but it does require saying more or less the same
thing in ways that are understood in different ways. They're all politicians, yes—very much including Obama. But that doesn't mean they're
all the same.

It was inevitable that the boggier reaches of the blogosphere would
eventually smell betrayal. In contrast, what bloggers call the MSM—the
mainstream media—seldom trades in the currency of moral indignation. Although the better newspapers have regular features devoted to
evaluating the candidates' proposals for workability, the MSM generally eschews value judgments about the merits. The MSM—especially
the cable news intravenous drip—prefers flip-flops.

Obama has been providing plenty of plastic for the flip-flop factories
with the adjustments he's been making as he retools his campaign for
the general election. Under headlines like "IN CAMPAIGN, ONE MAN'S
PRAGMATISM IS ANOTHER'S FLIP-FLOPPING," the big papers have been
assembling quite a list of matters on which the candidate has "changed
his position," including Iraq, abortion rights, federal aid to faith-based
social services, capital punishment, gun control, public financing of
campaigns, and wiretapping. Most of them are mere shifts of emphasis,
some are marginal tweaks, and a few are either substantive or nonexistent. Let's do a quick *tour d'horizon*.

On July 3, Obama remarked to reporters, vis-à-vis his projected visit
to Iraq, that he will "continue to refine" his policies in light of what
he learns there. The flip-flop frenzy exploded so quickly that Obama
called a second press conference that same day in an effort to tamp it
down, saying that while he "would be a poor commander in chief"
if he "didn't take facts on the ground into account," his intention to
withdraw American combat troops from Iraq within sixteen months

of his inauguration—which is to say less than two years from now—remains unchanged. *Flip-flop category: marginal tweak.*

The same week, Obama said he didn't think that "mental distress" alone was sufficient justification for a late-term abortion, prompting the president of the National Organization for Women to rebuke him for feeding the perception that women seek abortions because they're "having a bad-hair day." In *The Audacity of Hope*, Obama had written that

> the willingness of even the most ardent prochoice advocates to accept some restrictions on late-term abortion marks a recognition that a fetus is more than a body part and that society has some interest in its development.

The leading reproductive-rights group, NARAL Pro-Choice America, defended him, pointing out that his views are fully consistent with Roe v. Wade. *Flip-flop category: nonexistent.*

Obama also wrote that "certain faith-based programs" could offer "a uniquely powerful way of solving problems and hence merit carefully tailored support." Yet his recent call for an expansion of President Bush's program came as a shock to some, including the *Times*, which called the program a violation of the separation of church and state. If it is, it's a minor one, like grants to religiously affiliated colleges; in any event, this isn't a new position for Obama. *Flip-flop category: shift of emphasis.*

For twenty years, nominal support for the death penalty and its partner in crime, "gun rights," has apparently been mandatory for any Democrat wishing to have a serious chance to be elected president. Without enthusiasm, Obama has endorsed capital punishment throughout his political career. In his book, he wrote that "the rape and murder of a child" is "so heinous, so beyond the pale, that the community is justified in expressing the full measure of its outrage by meting out the ultimate punishment." But in demurring from last month's Supreme Court decision banning executions for child rape alone, he went further: "and" is not "or." As for the Court's radical decision conferring upon an individual the right to possess guns separate from service in a "well regulated militia," he did not, as reported, "embrace" it. But he did commend it for providing "much-needed guidance to local jurisdictions"—a distinctly Panglossian gloss. Still, if Obama becomes president the practical effect of these panders will be minimal. It's hard to imagine an Obama appointee to the Supreme Court voting with Justices Scalia and Thomas on issues like these. *Flip-flop category: substantive tweak.*

As for the last two items on the flip-flop list—well, it's a fair cop, as the Brits say. Obama's decision to refuse public funds for the general-election campaign was political hardball, a spikes-high slide at third base. He still favors public financing in principle, and he says he'll work to modernize it in practice. In a sense, his utterly unexpected success in raising tens of millions from small, no-strings contributors has created a kind of unofficial public finance system. But that success is a one-off, and the big contributors are still contributing big, with all that entails. He didn't change his "position," but he did break a promise.

Obama's U-turn on the Foreign Intelligence Surveillance Act last week was not so trivial. He had promised to filibuster it if it retained the provision immunizing telecom companies from lawsuits arising from the companies' compliance with administration requests—orders, really—to cooperate in patently illegal activity. The bill did retain that provision, and Obama voted not only for the bill but against the filibuster. Opinion is divided on the seriousness of the bill's threat to civil liberties. In the *Times* last week, the Open Society Institute's Morton H. Halperin, whose devotion to civil liberties is rivalled only by his knowledge of national security matters, called the bill "our best chance to protect both our national security and our civil liberties." Other civil libertarians see it as the death knell for the Fourth Amendment. But there can be little doubt that Obama's vote—which could not have affected the outcome—was influenced by worry about being branded as soft on terrorism. Unlike FISA, the Iraq war can't be repealed. But perhaps Obama will now take a more compassionate view of Hillary Clinton's vote to authorize it.

Meanwhile, McCain has been busily reversing his views in highly consequential ways. He opposed the Bush tax cuts because they favored the rich; now he supports their eternal extension. He was against off-shore oil drilling as not being worth the environmental damage it brings; now he's for it, and damn the costs. He was against torture, period; now he's against it unless the C.I.A. does it. He keeps flipping to the wrong flops. But he and Obama can both take comfort in what they're avoiding. If they were clinging to every past position, the flip-flop police would be busting them for stubbornness and rigidity in the face of changing circumstances. Bush all over again! Flip-flops are preferable to cement shoes, especially in summertime.

FOREIGNERS

July 25, 2008

Back in the nineteenth and twentieth centuries, candidates for president of the United States didn't have much truck with foreigners. Foreigners didn't vote, they lived on the other side of the ocean, and they spoke funny, most of 'em. (If a Frenchman is a man, Jim points out to Huck Finn, "why doan' he talk like a man?") Even after America's rise to global power, the only overseas travel seen as obligatory for a presidential hopeful was to what pols called the Three-I League—Ireland, Italy, and Israel, venues that had more to do with the lingering tribal identities of big-city ethnics than with anything as highfalutin as foreign policy. (Let us note, in the currently fashionable spirit of joke-explaining, that the baseball allusion is to a long-defunct Class B circuit made up of teams from Illinois, Indiana, and Iowa.) Nor did the incumbent get around much during the first fifty-four years of his life. "Bush's foreign travels," the Associated Press reported a few days after the Supreme Court awarded him custody of Air Force One, "have been limited to three visits to Mexico, two trips to Israel, a three-day Thanksgiving visit in Rome with one of his daughters in 1998, and a six-week excursion to China with his parents in 1975." Israel, check. Italy, check. He didn't bother with the third I.

In our post-9/11, post-unipolar, and soon-to-be-post-Bush world, staying home is not an option—especially if you're the "inexperienced" candidate and the opinion polls say that your war-hero opponent is better at foreign policy and national security than you are. Anyway, John McCain had spent months needling Barack Obama for not having lately visited the fourth I. So, last week, off to Iraq he went—and, while he was at it, he doubled and redoubled down, adding Afghanistan, Jordan, Israel, the West Bank, Germany, France, and Britain to his itinerary.

Just before the trip, a leading wire service summarized the prevailing view:

> WASHINGTON (Reuters)—U.S. Democratic presidential candidate Barack Obama's overseas trip will be a high-risk debut on the world stage—with the potential pitfalls at least as numerous as the likely rewards.

"On a trip like this, on a stage like this, there is no room for error," Tad Devine, a veteran Democratic operative, told ABC News. "He needs to make sure every word is right, every setting is proper, and that he makes absolutely no mistakes." And *Newsweek*'s Richard Wolffe predicted that the trip would be "an extraordinarily public test of a Presidential contender's mastery of world affairs."

Whether or not it was that, it was certainly a test of his mastery of political theatrics, his sure-footedness, and his willingness to take a calculated risk. On the first leg of the trip, Obama found himself in a military gym in Kuwait, a major staging point for Americans going to the war zones. The bleachers were packed with soldiers wearing fatigues. A basketball materialized. "I may not make the first one," he said, no doubt imagining what a metaphor-hungry press would make of a miss or, God forbid, a whole string of misses, "but I'll make one eventually." With a spring of his toes, he put the ball up. When it came down, *swish*.

It was the three-point shot heard round the world, and, for the Obama campaign, things only got better from there. As the candidate whirled through Afghanistan and Iraq—talking with troops, huddling with generals, conferring with presidents and prime ministers—the policy dominoes suddenly began toppling his way, flicked by unexpected fingers. Commanders on the ground in Afghanistan made known their belief that more NATO troops are badly needed there, as Obama has been arguing all along. The Bush administration sent an under secretary of state to a meeting in Geneva with Iran's chief nuclear negotiator, thereby edging toward the kind of direct diplomatic engagement with Tehran that Obama has been urging all along. The White House announced that President Bush and the Iraqi prime minister, Nouri al-Maliki, had agreed on the idea of a "time horizon" for withdrawing American troops from Iraq, thus seeming to endorse the general approach that Obama has been advocating (and his opponent just as firmly rejecting) all along. In an interview with *Der Spiegel*, Maliki went stunningly further. Asked to predict when most of the American troops will leave Iraq, he replied:

> As soon as possible, as far as we're concerned. U.S. presidential candidate Barack Obama talks about sixteen months. That, we think, would be the right time frame for a withdrawal, with the possibility of slight changes.

After four days of panicky spinning and backtracking from Washington and (at Washington's prodding) Baghdad, an audio recording of the interview—the published text of which, in any case, had been provided to Maliki's office in advance—surfaced, and its accuracy was confirmed. Maliki's spokesman, Ali al-Dabbagh, had the final word: "We cannot give any timetables or dates, but the Iraqi government believes the end of 2010 is the appropriate time for the withdrawal." By the time Obama's plane touched down in Germany, an utterly unanticipated consensus seemed to have emerged: besides having been right about the Iraq war's beginning (i.e., that it should not have had one), he is right, in broad outline, about the path to its ending.

There has been much discussion of whether it will prove politically advantageous for Obama to have addressed a mile-long crowd of two hundred thousand happy Berliners in the golden early-evening sunlight. Berliners are Germans, and Germans are foreigners, and since well before John Kerry was demonized for knowing how to speak French it has been axiomatic that heartland Americans don't like foreigners piping up about our elections, however much brainland Americans may disagree. Obama gained nothing in the polls during his nearly flawless, arguably triumphant grand tour. Still, after seven years during which, even among our closest allies, contempt for Bush bled into resentment of the country that returned him to office, one would have to be an awful grouch not to be gratified by the sight of a sea of delighted Europeans waving American flags instead of burning them and cheering an American politician instead of demonstrating against one.

Back home, one such grouch had ample reason to be grouchy. McCain's luck last week was as bad as Obama's was good. McCain rode in a golf cart with Bush Senior; Obama rode in a helicopter with General David Petraeus. Obama was hailed by the German multitudes; McCain, his planned photo op at an offshore rig preempted by an oil spill and rained out by Hurricane Dolly, held a press gaggle in front of Schmidt's Fudge Haus, in Columbus, Ohio. Obama got a big kiss (*"Obama? C'est mon copain!"*) from the new president of France, a dashing conservative with an exotic background and an unusual name; McCain stood athwart the cheese aisle of a supermarket, complaining. The presumptive Republican nominee had a right to be irritated by what he was complaining about: Obama's reluctance to admit that the surge in Iraq which he opposed has helped make the withdrawal from Iraq which he supports less problematic. But McCain had no right to accuse him, not once but repeatedly last week, of being willing to have his country "lose a war" if it would win him an election. That was shocking; that was unworthy. Obama drained a three-point shot; McCain committed a three-shot foul. The game is getting physical.

MCDOG BITES MAN

July 30, 2008

On the front page of today's *Washington Post*, peeking just above the fold, we find the following astounding headline:

MCCAIN CHARGE

AGAINST OBAMA

LACKS EVIDENCE

Not "Some Observers Say," not "Critics Claim," not "Provokes Controversy"—just a statement of ascertainable fact, minus the strenuous attempts to achieve "balance" between lies and truth that are customary when truth is suspected of having a liberal bias.

The lede of the story, by Michael D. Shear and Dan Balz, does not equivocate:

> For four days, Sen. John McCain and his allies have accused Sen. Barack Obama of snubbing wounded soldiers by canceling a visit to a military hospital because he could not take reporters with him, despite no evidence that the charge is true.

Wow.

A few excerpts from the rest:

The essence of McCain's allegation is that Obama planned to take a media entourage, including television cameras, to Landstuhl Regional Medical Center in Germany during his week-long foreign trip, and that he canceled the visit when he learned he could not do so. . . . In fact, there is no evidence that he planned to take anyone to the American hospital other than a military adviser, whose status as a campaign staff member sparked last-minute concern among Pentagon officials that the visit would be an improper political event.

Despite serious and repeated queries about the charge over several days, McCain and his allies continued yesterday to question Obama's patriotism by focusing attention on the canceled hospital visit.

McCain's advisers said they do not intend to back down from the charge, believing it an effective way to create a "narrative" about what they say is Obama's indifference toward the military.

"Some observers" (not me) might say that it isn't really news when a politician and his campaign lie. On the other hand, "some observers" (me) might say that it *is* news when a flagship of the "MSM" straightforwardly reports that a lie is a lie without using "some observers" as a ventriloquist's dummy. Actually, the big papers, to their credit, have been increasingly daring about doing exactly this sort of reporting lies as news. Still, it's a breakthrough when the report is presented on page 1, and as news, not "analysis." Good for the *Washington Post*.

One more thing. It is truly disgusting that McCain's people justify their lie by saying it's an "effective" way to create "a narrative." McCain's campaign is rapidly becoming a characterological tragedy disguised as a postmodern farce.

FOXY FUN WITH FRANK

July 31, 2008

Here's a rare and remarkable example of someone going seriously off message on Fox News. It happened a whole week ago, but it's still ringing in my ears.

The guest on *Hannity & Colmes* is Frank Luntz, the Gingrichian pollster and word technician whose services to the idle rich and their conservative court philosophers include renaming the inheritance tax the "death tax." Though Luntz has been guilty of occasional flashes of deviationism over the years, you'd expect him to toe the party line when the Nation's Future is at stake. But no.

A clip of Obama speaking in Berlin has just been shown, followed by clips of the famous one-liners from the Berlin speeches of J.F.K. ("Ich bin . . .") and Reagan ("Tear down . . ."). "How do these three speeches compare?" asks Alan Colmes.

LUNTZ: That's what's remarkable. This is political theatre at its best. Barack Obama clearly delivered one of the great speeches of his lifetime. The Europeans are watching very carefully, almost as much as Americans are, and you have to give him credit. Ronald Reagan was an experienced politico when he delivered his impressive speech back in 1987. John Kennedy had been president for over two years. Obama has done this with only being on the national and international stage for months or years.

Uh-oh. A minute or two later, after another clip:

LUNTZ: You have to give Obama credit for having the ability, the poise, and the presentation skills to be able to capture the hearts and the passion of almost two hundred and fifty thousand Berliners—and this is a guy, of course, who is just a candidate for president of the United States.

And:

LUNTZ: He spoke about America—and this is something that's very dangerous for a presidential candidate to do, where he addresses America in less than a perfect light—but notice how at the end he does something that his wife didn't do. Barack Obama talks not just what's wrong with America, but how much he loves it.

The slap at Michelle notwithstanding, Hannity is visibly squirming. Finally he can't contain himself.

HANNITY: Hey, Frank, it's Sean, good to see you.

You know, we are electing the president of the United States. We're not electing the president of Germany or Europe in general here. And I understand your point about words, but they are just words. This is just a speech here.

Let's make one other comparison that nobody's brought up at this point. You know, when Ronald Reagan went to Europe, there usually were large crowds protesting him. . . . President Bush, similarly, has not been loved by some of our European friends.

Is it maybe that he's liked so much because he supports European socialist ideas and that they agree with him on Iraq—they don't agree the surge has been successful?

LUNTZ: I think that they like him so much because he represents such a significant change. Part of the responsibility of a president is stagecraft. And part of stagecraft is to be able to capture the public's imagination and get them to dream dreams and get them to want to work together.

HANNITY: But nobody—wait a minute.

LUNTZ: There's an example.

HANNITY: Hang on a second. But nobody did that in this country better than Reagan. Nobody inspired a shining city on the hill, you know, the last great hope for man on this earth. That was Reagan. And, you know, Americans responded, but Europeans despised him.

LUNTZ: And, Sean, our goal should not be to be loved by the Europeans, and it shouldn't even be to be respected by the Europeans, because, in the end, there are times when you're right—America does have to do certain things on its own. But you cannot ignore the fact that the world community over the past week has been absolutely wowed by this individual.

HANNITY: Wait a minute.

LUNTZ: At a time when American popularity is at its low point.

HANNITY: Frank, could it be that Barack Obama shares Europe's contempt and criticisms of America? Could it be that they agreed with him on the war? Could it be that they bow at the altar of the United Nations? Could it be that they don't agree with Gitmo or tough interrogations? Could it be that they are more—they would talk to Ahmadinejad without preconditions? Could it all have to do with that his ideology is one of the European socialists?

LUNTZ: It does have something to do with his ideology, but in this election campaign—and it is very frustrating for conservatives—we are not choosing the candidate, necessarily, who we agree with on policy. We're choosing the candidate because of his attributes and his character traits. And what Obama has been able to do is transcend politics.

Wait a minute. *Wait a goddam minute!* Hannity is getting agitated. The segment is spinning out of control. He keeps trying to steer Luntz back onto the true path, but Luntz keeps saying things like, "Obama has been able to cut through at a time when Americans do not trust politicians."

Hannity makes one more try, then cuts his losses:

HANNITY: I guess what's frustrating—if there's anything that's frustrating to me, Frank, these are just words. He seems to agree with the European, anti-American sentiment and the belief in the United Nations. But I look at it this way. America's four percent of the world's population, but we pay ninety-six percent of the cost of keeping the entire planet sane and free. And you know what? That's what *I* would have said if I went to Europe.

LUNTZ: But, Sean, in the end, the American people do vote on words, and as an analyst of words, I can tell you that these were effective—not just for Europeans but for undecided voters in America.

HANNITY: All right, Frank. Always good to see you. Thanks for being with us.

Yeah, thanks. Thanks a load, toad. And don't let the door hit you on the way out.

RACE, LIES, AND VIDEOTAPE

August 6, 2008

I t's been a distressing few days for the faint of heart, among whom I count myself. The TV spots generated by McCain's new team, which is dominated by veterans of the Swift Boat slander factory and the Bush 2004 war room, seem to be "working," to use a favorite accolade of cable news moral philosophers. Two of the spots have been certified "effective" by experts: "Wounded Troops" and "Celebrity."

Both spots employ lies. The lie in "Celebrity"—an assertion that Obama wants to "raise taxes on electricity"—is relatively anodyne. (This is a routine type of Republican untruth; another McCain ad falsely accuses Obama of proposing to raise income taxes on people earning as little as $32,000 a year.) The lie in "Wounded Troops"—that Obama "canceled a visit with wounded troops" because "the Pentagon wouldn't allow him to bring cameras"—is poisonous and despicable.

But what is perhaps more deeply evil and unforgiveable in these ads is their use of visual cues to trigger feelings of racial revulsion assumed to be latent in a certain segment of the white electorate. In political advertising, as in commercial advertising, ad makers think through every millisecond. There is no such thing as inadvertence.

The cues are of varying degrees of subtlety. In the "Wounded

Troops" ad, when the narrator says of Obama, "He made time to go to the gym," we see a clip of Obama dribbling a basketball. There are pictures available of Obama using exercise equipment, so this is a conscious choice. Basketball is a "black" sport. Is it too much of a reach to imagine that in the minds of the McCain ad makers this "benefit" outweighed the cost of reminding viewers of Obama's famous three-pointer, which occurred seconds after the shot they used?

Perhaps. But no big leap is required to discern the meaning of the visual cue in "Celebrity." The intercutting of shots of the Berlin crowd chanting "Obama!" with pictures of Britney Spears and Paris Hilton has been defended on the grounds that Spears and Hilton symbolize the irrelevance of celebrity as a qualification for leadership—which they do, of course. But it cannot have escaped the ad makers' notice that they also symbolize white, blonde sexual availability. There are plenty of celebrities whose images would not have carried this supposedly inadvertent second meaning. But pictures of Tiger Woods and J. K. Rowling, or even Regis Philbin and Angelina Jolie (all of whom score high on the *Forbes* Celebrity 100, a list Britney and Paris don't even make), wouldn't have packed quite the same sucker punch, somehow.

It cannot be proved—and I, for one, don't believe—that the makers and beneficiaries of these ads are "racists" in the commonsense meaning of the term. After all, they are perfectly willing to use the "elitist" stereotype against Obama even though they themselves probably harbor no particular ill feelings toward elitists and, in fact, are elitists themselves. (Which is more "elitist," Obama's alleged fondness for arugula or McCain's $520 Ferragamo loafers?) But they display no awareness that exploiting race prejudice poses more danger to the American social fabric than exploiting hatred of people who like windsurfing or can speak French.

These McCain ads are pretty clearly part of a concerted strategy of provocation aimed at surfacing the "race issue," projecting the blame for its emergence on Obama (who has nothing to gain from injecting racial resentment into the campaign), and letting somebody else's latent racism do the rest. McCain's personal contribution to this ugly strategy has been to repeat his campaign's charge that it is Obama (!) who is "playing the race card." McCain was widely quoted last week as saying, "His comments were clearly the race card—everybody can read what he said, his remarks." That was lame enough, but McCain looked and sounded dazed and stricken for the long seconds it took him to pull himself together enough to croak out that quote. I prefer to think that it was McCain's conscience, not his septuagenarian hearing, that was giving him trouble. But feeling bad about doing something bad doesn't make the something bad something good. And a conscience isn't much good if all it does is make you sputter for a few moments on your way to administering a dose of poison.

Other than hitting back on the actual issues, especially the economy and the war, I'm not sure what Obama can do in response. It won't do his campaign any good to complain about racial subtexts, though I suppose it's marginally helpful (and quite admirable) when a decent Republican like David Gergen points them out.

I continue to believe that it was a big mistake for Obama to turn down McCain's proposal for a series of unmoderated face-to-face town-meeting-style debates. If the two men were regularly sharing a stage (and maybe a greenroom), I'm pretty sure Obama would have been able to shame his Senate colleague into cutting, or at least cutting down on, this kind of crap.

THE LARGER HALF

August 11, 2008

At the *American Prospect*, Adam Serwer offers a piece of extraordinarily astute analysis of what the McCain campaign is up to. Serwer's most striking insight:

> In a dispute about race, the McCain campaign knows it will end up with the larger half. *For the most part, most white people's experience with race isn't one of racial discrimination. They can only relate to racial discrimination in the abstract. What white people can relate to is the fear of being unjustly accused of racism.* This is the larger half. This is why allegations of racism often provoke more outrage than actual racism, because most of the country can relate to one (the accusation of racism) easier than the other (actual racism). *For this reason, in a political conflict over race, the McCain campaign has the advantage, because saying the race card has been played is actually the ultimate race card.*

Italics mine.

I think Serwer is exactly right about the precise kind of white resentment McCain is aiming to stir up. The racial imagery I've been waxing indignant about lately is just bait. The goal is not so much to stimulate white racism per se (though that would be a nice bonus) as it is to provoke *charges* of white racism. In fact, overt charges of white racism aren't even necessary for the strategy to work. All that was required was for Obama to make an indirect *allusion* to race—his remark that he doesn't look like the presidents on the currency—in order to trigger McCain's charge that *Obama* is the one who's "playing the race card."

It's a two-cushion bank shot—skillful, but with the same purpose as breaking your cue over the other guy's head. Is it "racist"? Well, it's not Ku Klux Klan racist. And it's not quite White Citizens' Council racist. It's just mainstream Republican racist, with a twist of McCain deniability. These guys aren't thugs. They're pool sharks.

OUR DROP, THEIR BUCKET

August 12, 2008

Ever since McCain switched—dare I say flip-flopped?—from being one of the loudest opponents of Bush's demand for more oil platforms off America's most beautiful coastlines to being its loudest advocate, Democrats have been slamming him for it. That's good. What's not so good is some of the arguments they're using.

It's a gimmick, the Dems keep saying. But who cares if it's a gimmick if it brings down energy prices?

It won't produce results for twenty years, they keep saying. But since when are Democrats opposed to long-term solutions?

It's a hoax, because we can't drill our way out of our energy problems, they say. But why shouldn't we drill *part* of our way out?

A better argument may be found in the *New York Times Magazine* in Deborah Solomon's crisp mini-interview with Robert Reich. The relevant Q's & A's:

> *What do you make of the argument that the only way to lessen our dependence on foreign oil is to tap more oil wells here—in Alaska and off the coasts of Florida and California?* When you consider that the oil we pump goes into a global oil market, offshore drilling makes no sense. We take the

environmental risk, but we'd have to share the negligible price gains with Chinese consumers and every other user around the world.

Then why do you think President Bush asked Congress last month to lift the longtime ban on offshore oil drilling? If I had to guess, I would say that President Bush is very close to the oil companies and wants whatever they want.

The point is easy to understand. We take all the risks. We pay all the costs. But we don't get all the benefits, such as they are. Once the oil comes out, sometime in the far future, it gets sold to whoever's buying at that day's price. The impact on price will be spread across the globe—which is why, as even the Bush administration's Department of Energy admits, that impact will be "insignificant."

It's a drop in the bucket, and it's not even our bucket. It's China's, India's, Europe's—everybody's. We get a thimbleful. But our wind and our sunlight aren't going anywhere. Aren't we better off putting our efforts into encouraging and harnessing *them*? When we're thinking long term, when we're planning for twenty years from now, shouldn't we be looking to get *away* from carbon-belching, icecap-melting, coast-destroying oil?

The underlying truth, though it may be a little too raw for campaign purposes, is that the price at the pump should be higher, not lower. The past few months of sharply rising fuel costs have done more to cut our oil profligacy than all the preceding years of high-minded exhortations. Unfortunately, all that extra cost is simply a transfer of wealth to the coffers of oil "producers" like Saudi Arabia, Iran, and Venezuela, with a few tens of billions skimmed off the top by ExxonMobil and the like.

Tom Friedman pointed out the other day that the Danes are paying ten dollars a gallon for gasoline. It's not a problem for them. That's because most of what they pay goes for taxes that have financed an energy policy so effective that Denmark now gets twenty percent of its electricity from wind (we get one percent) and zero percent of its fuel from the Middle East (down from ninety-nine percent twenty-five years ago). Now the Danes are getting ready to jack up gasoline taxes even more and use the proceeds to cut personal income taxes. They have this crazy idea that they should tax things they want to discourage, like gas guzzling, and ease up on taxing things they want to encourage, like people working.

But what do they know. They're just a bunch of foreigners. European socialists, too, probably.

SADDLE SORE

August 18, 2008

I had hoped for a more fluid, energetic performance from Barack Obama at Saturday night's Saddleback Church forum. It was not to be. Obama didn't seem to know how to go with the flow and make a real emotional connection with his audience, either in the room or beyond. He seemed a little out of sorts—tentative and wan and much too careful, introducing too many of his comments with a choked "y'know" and keeping his eyes downcast instead of locked on Warren's. He was wilted, not crisp. Or so he seemed to me.

I was especially disappointed by his answer on same-sex marriage. He said what he has often said before: that he sees marriage as a union of a man and a woman; that he supports civil unions that extend rights and obligations to same-sex couples; that under the Constitution marriage is a matter for the states and should remain so. It felt chilly and legalistic—not quite Dukakis on capital punishment for wife-murderers, but perilously close. He missed a chance to challenge his evangelical audience and connect with it by pointing out the human contradiction between sectarian doctrine and Christian compassion. Christian denominations take all manner of views of homosexuality, but it's hard to find a Christian these days who insists that simply *being* homosexual—having a gay or lesbian orientation—is sinful in and of itself. If two people love each other and wish to commit themselves to each other and are eager to take on the responsibilities and joys of family life, including the raising of children (biological or adopted) in a loving home, isn't that a good thing, not just for them and the children they give a home to, but for all of us? Obama said, "I think my faith is strong enough and my marriage is strong enough that I can afford those civil rights to others, even if I have a different perspective or a different view." But how helpful is it to imply that other people—people whose faith and/or marriages aren't so strong—are in danger of abandoning their faith or their marriage because gay people are permitted to get married?

There are observers I respect—Andrew Sullivan, for one, and members of my family with whom I watched the program, for two more—who saw thoughtfulness and humility where I saw hesitation and eggshell-walking and, watching McCain, saw pandering and bloviating where I saw shrewdness and confidence. If they're right, and I hope they are, I still wish that the thoughtfulness and humility had been accompanied by a bit more passion and force.

Everyone, me included, seems to agree that Rick Warren was the undisputed winner of the night. Granted, he isn't a particularly probing questioner. But at least he was polite, and he didn't commit any of the sins James Fallows enumerates in the current *Atlantic*, such as posing a "will you pledge tonight" question, or asking the kind of "gotcha" question that assumes that any change in a policy position is conclusive evidence of lack of principle. Warren, with his genial personality, his emphasis on happiness over hellfire, and his instinct for (relative) moderation, reminds me a little of the young Henry Ward Beecher, a fascinating biography of whom (*The Most Famous Man in America*, by Debby Applegate) I happen to be reading at the moment—not that they're in remotely the same league, of course. (Warren's willingness to admit the reality of global warming and his admonitions to his fellow evangelical heavies to quit demonizing Democrats are welcome, but he's still got a long way to go before he can match the content or courage of Beecher's stirring antislavery sermons.)

Today's evangelical Christianity may be thriving on TV and at the megachurch collection plate, but it has yet to find a cause worthy of its fervor. Its crusade on behalf of the unborn and unquickened—which, if successful, would make criminals out of actually existing women and doctors while doing less than nothing to relieve actual human suffering—is a sad waste. A century and a half ago, the great evangelical blockbuster was *Uncle Tom's Cabin*, by Beecher's sister Harriet. Now it's Warren's self-help manuals and the *Left Behind* series. This is a progression that offers meager evidence either for evolution or for intelligent design.

ATTACK-DOG DAYS

August 22, 2008

The week before the week before this week's scheduled gathering of the delegates and their media camp followers in Denver, the nominee-presumptive of the Democratic Party did something that is strongly recommended, and ought to be mandatory, for anyone who has just logged a year and a half's worth of eighteen-hour days travelling in airplanes, making speeches, shaking hands with tens of thousands of strangers, answering numbingly repetitive questions, fending off attacks on everything from his position on insurance mandates to his alleged similarity to Paris Hilton, and trying to remember what it feels like to get a good night's sleep: Barack Obama went on vacation.

He did this in Hawaii, one of the fifty United States of America. Not only is Hawaii amply supplied with beaches, sunshine, hotels, and other features useful to vacationers (tourism is the state's largest industry); it is also where Obama was born and went to high school, and it is the only place he can visit his eighty-five-year-old grandmother, who still occupies the apartment they shared when she was helping rear him. To summarize, Obama took a break. But he wasn't given one. "Going off this week to vacation in Hawaii does not make any sense whatsoever," Cokie Roberts, one of the resident sourpusses on ABC's *This Week with*

George Stephanopoulos, complained. "I know his grandmother lives in Hawaii, and I know Hawaii is a state, but it has the look of him going off to some sort of foreign, exotic place. He should be in Myrtle Beach, you know, if he's going to take a vacation at this time"—birthplace and grandma be damned.

On the other hand, the proposition that Obama vacationed in Hawaii is at least factually true. The same cannot be said for the contents of *The Obama Nation*, by Jerome R. Corsi, Ph.D., which, thanks to bulk purchases, has been the No. 1 *New York Times* best-seller for three weeks. The tired pun of the book's title is a rare instance of hard-right truth in labelling. On a foundation of small, medium-sized, and extra-large falsehoods, *The Obama Nation* erects a superstructure of innuendo, guilt by (often nonexistent) association, baseless speculation, and sinister-sounding but irrelevant digression. The result is an example of what used to be known, in the glory days of ideologically driven totalitarianism, as the Big Lie—in this case, a fabricated, alternate-universe Barack Obama, who, we are told or invited to infer, is a corrupt, enraged, anti-American, drug-dealing, anti-Israel, pseudo-Christian radical leftist, black militant, plagiarist, and liar, trained as a Muslim and mentored by a menagerie of Marxists, Communists, crypto-Communists, and terrorists.

The fabrications and distortions in *The Obama Nation* have been patiently enumerated and refuted by Media Matters and other watchdog Web sites; "Fight the Smears," a section of Obama's site, has a fairly complete compilation. The exercise is an absolutely necessary one, but the point-by-point approach can leave the impression of quibbling over details. The problem for Obama isn't little lies. It's the big one.

Corsi won his first dollop of fame four years ago, as the co-author of another best-selling tissue of lies, *Unfit for Command: Swift Boat Veterans Speak Out Against John Kerry*. The moral depravity of that book was matched by its physical slovenliness. It looked as if it had been laid out on a teenager's home computer, it was barely literate, and it was padded with large type, wide margins, and redundant appendixes. The sole raison d'être of its publisher, Regnery, is the promulgation of hard-right politics. *The Obama Nation*, on the other hand, has been published by Threshold Editions, an imprint of Simon & Schuster. It is a professional job, and it has evidently benefitted from professional help. In a typical passage, the harsh taste of poison is artificially sweetened by a dose of solemn, ersatz thoughtfulness:

> Our argument is that Obama's experience with Islam predisposes him to Islam in a way that is reflective of his political associates, his political advisors, and his specific policies regarding the Middle East. This is a very different argument than to claim Obama is a Muslim, something no one can prove one way or the other, except for Obama himself.

Corsi himself is a crackpot, a boor, and a bigot. He wrote a book last year accusing the Bush administration, the Council on Foreign Relations, and assorted liberals of plotting to subsume the United States into a North American superstate with its own currency, the "amero"; he helped fuel a theory, popular with slivers of the far right and the far left, that the World Trade Center collapse on 9/11 was caused by explosives planted in the buildings; on a malarial right-wing Web site called FreeRepublic.com, he called Hillary Clinton "a lesbo," Muslims "ragheads," and John Kerry, Bill Clinton, Katie Couric, and John Lennon "communists" ("a dead communist," in the Beatle's case), and wrote that "boy buggering in both Islam and Catholicism is okay with the Pope"—meaning John Paul II, whom he derided as "senile"—"as long as it isn't reported by the liberal press."

All of which is to say that Corsi is, or ought to be, a marginal figure. But Mary Matalin, the editor in chief of Threshold Editions, is not a marginal Republican. She is a former chief of staff of the Republican National Committee, and she served in the current administration as an Assistant to the President, the White House staff's shiniest title. Nor is Simon & Schuster—which, seventeen years ago, gave a book contract to a young man who had been elected the first African-American president of the *Harvard Law Review*—a marginal publisher. But its standards have evidently slipped now that, along with CBS, MTV, and Paramount, it is part of Sumner Redstone's National Amusements, Inc.

The Corsi book does its real damage on the air, via the sprawling conservative slander industry. The book, its author, and its claims are in heavy rotation on Fox News and the talk radio programs of Rush Limbaugh, Sean Hannity, Michael Savage, Laura Ingraham, and their hundreds of imitators. There is no Democratic equivalent, and, because these broadcasters have no formal connection with the Republican Party or with John McCain, their unending campaign of character assassination against Obama affords the party and its presumptive nominee the gift of deniability. Even so, McCain has increasingly embraced their methods. At the Veterans of Foreign Wars convention last week, he accused Obama of placing the nation's security below "the ambition to be president." Before the same audience the following day, Obama said he had "never suggested, and never will, that Senator McCain picks his positions on national security based on politics or personal ambition," adding, "I believe that he genuinely wants to serve America's national interest. Now it's time for him to acknowledge that I want to do the same."

That should clear up any doubts about whether Obama is a Christian. But, in politics, a soft answer does not always turn away wrath. At the Democratic Convention four years ago, John Kerry, heeding focus groups in which "negativity" was deplored, made the colossal mistake of discouraging discouraging words about George W. Bush. If the character of a campaign reflects the character of its candidate, then John McCain's character is not above criticism. In Denver this week, Obama and the Democrats had better hold McCain and the Republicans accountable, not only for the moral, strategic, and material disasters of the past eight years but also for the viciousness of their method of clinging to power. If they do, perhaps Barack Obama will be able to take his next vacation at Camp David.

THE LION

Denver, August 26, 2008

The Kennedy family occupies, for the moment, a place of equilibrium and purity. It is no longer at the center of a roiling drama of power and striving. Its younger members, including the nieces and nephews among them who have tried for and sometimes achieved elected office, have settled quietly into lives of service; they are not, for the moment, a threat to anybody else's ambitions.

The violent deaths of John and Robert, murders most foul and horrifying, tore the nation's heart as painfully as did the death of Abraham Lincoln, and the historical consequences of their deaths were arguably as baleful. Now the last brother, the only one to survive beyond the youthful cusp of maturity, is dying, too. Teddy was the youngest and the slowest, the one who relied the most abjectly on family connections for his advancement and who, at Chappaquiddick in 1969 and then with his doomed and damaging campaign for president in 1980, seemed destined to do the most to squander and tarnish the family legacy. Yet in the twenty-eight years since then he has gradually constructed a life of large and consistent accomplishment that has earned him a stature that, in its way, is as impressive as his brothers'.

His appearance at the convention last night was a surprise, at least to me. (I imagine the TV audience knew all about it.) A greater surprise was the strength of his voice and his message. This was no feeble invalid. Kennedy's energy was fully a match for that of the vast crowd. That he and his niece Caroline, who introduced him with great affection and respect, were there less to celebrate themselves and their past than to accelerate a future represented by Barack Obama, whom they plainly see as the inheritor of what they represent, kept the moment from becoming maudlin. The tears that streaked so many faces came from everywhere tears can come from: from joy and grief, from pride and sorrow, from love and hope, from a simple upwelling of mingled emotions. The lion roared one last time, and we were all his cubs.

THE ERA OF BILL AND HILL

Denver, August 28, 2008

The Clinton Era at the Democratic National Convention (and two days out of a four-day event is an era, maybe an epoch, possibly an age) dawned at 8:38 P.M., Mountain Time, on Tuesday. The opening act—a lapsed Republican, a retired admiral, a motley crew of governors—had come and gone, the houselights in the Pepsi Center had dimmed, and the introductory film unspooled. On the giant telescreens flanking and facing the lectern, a fuzzy black-and-white snapshot of Baby Hillary appeared. When the lights came up again, there she was, all blonde hair and burnt-peach gabardine, waving and smiling and striding and clapping.

High, high up in the cheap seats, a woman named Judi Lanza ("like Mario") listened to the speech. Lanza is a registered nurse from Goffstown, New Hampshire. Last fall, Hillary came to Lanza's house for a roundtable on health care. Lanza has pictures to prove it—Hillary in the Lanzas' dining room, flanked by Judi; her husband, Joseph, a retired cop turned truck driver; and their three grown kids, Joseph, Jr., Jennifer, and Jeffrey. Judi just missed getting to be a delegate, so she came to the convention on her own, as a volunteer. She listened hard. When Hillary said, "I will always remember the young man in a Marine Corps T-shirt who waited months for medical care," Judi teared up a little. And when Hillary said, "Those are the reasons I ran for president. Those are the reasons I support Barack Obama. And those are the reasons you should, too," Lanza—eyes fixed on the little screen of her video camera, a firm set to her round chin—nodded vigorously.

"I've been calling my friends, trying to convince them to go with Obama," Lanza said after the benediction. "I met her again, after she conceded, on her unity day, in New Hampshire. Him, too. She said she remembered me."

A couple of hours later, at a party thrown by MSNBC at the art-filled home of Scott Coors, a liberal outlier in a family that has funnelled mighty rivers of beer money to conservative think tanks, three media heavies, middle-aged men to a man, discussed the speech.

"It depends on what you compare it to," said Heavy No. 1. "It was pretty damn generous compared to Teddy in 1980."

"Yeah," said No. 2. "Teddy, like, turned his back on Carter. Might've cost him the election."

"It would've been nice if she'd made some argument for Obama besides that he's the nominee of the Democratic Party," said No. 3.

"Yeah, like something specific about him. Half her speech was about herself."

"Woulda, shoulda, coulda. Give her a break. Maybe the speech wasn't as good as it shoulda been, but it was a hell of a lot better than it coulda been. She did what she had to do. Maybe more."

"Bill, though. Tomorrow night."

"The big dog."

"Yeah. Supposedly it's the only speech the Obama people haven't vetted."

"No, Hillary's, too. But yeah, Bill. That's the key."

By the time the big dog rolled out onto the stage the next night, Obama's nomination had gone from presumptive to official. Relaxing in her seat near the New York standard, Rosina Rubin, a passionate Hillary delegate from Rockland County, was starting to feel better about the whole thing. The roll call hadn't been disruptive or divisive or any of that. It was first-rate theatre, and the moment when Clinton herself appeared on the floor and moved to nominate Obama by acclamation seemed to provide some of the promised catharsis.

After Bill's speech—which featured all the "shoulda"s Hillary's didn't—Rubin felt just fine. "That was electrifying," she said. "It's such a clichéd thing to say, but this feels like a cleansing, a healing that allows the page to be turned. I've talked to a lot of women who worked for Barack Obama. Somehow they weren't feeling the joy they should have. Something was missing. I think that's over. There's joy in the house."

BEING THERE

Denver, September 1, 2008

I am at a disadvantage when it comes to evaluating the recently concluded Democratic National Convention. I was there, you see. And the banal (and wonderful) reality of an American political convention is that there is no there there. There may not even be a there anywhere. But to the extent that there is a there, to the extent that a there exists, it's a there that hovers and shimmers as an overlapping, pulsing, unembodied electronic emanation casting its crackly glow over the nation and, more feebly, the planet.

This goes beyond the increasingly outdated distinction between experiencing a convention in person and experiencing it on television. A generation ago, the TV coverage varied slightly depending on whether you were watching ABC, NBC, or CBS, and slightly more if you threw PBS and radio into the mix, but basically the experience—the "there"—was pretty much the same for everybody outside the convention hall and its immediate environs. Now, of course, what with the cable news and cable nonnews broadcasts, the live bloggers, the non-live (but lively) bloggers, the video and audio webcasts, the newsgroups and chat rooms, the Web sites of newspapers, broadcasters, candidates, parties, and interest groups, the Huffingtons and Freepers and

TPMs, the text messages and cell phone snapshots—what with all that, the non-there there is even harder to pin down than the there there. A thousand conventions bloom. A million.

And if you do happen to be "there," i.e., spending half your time going to and from your distant hotel and worrying about who's got what credentials and inching through security checkpoints and getting patted down by the Secret Service? And, once inside the hall or its perimeter, relying on your own poor nervous system for input? Well, in that case, you arguably have less of an idea of what (if anything) of broad significance is actually "happening" at the convention than if you were back home with your laptop and your television, absorbing the jagged, jangly, digitized outputs of the nervous systems of unknown thousands of other people and their electronic extensions.

The closest approximation to sitting in the press gallery inside the convention hall, I guess, is the Warholian coverage offered by C-Span. But that, of course, lacks the three-dimensional, carnal corporality that comes from total immersion in an immense sea of human protoplasm. That's what a floor pass gets you. There is something to be said for being at the Battle of Austerlitz, fog of war or no fog of war, especially when you can still get the big picture by reading about it later in *War and Peace*—not that MSNBC, Fox, and CNN are exactly Count Leo Tolstoy. But still.

As George Packer points out, conventions "are about disorientation, estrangement, and fragmentation . . . unless you come for the parties." Which, of course, is exactly what you come for, because the whole damn thing is a party, a Party's party, and it's always a very good party. An American political convention is as much fun as a rock festival, a transatlantic ocean-liner voyage, a really good political science seminar, a Renaissance Faire, a college mixer, and a class reunion combined.

All of which is to repeat: I may be at a disadvantage in evaluating this convention. But evaluate it I will:

It was one of the best.

LET IT RAIN

September 5, 2008

A couple of weeks before August 28—the night that Barack Obama accepted the Democratic nomination for president, in a Denver football stadium—Stuart Shepard, the digital-media director of the lobbying arm of Focus on the Family, one of the most powerful organizations on the religious right, posed a question to his Internet viewers. "Would it be wrong," he asked, "to pray for rain?" Shepard's answer, apparently, was no, because he proceeded to do just that. He prayed for there to be rain—abundant rain, torrential rain, "rain of Biblical proportions"—in Denver on August 28. "I'm praying for unexpected, unanticipated, unforecasted rain that starts two minutes before the speech is set to begin," he said, adding, "I know there will probably be people who will pray for seventy-two degrees and clear skies, but this isn't a contest."

In the event, Obama gave his speech under clear skies with the thermometer at seventy-two degrees. It's hard to draw definitive conclusions from this about the efficacy of prayer. Still, Shepard and others who assume that the Almighty faxes meteorological talking points as a matter of routine must now be puzzling over what He meant last week by arranging for a hurricane just severe enough to disrupt the opening

of the Republican National Convention (and freshen the public's memories of the present administration's Katrina incompetence) but, merci-
fully, not so severe as to do too much damage to the innocent.

The Focus on the Family approach to divine intervention having
fizzled, John McCain needed a deus ex machina. The deus—or rather,
in this case, the dea—he found, sprung fully formed from the brow of
Rush Limbaugh, is the governor of Alaska, Sarah Palin. The machina is
"the base," the Christianist conservatives who have come to dominate
the Republican Party. Governor Palin ticks every box on the check-
list of the social right. She opposes abortion rights, even for women
and girls made pregnant by rape or incest. She thinks that creationism
should be taught alongside evolution in public schools. She does not
believe that global warming is caused by human activity. She supports
public funding for homeschooling. She is against stem cell research.
She opposes "explicit" sex education and supports the abstinence-only
kind, though she is surely aware of its indifferent record of success.

With the selection of Sarah Palin, McCain completes the job
of defusing the enmity (and forgoing the honor) he earned in 2000,
when he condemned Pat Robertson and Jerry Falwell as "agents of
intolerance." His motives in choosing her were entirely tactical and
mostly—the mot juste is that of Mike Murphy, once McCain's top
political aide, overheard by an errant microphone—cynical. Besides
placating the right, those motives included the short-term goal of pre-
empting the weekend news cycles that might otherwise have been
devoted to reviewing Obama's triumphant Democratic Convention.
The price that McCain paid, and that could sooner or later be exacted
from the nation, was the abandonment of what he had repeatedly
called his overriding requirement for a vice president: someone who
would be ready to take his place at a moment's notice—"you know,
immediately."

According to *Time*, Palin's acceptance address was drafted—by a former Bush White House speechwriter—before she was chosen and then
retailored to fit her. Like almost every major speech at that convention

(Mike Huckabee's being an exception), it substituted sarcasm for humor in its sneers at Obama. "I guess a small-town mayor is sort of like a community organizer, except that you have actual responsibilities," she said. "Al Qaeda terrorists still plot to inflict catastrophic harm on America, and he's worried that someone won't read them their rights," she said, a little chillingly. "Listening to him speak, it's easy to forget that this is a man who has authored two memoirs but not a single major law or even a reform, not even in the state senate," she said. This last was simply false; Obama's legislative record, both in Illinois and (given its brevity) in Washington, is impressive. (Also, it's McCain whose books have been "authored." Obama wrote his.) But the speech was well crafted and more than competently delivered, with even its most mean-spirited lines accompanied by perky smiles and girlish wrinklings of the nose. McCain's gamble, though shockingly irresponsible as an act of potential governance, is, for now, a political success: Palin attracted close to forty million television viewers, the crowd in the hall went wild for her, and a Rasmussen poll taken immediately afterward showed her with higher "positives" than any of the three men on the national tickets.

After that, it was inevitable that the presidential nominee's acceptance speech would be an anticlimax. But, if it did not excite, neither did it disgust. McCain was gracious to his opponent—"I wouldn't be an American worthy of the name if I didn't honor Senator Obama and his supporters for their achievement"—and his call to "comfort the afflicted" and "defend the rights of the oppressed" sounded interestingly like a community organizer's job description. The speech contained only one serious falsehood: the charge that Obama would "force families into a government-run health-care system where a bureaucrat stands between you and your doctor." It was withering in its rhetorical critique of McCain's own party. "We lost the trust of the American people when some Republicans gave in to the temptations of corruption," he said. "We lost their trust when we valued our power over our principles." He promised to bring Democrats and independents into his administration. He acknowledged the pain of America's sinking economy. But the sketchy solutions he proposed were indistinguishable from George W. Bush's.

At the end, McCain peered not into the future but forty years into the past. His retelling of his experience as a prisoner of war in Vietnam was powerful, and the lesson he drew from it—that it caused him "to learn the limits of my selfish independence"—was the very opposite of Republican boilerplate. But its backward-looking orientation—at one point, McCain described where he was when he learned about the Japanese attack on Pearl Harbor—underlined his age and, with it, the recklessness of the most important decision he has made as a candidate.

The speech made clear that it will not be enough for Obama and the Democrats simply to equate McCain with Bush. If McCain wins, he will, almost certainly, "change the tone," as Bush promised, falsely, to do eight years ago. In certain details, McCain may even change the policies, though there was little in his speech to encourage that hope. But he is seventy-two years old; if he is elected and reelected, he will be in his eighties by the end of his second term. If he does become our next president, then all of us, believers and nonbelievers alike, had better pray for his health.

GOTT MITT UNS

September 8, 2008

Mitt Romney's speech, on the final night of the G.O.P. convention last week, was so nutty that I can't help indulging in a fond look back at it before it recedes forever into the mists of time. These are a few of my favorite lines.

Last week, the Democrats talked about change. But let me ask you—what do you think Washington is right now, liberal or conservative?

If you get this one right, the rest of the quiz should be a snap. Now, think hard. Here's a hint:

Is a Supreme Court liberal or conservative that awards Guantanamo terrorists with constitutional rights? It's liberal!

Now you're cookin'. Some fine wordcraft here. A person imprisoned at Guantanamo is, ipso facto, a terrorist. Evidence not required; the imprisonment *is* the evidence. Persons shown to be terrorists by virtue of being held at Guantanamo are "awarded with"—sounds like "rewarded with," see?—constitutional rights. The rest of us "have" such rights. Up to a point.

Is government spending—excluding inflation—liberal or conservative if it doubles since 1980? It's liberal!

Let's see—1980. That was the year Ronald Reagan was elected president. Republicans have held the White House for twenty of the twenty-eight years since then. That's two-thirds of the time. It's liberal!

We need change all right—change from a liberal Washington to a conservative Washington! We have a prescription for every American who wants change in Washington—throw out the big-government liberals and elect John McCain!

How do you run an insurgent campaign against your own political self? Romney's answer is search and replace. Search for: *conservative*. Replace with: *liberal*. Or just stick *liberal* in when you need a bit of negative emphasis. Then you too can write sentences like the ones above, or this one:

This is no time for timid, liberal empty gestures.

It's time for timid, conservative empty gestures, such as doing the same things we've been doing for the past eight years. Or longer:

The right course is the one championed by Ronald Reagan thirty years ago, and by John McCain today.

The change we need.

Just like you, there has never been a day when I was not proud to be an American. We inherited the greatest nation in the history of the earth.

The early post-Palin polls suggest that the Republicans may get another four years in which to continue squandering that inheritance. But at least those of us who have also inherited beer distributorships won't have to pay "death taxes."

TIMING IS EVERYTHING

September 11, 2008

It has been generally assumed that the fact that John McCain is the candidate of the incumbent party is inimical to his chances of victory, on account of the undeniable unpopularity of that incumbent party.

I would like to offer an alternative view. The fact that John McCain is the candidate of the incumbent party is essential to his chances of victory, on account of the undeniable *incumbency* of that incumbent party.

You see, the order in which the parties hold their conventions is determined by which party holds the White House. The out party always goes first. The in party always goes second.

If the order of this year's conventions had been reversed, we would now be looking at a very different set of story lines. The final, reverberating impression left by the conventions would not have been Sarah Palin's everygal charm but Barack Obama's stirring specifics delivered to a cheering throng of eighty thousand under the lights. The TV commentaries, once the conventions were over, would have found time to contrast the Republicans' relentless negativity to the positive tone struck by the Democrats. Because the Republicans concentrated on personality while the Democrats stressed policy, the talking heads, who always go with whatever is most recent, might have found time to talk about what the candidates, if elected, might actually *do*.

Would McCain have picked Palin if he'd had to choose first? It's certainly possible that what pushed McCain over the Palin edge was the unfolding of the Democratic Convention, which was clearly a success by the time Bill Clinton finished speaking on Wednesday night. On the other hand, it was almost as clear before the conventions as it was after that McCain needed to do something dramatic. My guess is that he would have gone with Palin. His need for a "game changer" was almost as apparent before the Democrats convened as afterwards. And the factors that forced him to abandon his Lieberman fantasy would have been the same.

Would Obama have picked Hillary Clinton if he'd had the luxury of waiting till McCain had made his choice? Certainly not, of course, if he'd picked his running mate before both conventions. But if he hadn't, then conceivably, maybe even probably. But the magnitude of the Palin phenomenon might not have been so apparent, because it wouldn't have had time to fully take flight before getting stepped on by the festivities in Denver, which would have followed hard upon it.

Crucial to the advantages McCain reaped from the order of the conventions was the fact that they were held back-to-back. The Dems closed Friday night; the reporting teams and commentators emplaned immediately for Minneapolis–St. Paul; the Reps opened Tuesday morning.

For all practical purposes, this was unprecedented. Only twice since 1856, when the first Republican Convention nominated John C. Frémont, have there been back-to-back conventions—in 1916 and in 1956. From 1960 until this year, the gap between conventions has ranged from ten days to five weeks. In half of those twelve cycles, the gap was a month or more.

"History shows that a five-point convention bounce has been typical, no matter the particulars of the convention in terms of political party and incumbency/convention order," an analyst for the Gallup organization wrote last month, using data from 1964 to 2004. But this year, history is bunk. A convention bounce needs time to develop. No time, no bounce. Obama got neither. McCain got both.

One other scheduling factor that operates in McCain's favor, smaller but not entirely insignificant: the shortness of the post-convention campaign season. This is the first time ever in which a convention has slopped over into September. McCain's bounce, therefore, will likely take him correspondingly closer to the finish line.

PALINOPSIA

September 15, 2008

A neurologist friend, Dr. Richard Ransohoff, has drawn our attention to an early contribution to the suddenly burgeoning field of palinological studies.

It is hoped that this paper, published, in 1989, in the Swiss-based journal *European Neurology* (Vol. 29, No. 6) may illuminate the phenomenon, often seen in Republican patients, whereby failed Bush policies are retained in policy-processing areas of the brain long after these policies have demonstrated themselves to be abject failures.

The abstract of the paper follows.

PALINOPSIA AS AN EPILEPTIC PHENOMENON

Ch. Lefebre, H.W. Kölmel
Abteilung für Neurologie, Universitätsklinikum-Rudolf-Virchow,
Freie Universität Berlin

Eur Neurol 1989;29:323–327 (DOI: 10.1159/000116439)

The preservation or recurrence of images in the visual field after removal of the real stimulus is called "palinopsia" or "visual perseveration" which can be split up into three different types according to the latency between the real external stimulus and its apparent recurrence. For a long time it was subject of discussion whether the delusion is a sign of lacking cortical inhibition or of a cortical afterimage or part of an epileptic seizure. If there are different reasons for the three sorts of visual perseveration has not been answered yet. In our case report, however, it is possible to demonstrate a patient's post-traumatic lateralized long-latency visual perseveration for the first time as a clear-cut focal epileptic seizure which is approved by synchronous temporo-parietal epileptic discharges in the electroencephalogram.

So far, the only known treatment is a radical palinectomy, but without extensive follow-up therapy the delusionary policies may return in more virulent form with misleadingly different presenting symptoms, a condition known as McCain Syndrome.

(Referral: Dr. Donald Fagen, S.D.)

DRONING ON ABOUT PALIN

September 16, 2008

A reader writes:

> You might be interested and amused (but certainly not "intrigued")
> to learn that, in Ancient Greek, the word "Palin" means, more or less,
> "backwards." Not in the sense of slow or stupid, but, rather, in the
> sense of reversing direction. A "palindrome," for instance, is some-
> thing that "runs backwards" or, one might say, reverses itself.

By a similar logic, a "Palindrone" is an endlessly repeated reversal of
the truth, as in, "I told Congress, 'Thanks but no thanks' for that bridge
to nowhere."

(Reader J. P. Bernbach evidently knows his *New Yorker* history.
The sainted William Shawn, our editor from 1952 to 1987, forbade the
passive use of "intrigued" to mean interested, amused, or fascinated,
permitting it only in its active meaning of engaging in underhanded
scheming.)

A BUSY DAY

September 25, 2008

What a contrast yesterday. First, out comes McCain, looking drawn, jittery, and (to my admittedly jaundiced eye) guilty, with his announcement that he doesn't want to debate on Friday because the financial crisis is too awful for a thing like politics to occur. He reads his statement and exits quickly. A couple of hours later, Obama appears. He looks and sounds like a president of the United States. He is preternaturally calm. He explains the chronology of the day: he called McCain at 8:30, the call was returned at 2:30, they discussed the idea of putting out a joint statement about the crisis. He says not a word about postponing the debate.

Then, unlike McCain, Obama takes questions. It becomes a full-fledged press conference. He eventually mentions the postponement. He says that during their phone call McCain had said it was something that ought to be looked at, and he had replied that they should get their joint statement out first. He makes it clear, in an offhand way, that McCain had blindsided him, but he does it without rancor. Perhaps there was a miscommunication, he suggests generously. He stresses his agreement with McCain that the crisis is neither Republican nor Democratic but American. He outlines some conditions he would like to see attached to the bailout bill but adds that both parties should refrain from loading it up with extraneous desiderata. He mentions a couple of specific examples of Democratic pet causes, including bankruptcy protection, that he doesn't think should be in the bill. His manner with respect to the crisis is grave and businesslike, but he treats McCain's debate-postponement demand as a minor matter that need not be taken too seriously. He notes dryly that both candidates have big airplanes with their names emblazoned and can easily travel to Oxford, Mississippi. He suggests that a potential president ought to be able to cope with more than one problem at a time.

Obama handled the situation perfectly. He didn't have to point out that McCain's cheap gambit was a cheap gambit. Surrogates, supporters, and, perhaps, the press would do that for him. And by treating the debate-postponement ploy as a detail, he slipped the trap McCain had set for him: either be bullied into obeying McCain's order or be seen as putting politics above country. That's how I saw it, anyhow. I have no idea if "the American people" will agree. Dick Morris doesn't think so. On Bill O'Reilly's show on Fox News, Morris was bubbling over with glee at the brilliance of it all. McCain's maneuver, Morris said, was so clever it might have been orchestrated by Karl Rove himself. Maybe Morris is right. At the very least, McCain managed to prevent the cable chatterers from focusing on the news that his campaign manager had been on the Freddie Mac take right up to the moment last month when Freddie fell on his fanny.

A couple of hours later, Katie Couric, whose evening news program on CBS is said to have become the best of the big three, shows a few minutes of the interview she had taped that morning with Sarah Palin. Couric is both pleasanter and tougher than Charlie Gibson had been during the only other non-Fox interview the lady has condescended to give. For Palin, the interview excerpt begins badly. Couric asks about the campaign manager and the Freddie Mac payroll. Palin gives her answer, something about how her "understanding" is that the campaign manager had "recused himself." Couric rephrases the question.

Palin gives her answer again. It is nearly word for word the same as the first time. Chilling. The interview excerpt ends badly, too. Couric asks what, besides suggesting two years ago that there ought to be more oversight of the mortgage giants, McCain has ever done in his twenty-six years in Congress to change the way Wall Street does business. Palin points to McCain's call for more oversight of the mortgage giants. Couric asks again. Palin says fondly that McCain is a maverick. Politely, a third time, Couric asks for specific examples. Pertly, Palin says, "I'll try to find some and I'll bring 'em to ya."

In other news, President Bush gave a nationally televised speech.

FOREIGN COUNTRIES

September 26, 2008

The second installment of Katie Couric's interview with Sarah Palin aired last night. The topic was the great wide world. One exchange deserves special study. From the transcript provided by CBS:

COURIC: You've cited Alaska's proximity to Russia as part of your foreign policy experience. What did you mean by that?

PALIN: Alaska has a very narrow maritime border between a foreign country, Russia, and, on our other side, the land-boundary that we have with Canada. It's funny that a comment like that was kinda made to—I don't know, you know—reporters.

COURIC: Mocked?

PALIN: Mocked, yeah I guess that's the word, mocked.

COURIC: Well, explain to me why that enhances your foreign-policy credentials.

PALIN: Well, it certainly does, because our, our next-door neighbors are foreign countries, there in the state that I am the executive of. And there—

COURIC: Have you ever been involved in any negotiations, for example, with the Russians?

PALIN: We have trade missions back and forth, we do. It's very important when you consider even national-security issues with Russia. As
Putin rears his head and comes into the air space of the United States of
America, where do they go? It's Alaska. It's just right over the border. It
is from Alaska that we send those out to make sure that an eye is being
kept on this very powerful nation, Russia, because they are right next
to, they are right next to our state.

This seems to be a case of incoherence of thought leading to incoherence of syntax. Pronouns wander in search of antecedents like Arctic explorers in a blinding snowstorm. In the "Putin rears his head"
answer, jagged shards of the hasty briefings lately stuffed into Palin's
pretty head clang tinnily against one another. "We send those"—those?
those what?—"out to make sure that an eye is being kept on this powerful nation, Russia." Those what? We send what? My hunch is that
this alarming jumble must have something to do with the path that
Russian intercontinental missiles would take on their way to the lower
forty-eight and/or the air defense installations that NORAD maintains
in the state Palin is executive of. But who knows? The whole thing
reads like something rendered from the Finnish by Google Translate.

For a seventy-two-year-old cancer survivor to have placed this
person directly behind himself in line for the presidency was an act
of almost incomprehensible cynicism and irresponsibility. It makes
a cruel—what's the word?—mockery of his slogan. "Country First"
indeed.

P.S. In the *Seattle Times*, Hal Bernton reports that Governor Palin has
"balked" at opportunities to visit Russia on any of those "trade missions" she boasted of. Bernton writes:

Opportunities abound for Alaska governors to engage in Russian diplomacy, with the state host to several organizations focusing on Arctic

issues. Anchorage is the seat of the Northern Forum, an 18-year-old organization that represents the leaders of regional governments in Russia, as well as Finland, Iceland and Canada, Japan, China and South Korea.

Yet under Palin, the state government—without consultation—reduced its annual financial support to the Northern Forum from $75,000 to $15,000, according to Priscilla Wohl, the group's executive director. That forced the Forum's Anchorage office to go without pay for two months.

On the other hand, she has met Henry Kissinger and the president of Afghanistan.

OLE MISS

September 29, 2008

When the commentators came on after Friday night's first McCain-Obama debate at Ole Miss, I have to say I was puzzled. They were all saying that it was a draw, or that McCain had won "on points," or that McCain had dominated the first part, about the financial crises, and maybe Obama the last part, about Iraq and foreign policy.

I hadn't seen it that way. I was nervous as hell beforehand, of course, but by ten minutes into it I had relaxed and was enjoying the show. I turned to my wife and said, "Am I missing something, or is this incredibly one-sided? One-sided for Obama, I mean?"

That's how I felt all the way through. It seemed pretty obvious to me. One guy was focused, well-organized, calmly energetic, and, while treating his opponent with collegial good manners, firm and occasionally stern; the other guy was churlish, repeated himself, rambled, made feeble jokes we'd heard a thousand times before ("I'm not Miss Congeniality"), and committed minor gaffes, such as (twice) calling the financial crisis a fiscal crisis.

So why were the talking heads saying what they were saying? I have three theories.

1. The talking heads didn't give the debate their full attention. They were reading their BlackBerrys, trading quips with each other on the set or in the greenroom, making notes, and eyeing their colleagues to gauge their reactions. As a result, they missed the emotional thread.

2. The talking heads did notice that Obama was "winning," but were reluctant to say so in case "the American people," as represented by focus groups and quickie polls, turned out to disagree. Also, they were worried about being called "in the tank."

3. Since the talking heads are the ultimate high-information voters, they kept noticing "opportunities" for "knockout blows" that Obama was missing. Instead of judging Obama against McCain, they were judging the actually existing Obama against a sort of Obama Muppet, with they themselves, the talking heads, doing the ventriloquizing.

I was relieved, but also a little surprised, when the focus groups and insta-polls seemed to indicate a fairly clear Obama "victory." I shouldn't have been so surprised, given that the nonverbal valences—the way the two men comported themselves, the way they looked and sounded—were so obviously in Obama's favor. But after seeing McCain's numbers spike in the wake of the Palin pick, I had begun to mistrust the wisdom of the crowd. Also, I assumed that some of the points that I saw as counting for Obama would either go over the heads of the uninformed or be counted for McCain. McCain's confusing "fiscal" with "financial," for example— that was pretty appalling if you happen to know which is which, but what if you don't? Or when McCain disdainfully accused Obama of not knowing the difference between strategy and tactics—it was actually McCain who had gotten that one wrong, but if you happened to be ignorant of the difference yourself you might have thought, "A palpable hit!"

The commentariat was nearly unanimous in judging that McCain had "scored" on the "earmarks issue," but who knows? Maybe some unknown portion of the public understands that $18 billion or $24 billion worth of earmarks is chicken feed in a trillion–dollar budget and therefore wondered why McCain kept obsessing about it. The commentariat also liked McCain's aggressiveness, but the voters, or those designated by pollsters to stand in for them, did not seem to agree. A quick CNN poll of debate-watchers showed Obama beating McCain in eleven categories, from Iraq to likeability, while McCain prevailed in just two: terrorism and "spent more time attacking his opponent."

The McCain people were evidently channeling the commentators. While the debate was still going on, they posted a spot, made from clips from the still-in-progress confrontation, showing Obama saying three times that McCain was "right" or "absolutely right" about something or other, followed by the usual sneering voice saying, "Is Barack Obama ready to lead? No." By the end of the debate, Obama had said seven times that McCain was right. In other words, while McCain talked about his ability to "reach across the aisle," Obama actually did it. But he gave up nothing substantive. Each time Obama credited his opponent with being right, it was always about something anodyne, and it was always followed by a strong expression of disagreement. Obama's purpose, besides appearing gracious, polite, respectful, and open-minded, was to slice off from whatever McCain had said the part that he (and the audience, presumably) had no problem with, the better to isolate and obliterate the part he did have a problem with. (Incidentally, as Ezra Klein noted, how could McCain have "approved this message" if the message was sent while McCain was still fully occupied on the stage at Ole Miss?)

Partly thanks to Chris Matthews, who, post-debate, kept asking everyone he interviewed why McCain had refused to look Obama in the eye, McCain's churlishness became a story. I didn't particularly notice it at the time, but then I didn't take much notice of Gore's sighs in '00 or Bush Senior's glancing at his wristwatch in '92, either. Still, it's gratifying that what goes around comes around.

NUDGE NUDGE WINK WINK

October 3, 2008

Well, if what we want is a perky president (actuarial probabilities being what they are), the choice is clear: go whalin' with Palin! No doubt about it, she's as cute as a Goldwater button. And if by some chance she doesn't put McCain over the top, her next career move is obvious: co-hosting the perennially last-place CBS morning program. She could ace the cooking and celebrity segments, and by the time this campaign is over she'll even know enough about legislation and foreign policy and stuff like that to banter with Jeff Greenfield and handle serious interviews with people like Richard Holbrooke and Michael Beschloss. *The Early Show,* with Harry Smith and Sarah Palin.

Did she "win" last night? In a way. She stanched the bleeding. If her activities for the next month can be limited to charming the "base" at rallies, chatting with right-wing talk radio and Fox News hosts, and granting interviews to dim, carefully vetted "Eyewitness News" local anchors, she probably will do no further damage to the Republican ticket. Given the disasters of the last couple of weeks, that counts as victory. Maybe not Trafalgar-type victory, but Iraq-type. The surge has succeeded.

The choppy format, which discouraged follow-ups, saved her, along with Gwen Ifill's tendency to ask questions (Does the financial crisis show the best of Washington or the worst of Washington? What's scarier, a nuclear Iran or an unstable Afghanistan?) that could be answered with the word "both." Beyond the *Animal Farm* certainties—taxes bad, victory good—and the hockey-mom patter, Palin had nothing to say, but she said it without too much of the usual syntactical chaos. The talking points and the buzzwords (maverick, the people's side) got her through.

Most of the commentators, again, seemed to get it wrong, mainly because they were grading on a curve. Palin did "better than expected." On the other hand, she had been expected to do so poorly that she could hardly fail to do better than expected, i.e., she was expected to do better than expected, which means that she did about as well as expected. But according to the insta-polls, the electorate, as opposed to the expectorate, seems to have concluded that Biden "won," possibly because what the electorate was expecting was a debate between two candidates for vice president, not the raw materials for some arcane calculation of who exceeded whose expectations. Biden succeeded in making a case for the Obama-Biden ticket. Palin succeeded mainly in making a case that she, Palin, is a person of near-normal intelligence and greatly superior adorability.

BEYOND THE PALIN

October 10, 2008

Format isn't everything. John McCain's campaign specialty has been the "town hall," where the candidate wanders the stage, microphone in hand, answering questions from ordinary citizens and bantering with them. So his staff was happy that his second debate with Barack Obama, which took place last Tuesday evening, in Nashville, Tennessee, was structured according to his favorite style. McCain's town meetings have been one-man shows, based on a relationship between candidate and audience that falls somewhere between that of a celebrity to his fans and that of a king to his subjects—one important man and a roomful of the little people. But the dynamic changed when a second important man, particularly one who was elegantly calm and self-assured, was added to the mix. Afterward, in CNN's poll of independent debate-watchers, fifty-four percent thought Obama came out on top, while thirty percent picked McCain as the winner. A congenial set of rules, it seems, can't offset a talented opponent, much less a worldwide financial panic.

The Nashville town hall was an interlude of comparative comity, sandwiched between moldy slices of slander. Early in the general-election campaign, Obama was accused, for example, of favoring "painful tax increases on working American families," when in fact his tax hike would apply only to family incomes of more than a quarter million dollars a year. Perhaps that could be dismissed as a routine political stretcher. But Obama was also portrayed as a libertine who demanded that kindergartners be exposed to explicit descriptions of sexual intercourse (when in fact he proposed only to teach them to recognize inappropriate advances) and as a sexist boor who called the Republican vice presidential nominee a pig (when in fact he used a common simile that his opponent had a habit of using himself). None of this quite amounted to suggesting that the Democrat is a traitor or a facilitator of terror. That came after the financial crisis began and Obama took a small but persistent lead in the opinion polls.

Early this month, McCain moved nearly his entire advertising budget into negative territory. But "negative" hardly does justice to the mendacity of the campaign of vilification that bracketed Nashville. "Barack Obama has said that all we're doing in Afghanistan is air-raiding villages and killing civilians," Sarah Palin said the week before. "Such a reckless, reckless comment and untrue comment, again, hurts our cause." McCain's wife, Cindy—who in May had said, "My husband is absolutely opposed to any negative campaigning at all"—told a rally last week, "The day that Senator Obama decided to cast a vote to not fund my son while he was serving sent a cold chill through my body." A McCain television spot summed up the line of attack:

Who is Barack Obama? He says our troops in Afghanistan are [Obama's voice] "just air-raiding villages and killing civilians." How dishonorable. Congressional liberals voted repeatedly to cut off funding to our active troops, increasing the risk on their lives. How dangerous. Obama and congressional liberals. Too risky for America.

Here is what Obama actually said, fourteen months ago: "We've got to get the job done there, and that requires us to have enough troops so that we're not just air-raiding villages and killing civilians, which is

causing enormous pressure over there." He was calling for reinforce-
ments, not casting aspersions. And, as McCain must know, the one
Senate vote on which the charge of defunding the troops is based has a
mirror image. In May of 2007, Obama voted against a troop-funding
bill because it did not include steps toward withdrawal from Iraq; two
months earlier, McCain had voted against one because it did. In neither
case did their parliamentary maneuverings pose the slightest risk to the
life of a single soldier.

Enter Bill Ayers, the former Weatherman, now a college professor and a pillar of the Chicago education-reform establishment. Palin
again, a few days ago: "Our opponent is someone who sees America
as imperfect enough to pal around with terrorists who targeted their
own country." At the end of the nineteen-sixties, when Bill Ayers was
a leader of the New Left's most destructive, self-destructive, and delusional splinter, Barack Obama was a small boy living with his mother
in Indonesia. The fact that thirty years later Obama and Ayers sat on
a couple of the same nonprofit boards tells us no more about Obama's
politics and character than does the fact that another member of one of
those boards was Arnold R. Weber, the former president of the Civic
Committee of the Commercial Club of Chicago and a donor of fifteen
hundred dollars to the McCain campaign. Ayers and Obama are not
now, nor have they ever been, pals.

The Obama campaign has been spending money on negativity, too,
of course—about a third of its advertising outlay. And a few of their
ads have been purposely misleading. For example, an Obama radio spot
says of McCain, "He's opposed stem cell research." (That too-clever use
of a contraction allows the line to be more truthy than true: McCain
flip-flopped on embryonic stem cell research in 2001.) But there is no
equivalence between the two campaigns. If there were, Obama's ads
would be "raising questions" about the other ticket's "associations."
For example, Todd Palin was a registered member of the Alaskan Independence Party—to which his wife, as governor, has sent friendly
greetings—between 1995 and 2002. Four years before Todd joined, the

A.I.P.'s founder, Joe Vogler, declared, "The fires of hell are frozen glaciers compared to my hatred for the American government," and added, referring to the Stars and Stripes, "I won't be buried under their damned flag!" (Sure enough, in 1995, Vogler, after being murdered in connection with an informal transaction involving plastic explosives, was buried in Canada.) Good material for an attack ad there, no? Ditto the fact that during the early nineteen-eighties John McCain sat on the advisory board of General John Singlaub's U.S. Council for World Freedom— the American outpost of the World Anti-Communist League, a sort of clearing house for former Nazi collaborators, Central American death squad leaders, and assorted international thugs. And, unlike Obama's alleged palship with Ayers, these things are true.

The Obama campaign hasn't gone there, for which it deserves no special credit; it has more to gain from sticking to the realities of the economy and the war. But the other side has been late in having second thoughts. This became frighteningly obvious in recent days, as the rallies McCain and Palin have held around the country turned into bloodcurdling hate-fests. The shouts of supporters in response to the candidates' attacks on Obama—"Traitor!" "Terrorist!" "Kill him!"—were uttered without rebuke. On CNN the other night, Anderson Cooper asked David Gergen, the soul of moderate concerned citizenship, about "all this anger out there." Gergen replied, "We've seen it in a Palin rally. We saw it at the McCain rally today. . . . There is this free-floating sort of whipping-around anger that could really lead to some violence. I think we're not far from that." Suddenly, McCain seems to be worried, too. "I admire Senator Obama and his accomplishments," he told a restive crowd in Lakeville, Minnesota, last Friday. "I will respect him, and I want everyone to be respectful." The crowd—the mob—booed. If McCain loses, or even if he wins, his campaign will be remembered as a tragedy in the Aristotelian sense, in which a hero is ruined through some terrible choice of his own. One can only hope that the tragedy will be his alone, and not the nation's.

VOTER-FRAUD FRAUD

October 15, 2008

The idea that Democrats try to win elections by arranging for hordes of nonexistent people with improbable names to vote for them has long been a favorite theme of Rove-era Republicans. Now it's become a desperate obsession.

Consider today's fund-raising e-mail from Robert M. (Mike) Duncan, chairman of the Republican National Committee. Some snippets:

> Every election, it's the same old song and dance from the Democrats and their liberal allies when it comes to donor and vote fraud.
>
> They will soon be trying to pad their totals at ballot boxes across the country with votes from voters that do not exist. From Ohio and Florida to Wisconsin and Nevada, there are reports of fraudulent voter registration forms being submitted by the Association of Community Organizations for Reform Now (ACORN), a liberal group that is dedicating its resources to electing the Obama-Biden Democrats.

The e-mail climaxes with this pledge, which one hopes is delivered with a Sarah Palin wink: "We will not stand for the stealing of the election—the tainting of our democracy—by those who wish to subvert the rule of law."

ACORN has become the 24/7 story on Fox News, too, on account of reports that it has submitted several thousand phony registration forms to local boards of elections. These reports appear to be true. Nevertheless, the "scandal," as Fox calls it, is itself on its face as phony as Mickey Mouse's social security number.

During this election cycle, the *Times* reported today, ACORN has deployed thirteen thousand mostly paid workers, who have registered 1.3 million new voters. One or two percent of these workers turned in sheaves of forms that they filled out themselves with fake names and bogus addresses, and, even though at least a hundred of these workers have already been fired, the forged forms have been submitted to election boards.

Sounds suspicious—unless you know that groups like ACORN are *required by law* to submit them, even if they're obvious fakes. This is to prevent funny business, such as trashing forms that look like they might be Republican (or Democratic, as the case may be).

Sounds suspicious—unless you know that ACORN normally sorts through forms, flags those that look fishy, and submits the fishy ones in a separate pile for the convenience of election officials.

Sounds suspicious—until you reflect that the motivation of the misbehaving registration workers is almost always to look like they've been doing more work than they really have, and that the victim of the "fraud" is actually the organization they're working for.

Sounds suspicious—unless you know that even if one of these fake forms results in a nonexistent person actually being registered, now under the Help America Vote Act of 2002, "any voter who has not previously voted in a federal election" must provide identification in order to actually cast a ballot. This will make it tough for Mickey Mouse, even if registered, to vote, no matter how big, round, or black his ears. Likewise, members of the Duck family (Donald, Daisy, Huey, Dewey, and Louie) who turn up at the polling place will have a hard time getting into the voting booth. (Uncle Scrooge might be able to bribe his way in, but he's voting Republican anyway.)

Sounds suspicious—unless you know that despite all the hysteria, from 2002 to 2005, only twenty people in the entire United States of America were found guilty of voting while ineligible and only five of voting more than once. By contrast, consider the lede on a newspaper story published a week ago today:

> Tens of thousands of eligible voters in at least six swing states have been removed from the rolls or have been blocked from registering in ways that appear to violate federal law, according to a review of state records and Social Security data by the *New York Times*.

And take it from Sarah Palin: the *Times* is "hardly ever wrong."

CIRCLING THE DRAIN

October 16, 2008

'm beginning to suspect that "the people" approach these debates more seriously than do "the pundits," including yours truly. Last night, I fretted that McCain was doing better and Obama worse than—well, better and worse, respectively, than I had hoped, even expected, they'd do. Obama too often smiled broadly during McCain's answers, which I yelled at the screen to tell him to quit doing. Obama has an amazing smile—he shows more teeth than Anne Hathaway—but his is a smile that should be deployed sparingly, and never sarcastically.

Then came the IM from the Oracle at Delphi, a.k.a. the focus groups and quickie polls. These showed that by the usual 2–1 margins, "the people" called it for Obama. The biggest surprise was the Fox News focus group. Frank Luntz asked the group if any of them had made up their minds during the debate. Four raised their hands.

LUNTZ: Who did you go to?
UNDECIDED VOTER #1: I lean more toward Obama.
UNDECIDED VOTER #2: Obama.
UNDECIDED VOTER #3: Obama.
UNDECIDED VOTER #4: Obama.

LUNTZ: This is a good night for Barack Obama.

BRIT HUME: All right, Frank. Very interesting. Thanks very much.

To make matters worse, Charles Krauthammer gave his analysis, which was that "Obama won resoundingly." Charles didn't look especially happy about having to say this, but he said it and kept saying it. He explained that McCain's only chance had been to "force a huge error on the part of the opposition, and Obama is a guy that does not commit huge errors. He simply doesn't." More from Charles:

KRAUTHAMMER: Obama, as usual, is remarkably unruffled. You could have had a grenade go off in the back of the room, and Obama would have smoothly spoken right through it. And that is his gift. He is a man of remarkable self-containment. And even on Palin, he was given an opening. Did you see his discipline on Palin? He did not say a single word attacking her, knowing it could only alienate a lot of people and would not advance his cause. It is that discipline and self-containment which I think is his greatest asset, and he deployed it remarkably tonight.

BRIT HUME: Charles, thank you very much.

Brit is well brought up. He knows it is always polite to say thank you.

The word ahead of time had been that McCain needed a "game changer," and presumably Joe the Plumber was going to be it. I remember seeing Joe on some cable network or other a few days ago, in a report on an Obama campaign event. Obama met him on a rope line and tried to persuade him of the virtues of his middle-class tax cut. The guy wasn't having any. (Now we know why: Joe, who looks like Henry Paulson on beer, is a stalwart Republican.)

I imagine somebody at McCain headquarters saw the same clip, checked Joe out to make sure he was politically correct (though the vetting was no more rigorous than Sarah Palin's), and gave the candidate a memo. As a result, Samuel J. (Joe) Wurzelbacher, of Toledo, Ohio, is the most famous nonmetaphorical plumber since George Meany. The problem was that McCain mentioned Joe the Plumber so many times that it became a running joke that, as of this writing, is still running, with McCain as the butt.

My eyes were pretty much riveted on Obama during the debate, so I missed McCain's bizarre repertoire of Yosemite Sam–like facial expressions—which, I now realize after reviewing the video clips, were a lot more unpleasant than the Democrat's arguably smug smiles. But I like to think that McCain's real problem, especially during the last half, was substance.

Obama was able, for example, to give a reasonably complete description of his tax and health-care proposals. McCain tangled himself up in a Reaganite ideology that has never looked more threadbare. Instead of American English, he spoke a dialect of Heritage Foundation–speak, sprinkling his disjointed answers with winger shorthand: "trial lawyers," "capital gains," "class warfare," airquote health of the mother unairquote. Obama, in his rope-line chat with Joe, had said casually, "I think that when you spread the wealth around, it's good for everybody," and McCain evidently thought that just contemptuously repeating the phrase "spread the wealth," as he did nine times, would be enough to expose Obama as a dangerous redistributionist. McCain failed to consider that after eight years of skyrocketing hedge-fund payoffs and declining real wages climaxing in a massive prospective shrinking in the whole economy, a little wealth-spreading might not sound as threatening to Main Street as it does to K Street.

Here, by the way, is the context of Obama's call to "spread the wealth," which came at the end of his long, lucid explanation, for Joe's benefit, of why tweaking the tax burden slightly in favor of the nonrich might be good for the economy as a whole:

> I do believe for folks like me who have worked hard, but frankly also been lucky, I don't mind paying just a little bit more than the waitress

that I just met over there who's—things are slow and she can barely make the rent. Because my attitude is that if the economy's good for folks from the bottom up, it's gonna be good for everybody. If you've got a plumbing business, you're going to be better off if you've got a whole bunch of customers who can afford to hire you, and right now I think everybody's so pinched that business is bad for everybody, and I think when you spread the wealth around, it's good for everybody.

It's called progressive taxation, and, tattered though it is, it's the only thing standing between us and a final descent into pure late-Roman-Empire-type plutocratic decadence.

HAIL, HAIL COLOMBIA

October 17, 2008

Barack Obama may have gone to Columbia, but John McCain went to Colombia.

One of the most curious, and little-remarked, features of this week's presidential debate was that the only foreign country to get more than cursory treatment was Colombia, known to most television-watching, non-García Márquez-reading North Americans as a land of rich drug lords, leftist guerrillas, rightist death squads, and ubiquitous coca plantations.

It was McCain who brought the subject up, after he and Obama had traded barbs about NAFTA, the North American Free Trade Agreement:

McCAIN: Let me give you another example of a free trade agreement that Senator Obama opposes. Right now, because of previous agreements, some made by President Clinton, the goods and products that we send to Colombia, which is our largest agricultural importer of our products, is—there's a billion dollars that we—our businesses have paid so far in order to get our goods in there.

Because of previous agreements, their goods and products come into our country for free. So Senator Obama, who has never traveled south of our border, opposes the Colombia Free Trade Agreement. The same country that's helping us try to stop the flow of drugs into our country that's killing young Americans. . . .

Free trade with Colombia is something that's a no-brainer. But maybe you ought to travel down there and visit them and maybe you could understand it a lot better.

OBAMA: Let me respond. Actually, I understand it pretty well. The history in Colombia right now is that labor leaders have been targeted for assassination on a fairly consistent basis and there have not been prosecutions.

And what I have said, because the free trade—the trade agreement itself does have labor and environmental protections, but we have to stand for human rights and we have to make sure that violence isn't being perpetrated against workers who are just trying to organize for their rights, which is why, for example, I supported the Peruvian Free Trade Agreement which was a well-structured agreement.

But I think that the important point is we've got to have a president who understands the benefits of free trade but also is going to enforce fair trade agreements and is going to stand up to other countries.

Obama then talked for several minutes about the need to strengthen the U.S. automobile industry and induce it to build fuel-efficient cars. But McCain still wanted to talk about Colombia. As soon as he got the floor back, he returned to his strange preoccupation:

McCAIN: Well, let me just say that that this is—he—Senator Obama doesn't want a free trade agreement with our best ally in the region but wants to sit down across the table without precondition to—with Hugo Chávez, the guy who has been helping FARC, the terrorist organization.

Free trade between ourselves and Colombia: I just recited to you
the benefits of concluding that agreement, a billion dollars of American dollars that could have gone to creating jobs and businesses in the
United States, opening up those markets.

This is not a new obsession for McCain. Puzzlingly, the first thing
he did after he clinched the Republican nomination, at the beginning
of July, was to get on a plane and go to . . . Colombia. Or maybe not
so puzzlingly. In the second paragraph of the *New York Times* story pre-
viewing the trip, Larry Rohter wrote:

Since 1998, the lobbying firm headed until recently by Charlie Black,
one of Mr. McCain's closest confidants, has earned more than $1.8
million representing the Occidental Petroleum Corporation, the leading foreign producer of gas and oil in Colombia. The lobbying firm,
BKSH & Associates, has also represented Colombian textile and apparel
manufacturers and a former foreign minister and presidential candidate
who is also a prominent businesswoman.

The *Times* went on to note that human rights groups have accused
Occidental of complicity in the killing of peasants and labor leaders
believed (erroneously, in the case of the labor leaders) to be affiliated
with guerrilla groups.

The week before McCain left for Colombia, Carl H. Linder, Jr., who
made billions as the C.E.O. of Chiquita Brands International, hosted a
fund-raiser for McCain at his home in Cincinnati, Ohio. It raised $2
million—a lot of money, though not much compared to the $25 mil-
lion fine Chiquita paid for paying, under Linder's leadership, more millions to the United Self-Defense Forces of Colombia, a bloodthirsty
paramilitary group which the State Department officially classified as
a terrorist organization. But, as Nico Pitney pointed out at the time
in a well-documented report at the Huffington Post, Chiquita was an
equal-opportunity terror funder in Colombia: it also made payments to

leftist guerrilla groups, including the notorious FARC. Nothing to do with ideology, of course. Just a routine business expense.

Besides Black, at least four other McCain staffers or major fund-raisers, including the campaign's finance director and a former national finance chairman, have earned tidy sums lobbying for the Colombia Free Trade Agreement.

But John McCain is an honorable man. Therefore, it is inconceivable that any of these "associations," to use one of his favorite words, had anything to do with the Republican nominee's extraordinary solicitude for the Colombia trade pact, let alone the way he rolled his eyes when Obama spoke of the murder of Colombian labor leaders.

SEALS OF APPROVAL

October 18, 2008

When I was a newsprint-besotted kid, in the 1950s, just about every big and middle-sized American city had at least one newspaper that performed the function talk radio does today: the relentless promulgation of crude reactionary lunacy. The Hearst chain was everywhere; its nationally syndicated columnists included, most prominently, the odiously talented Westbrook Pegler, the Rush Limbaugh of his day, whose anonymous corpse was recently exhumed by Sarah Palin's speechwriter to ventriloquize her praise of the small-town mentality. But the two giants of unhinged editorial-page right-wingery, back then, were the *Los Angeles Times* and the *Chicago Tribune*. (The *Tribune*'s New York cousin, the *Daily News*, ran a close third.)

That was a long time ago, especially in the case of the *L.A. Times*, whose editorial-page editors emeriti now include the great acerbic liberal Michael Kinsley. Even so, it was a pleasant surprise to read the *Times*'s endorsement of Obama. The *Chicago Tribune*'s was more startling: the paper's editorial stance remains conservative, though much more moderately so than in the days of Colonel McCormick. Never before in its one-hundred-and-sixty-one-year history has it backed a Democratic nominee for president. Better still, the *Trib*, Obama's hometown paper, is in a position to vouch for him personally:

> Many Americans say they're uneasy about Obama. He's pretty new to them.
>
> We can provide some assurance. We have known Obama since he entered politics a dozen years ago. We have watched him, worked with him, argued with him as he rose from an effective state senator to an inspiring U.S. senator to the Democratic Party's nominee for president.
>
> We have tremendous confidence in his intellectual rigor, his moral compass and his ability to make sound, thoughtful, careful decisions. He is ready. . . .
>
> We know first-hand that Obama seeks out and listens carefully and respectfully to people who disagree with him. He builds consensus.

Each of these endorsements ends on an unusually lyrical note. The *Times*:

> We may one day look back on this presidential campaign in wonder. We may marvel that Obama's critics called him an elitist, as if an Ivy League education were a source of embarrassment, and belittled his eloquence, as if a gift with words were suddenly a defect. In fact, Obama is educated and eloquent, sober and exciting, steady and mature. He represents the nation as it is, and as it aspires to be.

The *Tribune*:

> It may have seemed audacious for Obama to start his campaign in Springfield, invoking Lincoln. We think, given the opportunity to

hold this nation's most powerful office, he will prove it wasn't so audacious after all. We are proud to add Barack Obama's name to Lincoln's
in the list of people the *Tribune* has endorsed for president of the
United States.

Strong stuff.

ENDORSEMENT ENDORPHIN

October 20, 2008

s there a living American whose endorsement would have meant more to the candidacy of Barack Obama than Colin Powell's? I'm not asking rhetorically—I'd really like to know. Nancy Reagan? Bush the Elder? Henry Kissinger?

How about a revered sports figure? There aren't too many of those any more in this growth-hormone era. Misty May-Treanor and Kerri Walsh? Michael Jordan? Bobby Orr? Tiger Woods? (Or would he just be Powell without the substance?) Some icon of popular culture, then? Bruce Springsteen, Tony Bennett, Stevie Wonder, Oprah Winfrey? (No, Obama's got them already.) Clint Eastwood? Dolly Parton? Or a twofer like Arnold Schwarzenegger? Even if you expand the field to include the six billion people who aren't Americans, you're hard put. The Dalai Lama? Pope Benedict XVI? Anyone?

It wasn't just the "who" of Powell's endorsement, i.e., a résumé that includes service as Reagan's national security adviser, Bush the Elder's chairman of the Joint Chiefs of Staff, and Bush the Younger's secretary of state and a history of loyal Republicanism from the Nixon years until, literally, yesterday. (Powell, the most famous black Republican since Frederick Douglass, maxed out as a McCain contributor during the current electoral cycle and was mentioned as a possible running mate.) It was the force and focus of what he said.

Powell's presentation on *Meet the Press* had the casualness of an interview but the structure and pointedness of an argument crafted into a speech. He began by laying out the issues he regards as important: the global economy; Iraq and Afghanistan; the need for better relations with allies and for being "willing to talk to people who we have not been willing to talk to before"; the need for leadership on energy, global warming, and the environment; the plight of the poorest countries, which he linked to the problem of terrorism. Only then did he turn to his choice for president, making it explicit only after expressing his affection for McCain.

He said that the financial crisis had constituted a kind of "final exam" for the two candidates, one that Obama had passed and McCain had failed. He cited McCain's choice of Sarah Palin as having "raised some question in my mind as to the judgment that Senator McCain made." He praised the contrasting "steadiness" and "intellectual vigor" of Obama, adding:

> On the Republican side over the last seven weeks, the approach of the Republican Party and Mr. McCain has become narrower and narrower. Mr. Obama, at the same time, has given us a more inclusive, broader reach into the needs and aspirations of our people. He's crossing lines—ethnic lines, racial lines, generational lines. He's thinking about all villages have values, all towns have values, not just small towns have values.

General Powell—who is from a small town called the Bronx—then offered a devastating, definitive critique of what he called "this Bill Ayers situation":

> Why do we have these robocalls going on around the country trying to suggest that, because of this very, very limited relationship that Senator

Obama has had with Mr. Ayers, somehow, Mr. Obama is tainted? What they're trying to do is connect him to some kind of terrorist feelings. And I think that's inappropriate.

The emotional climax of Powell's argument came next. It turned on the death of a twenty-year-old Muslim American soldier, and it happens to have been prompted by a photo essay in the magazine I work for, so I can't help feeling some institutional pride.

And his conclusion:

So, when I look at all of this and I think back to my Army career, we've got two individuals. Either one of them could be a good president. But which is the president that we need now? Which is the individual that serves the needs of the nation for the next period of time? And I come to the conclusion that because of his ability to inspire, because of the inclusive nature of his campaign, because he is reaching out all across America, because of who he is and his rhetorical abilities—and we have to take that into account—as well as his substance—he has both style and substance—he has met the standard of being a successful president, being an exceptional president. I think he is a transformational figure. He is a new generation coming into the world, onto the world stage, onto the American stage. And for that reason I'll be voting for Senator Barack Obama.

All of it said calmly and gravely, without a single hesitation, and without notes—a stunning performance. Notwithstanding the conventional platitudes about how endorsements don't really matter, this one does.

SHOOTING THEMSELVES
IN THE MANOLO BLAHNIKS

October 22, 2008

This morning's sugary breakfast treat is the news that—well, linger, if you will, over the first few paragraphs of Politico's story:

> The Republican National Committee has spent more than $150,000 to clothe and accessorize vice presidential candidate Sarah Palin and her family since her surprise pick by John McCain in late August.
>
> According to financial disclosure records, the accessorizing began in early September and included bills from Saks Fifth Avenue in St. Louis and New York for a combined $49,425.74.
>
> The records also document a couple of big-time shopping trips to Neiman Marcus in Minneapolis, including one $75,062.63 spree in early September.
>
> The RNC also spent $4,716.49 on hair and makeup through September after reporting no such costs in August.

Predictably, this has produced a freshet of populist outrage. On MSNBC's *Morning Joe* today, Mika and the gang were marvelling over the sheer volume of indignant e-mails.

Naturally I am delighted to see the Hockey Mom and her handlers hoist on their own small-town, anti-"elitist" petard—karma is a fine and beautiful thing. Still, I have to say, in my capacity as a moral arbiter, that I see nothing wrong with this expenditure. Nothing, that is, apart from the political stupidity of charging the bill to the RNC rather than to, say, Cindy McCain's personal American Express card, on which, in any given month, $150K would be a mere rounding error.

Clothes are superficial. Clothes are about image, about—literally—appearances. But then so is most of what campaigns spend money on. All of Sarah's *schmattes* cost less than showing a single thirty-second spot a single time on a single network during prime time. Forking a little dough over to Neiman Marcus is no worse than forking a lot of dough over to NBC, or, for that matter, to some polling firm so it can focus-group the emotional valence of phrases like "too risky" and "not ready."

Sarah may not sound so great in the talking points for which she has been custom-fitted at campaign expense, but she looks absolutely mahvellous in those outfits. Also, her clothes are one hundred percent positive and zero percent negative. Morally, it's money well spent.

LIKE, SOCIALISM

October 24, 2008

S ometimes, when a political campaign has run out of ideas and senses
that the prize is slipping through its fingers, it rolls up a sleeve and
plunges an arm, shoulder deep, right down to the bottom of the barrel.
The problem for John McCain, Sarah Palin, and the Republican Party
is that the bottom was scraped clean long before it dropped out. Back
when the polls were nip and tuck and the leaves had not yet begun to
turn, Barack Obama had already been accused of betraying the troops,
wanting to teach kindergartners all about sex, favoring infanticide, and
being a friend of terrorists and terrorism. What was left? The anticli-
mactic answer came as the long presidential march of 2008 staggered
toward its final week: Senator Obama is a socialist.

"This campaign in the next couple of weeks is about one thing,"
Todd Akin, a Republican congressman from Missouri, told a McCain
rally outside St. Louis. "It's a referendum on socialism." "With all
due respect," Senator George Voinovich, Republican of Ohio, said,
"the man is a socialist." At an airport rally in Roswell, New Mexico,
a well-known landing spot for space aliens, Governor Palin warned
against Obama's tax proposals. "Friends," she said, "now is no time to
experiment with socialism." And McCain, discussing those proposals,

agreed that they sounded "a lot like socialism." There hasn't been so much talk of socialism in an American election since 1920, when Eugene Victor Debs, candidate of the Socialist Party, made his fifth run for president from a cell in the Atlanta Federal Penitentiary, where he was serving a ten-year sentence for opposing the First World War. (Debs got a million votes and was freed the following year by the new Republican president, Warren G. Harding, who immediately invited him to the White House for a friendly visit.)

As a buzzword, "socialism" had mostly good connotations in most of the world for most of the twentieth century. That's why the Nazis called themselves national socialists. That's why the Bolsheviks called their regime the Union of Soviet Socialist Republics, obliging the socialist and social democratic parties of Europe (and America, for what it was worth) to make rescuing the "good name" of socialism one of their central missions. Socialists—one thinks of men like George Orwell, Willy Brandt, and Aneurin Bevan—were among Communism's most passionate and effective enemies.

The United States is a special case. There is a whole shelf of books on the question of why socialism never became a real mass movement here. For decades, the word served mainly as a cudgel with which conservative Republicans beat liberal Democrats about the head. When Barry Goldwater and Ronald Reagan accused John F. Kennedy and Lyndon Johnson of socialism for advocating guaranteed health care for the aged and the poor, the implication was that Medicare and Medicaid would presage a Soviet America. Now that Communism has been defunct for nearly twenty years, though, the cry of socialism no longer packs its old punch. "At least in Europe, the socialist leaders who so admire my opponent are upfront about their objectives," McCain said the other day—thereby suggesting that the dystopia he abhors is not some North Korean–style totalitarian ant heap but, rather, the gentle social democracies across the Atlantic, where, in return for higher taxes and without any diminution of civil liberty, people buy themselves excellent public education, anxiety-free health care, and decent public transportation.

The Republican argument of the moment seems to be that the difference between capitalism and socialism corresponds to the difference between a top marginal income tax rate of 35 percent and a top marginal income tax rate of 39.6 percent. The latter is what it would be under Obama's proposal, what it was under President Clinton, and, for that matter, what it will be after 2010 if President Bush's tax cuts expire on schedule. Obama would use some of the added revenue to give a break to pretty much everybody who nets less than a quarter of a million dollars a year. The total tax burden on the private economy would be somewhat lighter than it is now—a bit of elementary Keynesianism that renders doubly untrue the Republican claim that Obama "will raise your taxes."

On October 12, in conversation with a voter forever to be known as Joe the Plumber, Obama gave one of his fullest summaries of his tax plan. After explaining how Joe could benefit from it, whether or not he achieves his dream of owning his own plumbing business, Obama added casually, "I think that when you spread the wealth around, it's good for everybody." McCain and Palin have been quoting this remark ever since, offering it as prima facie evidence of Obama's unsuitability for office. Of course, all taxes are redistributive, in that they redistribute private resources for public purposes. But the federal income tax is (downwardly) redistributive as a matter of principle: however slightly, it softens the inequalities that are inevitable in a market economy, and it reflects the belief that the wealthy have a proportionately greater stake in the material aspects of the social order and, therefore, should give that order proportionately more material support. McCain himself probably shares this belief, and there was a time when he was willing to say so. During the 2000 campaign, on MSNBC's *Hardball*, a young woman asked him why her father, a doctor, should be "penalized" by being "in a huge tax bracket." McCain replied that "wealthy people can afford more" and that "the very wealthy, because they can afford tax lawyers and all kinds of loopholes, really don't pay nearly as much as you think they do." The exchange continued:

YOUNG WOMAN: Are we getting closer and closer to, like, socialism and stuff? . . .

MCCAIN: Here's what I really believe: That when you reach a certain level of comfort, there's nothing wrong with paying somewhat more.

For her part, Sarah Palin, who has lately taken to calling Obama "Barack the Wealth Spreader," seems to be something of a suspect character herself. She is, at the very least, a fellow-traveller of what might be called socialism with an Alaskan face. The state that she governs has no income or sales tax. Instead, it imposes huge levies on the oil companies that lease its oil fields. The proceeds finance the government's activities and enable it to issue a four-figure annual check to every man, woman, and child in the state. One of the reasons Palin has been a popular governor is that she added an extra twelve hundred dollars to this year's check, bringing the per-person total to $3,269. A few weeks before she was nominated for vice president, she told a visiting journalist— Philip Gourevitch, of this magazine—that "we're set up, unlike other states in the union, where it's collectively Alaskans own the resources. So we share in the wealth when the development of these resources occurs." Perhaps there is some meaningful distinction between spreading the wealth and sharing it ("collectively," no less), but finding it would require the analytic skills of Karl the Marxist.

Addendum: Like, Confiscation

Since writing "Like, Socialism," I've seen numerous e-mails along these lines:

I may not be Karl the Marxist (whoever that is), but even I can easily see the distinction (which evades Mr. Hertzberg) between sharing the proceeds of a common asset, like a state's mineral rights, and spreading the wealth by confiscating (i.e., taxing) part of what some individuals

have produced and giving it to others. The proceeds of government
leases of drilling prospects are quite different from Hertzberg's paycheck. If he can't see that, why not share his entire paycheck with us?

I see the distinction, too, but I don't see much of a difference. What
I dispute is the flat characterization of personal income as "what some
individuals have produced." Part of my gross income reflects my individual efforts, of course, but part of it reflects the social and political arrangements that make it possible for me to have a paycheck to
begin with. That's the part that's withheld for taxes. I don't regard
this as "confiscation," any more than I regard my other monthly bills
that way.

In a democratic society, government is as much a "common asset"
as the oil under the tundra. We all "share the proceeds," such as roads,
police protection, the Smithsonian Institution, and not getting con-
quered by foreign armies. And all taxes redistribute the wealth from
some individuals to others, whether the others are defense contractors,
firefighters, chicken inspectors, destitute mothers, or Chinese (and,
lately, American) bankers.

It is fervently to be hoped that market idolatry—the belief that the
market is the only truly valuable institution of society and everything
else is a parasite on it—is on the way out. "Taxes are what we pay for
a civilized society," Mr. Justice Holmes is said to have said. "Freedom
ain't free," sing the poets of Nashville. Right they are. And neither is
civilization.

DIVIDED WE FALL

October 28, 2008

As the days dwindle down to a precious few, one of John McCain's last-minute arguments is that it would be a terrible thing for both of the elected branches of the federal government to be controlled by the same party. McCain never made that argument before this year, of course, and he would not be making it now if the Republicans were in a position to win both houses of Congress next Tuesday.

Still, nominally disinterested, chronically centrist types make essentially the same argument. "Voters in America are increasingly independent and don't trust any political party fully," Larry J. Sabato, the U.Va. political scientist and quotemeister, has said. "They don't want to give all of the political power to one party." Cokie Roberts, broadcasting's queen of the conventional wisdom, puts it this way: "For much of the last half-century, Americans have chosen divided government for good reason: We like it."

Do we really like it? And have we ever really "chosen" it?

In the real world, most ticket-splitting is an artifact of the advantages of congressional incumbency. Voters use the presidential ballot to express their political preference regarding the direction they want for the country. But they may vote for good old Congressman Thing because they know him or because he has enough seniority to bring goodies to the district or because they never heard of the other guy or because his office helped out with that Social Security problem Aunt Tillie was having.

One academic study, based on a regression analysis of 1992 and 1996 election data, finds that voters who split their tickets because they are consciously seeking to divide power and balance policy make up about twenty percent of the electorate. In other words, eighty percent of the electorate prefers to have the government dominated by one party—their own.

This doesn't mean that it's pointless for McCain to make the argument he's making. Every little bit helps. But, please, no more complacent lectures about how divided government is something that "we like."

HIS FINEST HALF HOUR

October 30, 2008

Last night's Obama infomercial was a good deal better than I expected: excellent production values (take a bow, Davis "An Inconvenient Truth" Guggenheim), astute choices of families to represent the problems Obama proposes to address, a ratio of fluff to substance that was on the high side but still within the parameters of civic responsibility, a good selection of talking heads (including the C.E.O. of Google, whose support of Obama was news to me), not-bad Ken Burns-y music, and, of course, the dulcet-toned narrator. (Obama could make an excellent living as a voice-over artist.)

There was some preemptive criticism from Republicans and commentators to the effect that it was presumptuous of Obama to use his bulging bank account to commandeer a whole half hour of television time on three broadcast networks plus several basic-cable ones. He should wait till he's actually president before he struts around making "addresses to the nation." He was overdoing the pretend stuff, like when his campaign experimented with that faux presidential seal. And so on.

Actually, back in the days when there was no Internet, no national newspapers, no nothing except three networks and a maximum of four unaffiliated television stations in any given market, buying a big block of TV time within a few days of the election was routine. The first political advertisement on the new medium ran in 1952, when Adlai Stevenson bought a half hour on CBS, displacing *I Love Lucy*. Bad idea. (To make matters worse, Adlai's speech ran long, so he was cut off in mid-sentence. Embarrassing.)

What about the supposedly outrageous expense? Well, according to TVweek.com, the Obama campaign spent $775,000 for the half hour on NBC and $961,000 for the half hour on CBS. That makes a total for those two networks of $1,736,000.

Obama's half hour was the equivalent of sixty thirty-second commercials. The average price of a thirty-second prime-time ad on NBC is $102,928. On CBS it's $116,729. Therefore, to buy a half hour in thirty-second increments—the usual procedure, at which no one bats an eye—on both networks would cost . . . let's see . . . $13,179,420.

Thirteen million dollars. With enough left over for an extra thirty-second spot plus carfare. Compared to a million seven.

Am I wrong in thinking that this was a bargain? Or even that it might even be regarded as evidence that an Obama administration might be able to rein in the budget by increasing efficiency and getting rid of waste, fraud, and abuse?

Most good-government types agree that the thirty-second-spot approach makes for deplorable distortions. Almost as many agree that granting candidates extended blocks of uninterrupted TV time would be a lot better. Like the Obama campaign's success in financing a campaign from millions of small contributors who can't be suspected of trying to buy access, its decision to put on a half-hour presentation of its policy proposals approximates an important goal of reformers—and does it through the "private sector" rather than through government action. Remind me: who's the conservative in this election?

One more thing about last night. Like Sarah Palin's wardrobe, the Barack Obama Show was sharp, beautifully designed, and one hundred percent positive.

HARTTHROB

November 1, 2008

I n the fall of 1980, I debated the issues of the day with Jeffrey Hart at Rockland Community College in Suffern, New York, a mile or two from the house I grew up in. I was the surrogate for my then boss, President Jimmy Carter. Hart was the surrogate for his old friend, conservative-movement comrade, and speechwriting customer Ronald Reagan.

Hart bested me that day, as his candidate was to best mine a month or so later. But he did it—to use a favorite word of his editor and colleague at *National Review*, Wm. F. Buckley, Jr.—cordially. He did not humiliate me more than was necessary, for which I remain grateful. Although he looked like a stereotypical liberal academic of the 1950s (bow tie, sweater vest, leather elbow patches, pipe and matches), there was nothing noticeably liberal about the ideological and political content of what he was saying.

Hart has been an important paternal presence in conservative circles for half a century. Now seventy-eight, he is a professor emeritus at Dartmouth. The *Dartmouth Review*, the first and hardiest of the "underground" conservative student papers, held its earliest editorial meetings in his living room. He mentored several future stars of conservative opinion-mongering, including Dinesh D'Souza, Gregory Fossedal, and Laura Ingraham.

Hart is a Burkean. His disenchantment with the anti-intellectual, Christianist, and imperial-triumphalist strains of the conservative movement has been growing for some time. This year he is an Obama-con. Thus, for the moment, we find ourselves on the same side, albeit for different (though sometimes overlapping) reasons.

Here's Hart in today's Daily Beast, Tina Brown's recently launched Web site:

> Republican President George W. Bush has not been a conservative at all, either in domestic policy or in foreign policy. He invaded Iraq on the basis of abstract theory, the very thing Burke warned against. Bush aimed to turn Iraq into a democracy, "a beacon of liberty in the Middle East," as he explained in a radio address in April 2006.
>
> I do not recall any "conservative" publication mentioning those now memorable words "Sunni," "Shia," or "Kurds." Burke would have been appalled at the blindness to history and to social facts that characterized the writing of those so-called conservatives.
>
> Obama did understand. In his now famous 2002 speech, while he was still a state senator in Illinois, he said: "I know that a successful war against Iraq will require a US occupation of undetermined length, of undetermined cost, with undetermined consequences. I know that an invasion of Iraq without a clear rationale and without international support will fan the flames of the Middle East, and encourage the worst, rather than the best, impulses of the Arab world, and strengthen the recruitment arm of al Qaeda. I'm not opposed to all wars. I'm opposed to dumb wars."
>
> Burke would have agreed entirely, and admired the cogency of so few words. And one thing I know is that both Nixon and Reagan would have agreed. Both were prudential and successful conservatives. But all the organs of the conservative movement followed Bush over the cliff—as did John McCain.

Hart concludes his essay with some observations on embryonic stem cell research, to which, as he notes, "the conservative movement publications, following Bush, have been fiercely opposed."

> Such opposition required a belief that a cluster of cells (the embryo) the size of the period at the end of this sentence is as important (more important?) than a seriously ill human being.
>
> I myself cannot fathom such a mentality. . . .
>
> Recently, Harvard announced a program that will be part of a multi-billion dollar science center to be established south of the Charles River, and will be able to supply stem cells to other laboratories. I call that Pro-Life.
>
> This analysis could be extended, but it seems clear to me that Obama is the conservative in the 2008 election.

It seems equally clear to me that Obama is also the liberal in the 2008 election. In truth, Obama is the only candidate in the 2008 election who thinks seriously enough and analytically enough to be considered either a conservative or a liberal.

As for Hart, he's not opposed to all conservatives. He's opposed to dumb conservatives. Substituting "liberals" for "conservatives," I concur. Perhaps this could be the basis for an Unpopular Front.

ELECTION DAY, ELECTION NIGHT

November 4, 2008

I vote at Public School 165, on West 109th Street, between Broadway and Amsterdam Avenue. It's an oldish building, dingy and utilitarian but with some of the dignified solidity that marked public works in the age of Roosevelt and LaGuardia. You walk through a high gate and across a concrete courtyard right into the gym. When we arrived— we being me, my wife (who can't vote because she's not an American citizen), and our son (who can't vote because he's ten)—the gym was full of snaking lines of people. We happily weaved our way to the line corresponding to our election district on the other side of the room. It was 7:30 in the morning.

In that room four years ago, the mood was warily hopeful, but with a jangly, jumpy edge. This time it was serene, as serene as the man almost everyone there had come to vote for. It was friendly. It was mellow. Kindness and consideration all around. The poll workers smiled and made gentle jokes. Our line was one of the shorter ones—maybe fifteen minutes.

I've always loved the experience of voting. For an unchurched secularist like me, it's the closest I'm likely to get to the feeling of sacred

solidarity which I imagine believers derive from their religious ritu-
als. It's especially satisfying in New York on account of our ancient
voting machines. No punch cards or touchscreens or spindly little
aluminum-and-plastic booths that look like they'd tip over at the
slightest push. Our machines weigh eight hundred pounds. They're
tall, the size and shape of a confessional. You go behind a calf-length
curtain and pull a big three-foot-long lever from left to right, like a
gondolier's oar. It goes Chunk! The candidates are laid out before you
in neat columns, with an inch-long black teardrop-shaped lever next to
each name. You snap the levers down. Chunk chunk chunk! You survey your work. You pull the oar back from right to left. Chunk! Most
satisfying. I let my son pull the little black levers, as I did in 2000, when
he was two, and 2004, when he was six. This time he was tall enough
to reach the Obama lever on tiptoes, without a boost. Next time he'll
be too big to come into the booth with me. But the time after that he'll
be able to go in alone.

This is the last election we'll have our magnificent machines, which
are slated to give way to some sort of third-rate technology. But the
human pleasure of this beautiful civic ceremony will remain. God bless
the Upper West Side and the United States of America.

Later

Like a lot of people, I've followed the Obama phenomenon with the
tracks of my tears since the beginning—that is, since that astounding
keynote address at the Democratic National Convention in Boston
on Tuesday, July 27, 2004. Correcting for the fact that with advanc-
ing age one tends to become less susceptible to sudden and/or overwhelming passions, I've never been as emotionally invested in the
fortunes of a politician as I've been in Obama's. The only possible
exception is Robert Kennedy, in 1968, when the feelings aroused in

many post-adolescents (like me) by the candidate's personal qualities (young, handsome, intense, relatively long-haired) were amplified by the poetical-tragical-romantic story of his personal transformation (from ruthless enforcer to openhearted idealist, propelled by grief) and the dramatic sweep of the events in which we were all embedded (a worldwide youth uprising, the Prague Spring, *Mai Soixante-Huit*, the civil rights revolution, Vietnam). This time the battle lines were somber and businesslike, not "cultural" (and countercultural). This time, solidarity cut across generational lines and "lifestyle" preferences. Obama summoned us to a singleness of nationhood ("the *United* States of America"), not to a "struggle" against some shadowy enemy like "the system" or "the power structure."

Having wept and/or teared up on so many occasions during the campaign, I was expecting major waterworks. They came, but it took a while. We were watching with friends in an East Side hotel suite, and when the networks declared Obama the victor we felt a need for humanity en masse. So the three of us (our ten-year-old son was with us, every inch of the way) hopped a cab and decided to detour a few blocks north on our way home.

People, naturally, were dancing in the streets. On upper Madison Avenue, north of 110th Street, exuberant knots of teenagers frolicked and waved. When we stopped at a traffic light, our driver clicked the door locks and rolled up the windows. We rolled them right down again. A dreadlocked young man ran straight for us, followed by his friends, chanting, "O-ba-ma! O-ba-ma!" He reached into the cab and slapped palms with us one by one.

We got out at 125th Street and headed west. The cops had closed the street off at Fifth Avenue. Every horn was honking, and it had nothing to do with traffic frustration. At the plaza in front of the New York State office building, at Adam Clayton Powell Jr. Boulevard, a.k.a. Seventh Avenue, where a jumbotron had been set up, people filled every square foot for blocks in every direction. The crowd was a photographic negative of the population of the United States: mostly black, ten or twelve percent white, lots of in between. When Obama appeared on the giant screen and his voice came through the speakers, the crowd quieted and listened. People murmured and nodded and many faces were wet.

Afterwards, we joined the flow west toward the Broadway subway, which comes out of the ground and passes high overhead on a trestle at 125th Street. In the doorways of apartment buildings people stood and watched the parade and exchanged smiles and V-signs and thumbs-ups. Teenage girls skipped along, slapping every palm within reach. Couples embraced. A big man ran past us exultantly; he had wrapped himself in an American flag like a shawl. At the corner of Morningside Avenue, the bells in the tower of a parish church, St. Joseph of the Holy Family, began to peal—the ancient sound of communal celebration, the sound of good news. They pealed and pealed and pealed.

That did it. Waterworks at last.

OBAMA WINS

November 7, 2008

At the *Times*, it is house style to refer to a successful presidential nominee by his full name in the lead of the main story the morning after the election. He may be Bill or Jimmy on his campaign posters, but in the newspaper of record on that one momentous occasion he is William Jefferson or James Earl, Jr. So say it loud and say it proud: Barack Hussein Obama, president-elect of the United States. Of the United States of America, as he himself liked to say on the stump—always, it seemed, with a touch of awe at the grandeur and improbability of it all.

Barack Hussein Obama: last week, sixty-five million Americans turned a liability—a moniker so politically inflammatory that the full recitation of it was considered foul play—into a global diplomatic asset, a symbol of the resurgence of America's ability to astonish and inspire. In the convention keynote speech that made him instantly famous four years ago, Obama called himself "a skinny kid with a funny name." Funny? Not really. "Millard Fillmore"—now, that's funny. The *Times* contented itself with referring to the candidate's "unusual name." Unusual? Unusual would be, say, "Dwight D. Eisenhower." Ten weeks from now, the president of the United States will be a person whose first name is a Swahili word derived from the Arabic (it means "bless-ing"), whose middle name is that not only of a grandson of the Prophet Muhammad but also of the original target of an ongoing American war, and whose last name is a perfect rhyme with "Osama." That's not a name, it's a catastrophe, at least in American politics. Or ought to have been.

Yet Barack Obama won, and won big. Democrats have now achieved pluralities in four of the last five presidential elections. But Obama's popular vote was an outright majority—a little more than fifty-two percent, at the latest reckoning, the largest share for a nominee of his party since Lyndon Johnson's in 1964. Obama made significant gains compared with John Kerry, four years ago, in nearly every category that exit polls record: black folks but also white folks; liberals but also conservatives; women but also men. His gains were especially striking among Latinos, the very poor and the very well-off, Catholics and the unchurched, and the two groups most likely to be concerned about the future: young people and the parents of children living at home. And although the Obama wave does not seem to have brought with it a filibuster-proof Senate, it did sweep into office enough new members of both houses of Congress to offer him the hope of a governing legisla-tive majority.

This election was so extraordinary in so many ways that its mean-ing will take many years to play out and many more to be understood. But there is already the feel of the beginning of a new era. As in 1932 and 1980, a crisis in the economy opened the way for the rejection of a reigning approach to government and the forging of a new one. Emphatically, comprehensively, the public has turned against con-servatism at home and neoconservatism abroad. The faith that unfet-tered markets and minimal taxes on the rich will solve every domestic problem, and that unilateral arrogance and American arms will solve every foreign one, is dead for a generation or more. And the electoral strategy of "cultural" resentment and fake populism has been dealt a grievous blow.

Obama is young, educated, focussed, reassuring, and energetic. He is as accomplished a writer as he is a speaker. His campaign was a marvel of discipline, organization, and prescience. He has, as a conservative critic acknowledged, "a first-class intellect and a first-class temperament." We have had these qualities in our presidents before, if rarely all in the same person. But Obama's most visible attribute, the only one mentioned in that *Times* lead, is unique, even revolutionary: the color of his skin. As surely as Appomattox, the post-Civil War constitutional amendments, Brown v. Board of Education, and the Civil Rights and Voting Rights acts of the nineteen-sixties, Obama's election is a giant victory in the long struggle against what an earlier generation of Republicans called the Slave Power and its long legacy of exclusion and hate.

During the campaign, Obama's "exoticism"—both real (his childhood in Jakarta) and imagined ("he's a Muslim")—served bigots as a cover for racism. But it was a shield as well as a vulnerability. It set him apart from the stereotypes of racial prejudice. It broadened rather than narrowed his "otherness." His absent father was Kenyan; if the son's line of descent includes American slaves, they are hidden on his mother's side, as they are in the lineage of myriads of this country's white citizens. His upbringing in his mother's far-flung world and the polyglot Hawaii of his white grandparents gave him the perspective of both an outsider and an insider. His search for identity—the subject of his book *Dreams from My Father*, now assured of a place in the American literary canon—made him a profound student of the American dilemma. In his Philadelphia speech of March 18, 2008, prompted by the firestorm over his former pastor, he treated the American people as adults capable of complex thinking—as his equals, you might say. But what made that speech special, what enabled it to save his candidacy, was its analytic power. It was not defensive. It did not overcompensate. In its combination of objectivity and empathy, it persuaded Americans of all colors that he understood them. In return, they have voted to make him their president.

A generation ago, few people anywhere imagined that they would witness the dissolution of Soviet totalitarianism, or the inauguration of Nelson Mandela as president of a multiracial South African democracy, or the transformation of China into a fearsome engine of capitalist commerce. Nor did Americans of an age to remember Selma and Montgomery and Memphis imagine that they would live to see an African-American elected president of the United States. It has happened. No doubt there will be disappointments and difficulties ahead; there always are. But a few months from now a blue-and-white Boeing 747 emblazoned UNITED STATES OF AMERICA will touch down on a tarmac somewhere in Europe or Asia or Africa, the door will open, and out will step Barack and Michelle Obama. That is something to look forward to.

APPENDIX

I n its issue of October 13, 2008, the New Yorker endorsed Barack Obama. This was the second time the magazine had "officially" supported a candidate for president; the first was four years earlier, when, in the November 1, 2004, issue, it recommended a vote for Senator John Kerry.

The New Yorker does not normally carry "editorials." The weekly "Comment" essay is a second cousin of the genre; the opinions expressed in "Comment" almost invariably fall somewhere within the boundaries of a broad consensus shared by the half-dozen or more writers who regularly or occasionally contribute to it, but it is not formally an expression of the views of anyone but the person whose name appears beneath it.

This endorsement, like its predecessor, was signed "The Editors," and it was a truly collaborative effort. Its principal drafters were David Remnick, the magazine's editor, and myself, but a number of other members of the staff contributed ideas or paragraphs to it, including Virginia Cannon, John Cassidy, Steve Coll, Henry Finder, Adam Gopnik, Elizabeth Kolbert, Nicholas Lemann, George Packer, Jeffrey Toobin, and Dorothy Wickenden. The week it was published, it occupied the whole of "The Talk of the Town."

—H.H.

THE CHOICE

Never in living memory has an election been more critical than the one fast approaching—that's the quadrennial cliché, as expected as the balloons and the bombast. And yet when has it ever felt so urgently true? When have so many Americans had so clear a sense that a presidency has—at the levels of competence, vision, and integrity—undermined the country and its ideals?

The incumbent administration has distinguished itself for the ages. The presidency of George W. Bush is the worst since Reconstruction, so there is no mystery about why the Republican Party—which has held dominion over the executive branch of the federal government for the past eight years and the legislative branch for most of that time—has little desire to defend its record, domestic or foreign. The only speaker at the Convention in St. Paul who uttered more than a sentence or two in support of the president was his wife, Laura. Meanwhile, the nominee, John McCain, played the part of a vaudeville illusionist, asking to be regarded as an apostle of change after years of embracing the essentials of the Bush agenda with ever-increasing ardor.

The Republican disaster begins at home. Even before taking into account whatever fantastically expensive plan eventually emerges to help rescue the financial system from Wall Street's long-running pyramid schemes, the economic and fiscal picture is bleak. During the Bush administration, the national debt, now approaching ten trillion dollars, has nearly doubled. Next year's federal budget is projected to run a half-trillion-dollar deficit, a precipitous fall from the seven-hundred-billion-dollar surplus that was projected when Bill Clinton left office. Private-sector job creation has been a sixth of what it was under President Clinton. Five million people have fallen into poverty. The number of Americans without health insurance has grown by seven million, while average premiums have nearly doubled. Meanwhile, the principal domestic achievement of the Bush administration has been to shift the relative burden of taxation from the rich to the rest. For the top one per cent of us, the Bush tax cuts are worth, on average, about a thousand dollars a week; for the bottom fifth, about a dollar and a half. The unfairness will only increase if the painful, yet necessary, effort to rescue the credit markets ends up preventing the rescue of our health-care system, our environment, and our physical, educational, and industrial infrastructure.

At the same time, a hundred and fifty thousand American troops are in Iraq and thirty-three thousand are in Afghanistan. There is still disagreement about the wisdom of overthrowing Saddam Hussein and his horrific regime, but there is no longer the slightest doubt that the Bush administration manipulated, bullied, and lied the American public into this war and then mismanaged its prosecution in nearly every aspect. The direct costs, besides an expenditure of more than six hundred billion dollars, have included the loss of more than four thousand Americans, the wounding of thirty thousand, the deaths of tens of thousands of Iraqis, and the displacement of four and a half million men, women, and children. Only now, after American forces have been fighting for a year longer than they did in the Second World War, is there a glimmer of hope that the conflict in Iraq has entered a stage of fragile stability.

The indirect costs, both of the war in particular and of the administration's unilateralist approach to foreign policy in general, have also been immense. The torture of prisoners, authorized at the highest level, has been an ethical and a public-diplomacy catastrophe. At a moment when the global environment, the global economy, and global stability all demand a transition to new sources of energy, the United States has been a global retrograde, wasteful in its consumption and heedless in its policy. Strategically and morally, the Bush administration has squandered the American capacity to counter the example and the swagger of its rivals. China, Russia, Iran, Saudi Arabia, and other illiberal states have concluded, each in its own way, that democratic principles and human rights need not be components of a stable, prosperous future. At recent meetings of the United Nations, emboldened despots like

Mahmoud Ahmadinejad of Iran came to town sneering at our predicament and hailing the "end of the American era."

The election of 2008 is the first in more than half a century in which no incumbent president or vice president is on the ballot. There is, however, an incumbent party, and that party has been lucky enough to find itself, apparently against the wishes of its "base," with a nominee who evidently disliked George W. Bush before it became fashionable to do so. In South Carolina in 2000, Bush crushed John McCain with a sub-rosa primary campaign of such viciousness that McCain lashed out memorably against Bush's Christian-right allies. So profound was McCain's anger that in 2004 he flirted with the possibility of joining the Democratic ticket under John Kerry. Bush, who took office as a "compassionate conservative," governed immediately as a rightist ideologue. During that first term, McCain bolstered his reputation, sometimes deserved, as a "maverick" willing to work with Democrats on such issues as normalizing relations with Vietnam, campaign-finance reform, and immigration reform. He co-sponsored, with John Edwards and Edward Kennedy, a patients' bill of rights. In 2001 and 2003, he voted against the Bush tax cuts. With John Kerry, he co-sponsored a bill raising auto-fuel efficiency standards and, with Joseph Lieberman, a cap-and-trade regime on carbon emissions. He was one of a minority of Republicans opposed to unlimited drilling for oil and gas off America's shores.

Since the 2004 election, however, McCain has moved remorselessly rightward in his quest for the Republican nomination. He paid obeisance to Jerry Falwell and preachers of his ilk. He abandoned immigration reform, eventually coming out against his own bill. Most shocking, McCain, who had repeatedly denounced torture under all circumstances, voted in February against a ban on the very techniques of "enhanced interrogation" that he himself once endured in Vietnam—as long as the torturers were civilians employed by the C.I.A.

On almost every issue, McCain and the Democratic Party's nominee, Barack Obama, speak the generalized language of "reform," but only Obama has provided a convincing, rational, and fully developed vision. McCain has abandoned his opposition to the Bush-era tax cuts and has taken up the demagogic call—in the midst of recession and Wall Street calamity, with looming crises in Social Security, Medicare, and Medicaid—for more tax cuts. Bush's expire in 2011. If McCain, as he has proposed, cuts taxes for corporations and estates, the benefits once more would go disproportionately to the wealthy.

In Washington, the craze for pure market triumphalism is over. Treasury Secretary Henry Paulson arrived in town (via Goldman Sachs) a Republican, but it seems that he will leave a Democrat. In other words, he has come to see that the abuses that led to the current financial crisis—not least, excessive speculation on borrowed capital— can be fixed only with government regulation and oversight. McCain, who has never evinced much interest in, or knowledge of, economic questions, has had little of substance to say about the crisis. His most notable gesture of concern—a melodramatic call last month to suspend his campaign and postpone the first presidential debate until the government bailout plan was ready—soon revealed itself as an empty diversionary tactic.

By contrast, Obama has made a serious study of the mechanics and the history of this economic disaster and of the possibilities of stimulating a recovery. Last March, in New York, in a speech notable for its depth, balance, and foresight, he said, "A complete disdain for pay-as-you-go budgeting, coupled with a generally scornful attitude towards oversight and enforcement, allowed far too many to put short-term gain ahead of long-term consequences." Obama is committed to reforms that value not only the restoration of stability but also the protection of the vast majority of the population, which did not partake of the fruits of the binge years. He has called for greater and more programmatic regulation of the financial system; the creation of a National Infrastructure Reinvestment Bank, which would help reverse the decay of our roads, bridges, and mass-transit systems, and create millions of jobs; and a major investment in the green-energy sector.

On energy and global warming, Obama offers a set of forceful proposals. He supports a cap-and-trade program to reduce America's carbon emissions by eighty per cent by 2050—an enormously ambitious goal, but one that many climate scientists say must be met if atmospheric carbon dioxide is to be kept below disastrous levels. Large emitters, like utilities, would acquire carbon allowances, and those which emit less carbon dioxide than their allotment could sell the resulting credits to those which emit more; over time, the available allowances would decline. Significantly, Obama wants to auction off the allowances; this would provide fifteen billion dollars a year for developing alternative-energy sources and creating job-training programs in green technologies. He also wants to raise federal fuel-economy standards and to require that ten per cent of America's electricity be generated from renewable sources by 2012. Taken together, his proposals represent the most coherent and far-sighted strategy ever offered by a presidential candidate for reducing the nation's reliance on fossil fuels.

There was once reason to hope that McCain and Obama would have a sensible debate about energy and climate policy. McCain was one of the first Republicans in the Senate to support federal limits on carbon dioxide, and he has touted his own support for a less ambitious cap-and-trade program as evidence of his independence from the White House. But, as polls showed Americans growing jittery about gasoline prices, McCain apparently found it expedient in this area, too, to shift course. He took a dubious idea—lifting the federal moratorium on offshore oil drilling—and placed it at the very center of his campaign. Opening up America's coastal waters to drilling would have no impact on gasoline prices in the short term, and, even over the long term, the effect, according to a recent analysis by the Department of Energy, would be "insignificant." Such inconvenient facts, however, are waved away by a campaign that finally found its voice with the slogan "Drill, baby, drill!"

The contrast between the candidates is even sharper with respect to the third branch of government. A tense equipoise currently prevails among the Justices of the Supreme Court, where four hard-core conservatives face off against four moderate liberals. Anthony M. Kennedy is the swing vote, determining the outcome of case after case.

McCain cites Chief Justice John Roberts and Justice Samuel Alito, two reliable conservatives, as models for his own prospective appointments. If he means what he says, and if he replaces even one moderate on the current Supreme Court, then Roe v. Wade will be reversed, and states will again be allowed to impose absolute bans on abortion. McCain's views have hardened on this issue. In 1999, he said he opposed overturning Roe; by 2006, he was saying that its demise "wouldn't bother me any"; by 2008, he no longer supported adding rape and incest as exceptions to his party's platform opposing abortion.

But scrapping Roe—which, after all, would leave states as free to permit abortion as to criminalize it—would be just the beginning. Given the ideological agenda that the existing conservative bloc has pursued, it's safe to predict that affirmative action of all kinds would likely be outlawed by a McCain Court. Efforts to expand executive power, which, in recent years, certain Justices have nobly tried to resist, would likely increase. Barriers between church and state would fall; executions would soar; legal checks on corporate power would wither—all with just one new conservative nominee on the Court. And the next president is likely to make three appointments.

Obama, who taught constitutional law at the University of Chicago, voted against confirming not only Roberts and Alito but also several unqualified lower-court nominees. As an Illinois state senator, he won the support of prosecutors and police organizations for new protections against convicting the innocent in capital cases. While McCain voted to continue to deny habeas corpus rights to detainees, perpetuating the Bush administration's regime of state-sponsored extra-legal detention, Obama took the opposite side, pushing to restore the right of all U.S.-held prisoners to a hearing, affirming America's founding principles. The judicial future would be safe in his care.

———

In the shorthand of political commentary, the Iraq war seems to leave McCain and Obama roughly even. Opposing it before the invasion, Obama had the prescience to warn of a costly and indefinite occupation and rising anti-American radicalism around the world; supporting it, McCain foresaw none of this. More recently, in early 2007 McCain risked his presidential prospects on the proposition that five additional combat brigades could salvage a war that by then appeared hopeless. Obama, along with most of the country, had decided that it was time to cut American losses. Neither candidate's calculations on Iraq have been as cheaply political as McCain's repeated assertion that Obama values his career over his country; both men based their positions, right or wrong, on judgment and principle.

President Bush's successor will inherit two wars and the realities of limited resources, flagging popular will, and the dwindling possibilities of what can be achieved by American power. McCain's views on these subjects range from the simplistic to the unknown. In Iraq, he seeks "victory"—a word that General David Petraeus refuses to use, and one that fundamentally misrepresents the messy, open-ended nature of the conflict. As for Afghanistan, on the rare occasions when McCain mentions it he implies that the surge can be transferred directly from Iraq, which suggests that his grasp of counterinsurgency is not as firm as he insisted it was during the first presidential debate. McCain always displays more faith in force than interest in its strategic consequences. Unlike Obama, McCain has no political strategy for either war, only the dubious hope that greater security will allow things to work out. Obama has long warned of deterioration along the Afghanistan-Pakistan border, and has a considered grasp of its vital importance. His strategy for both Afghanistan and Iraq shows an understanding of the role that internal politics, economics, corruption, and regional diplomacy play in wars where there is no battlefield victory.

Unimaginably painful personal experience taught McCain that war is above all a test of honor: maintain the will to fight on, be prepared to risk everything, and you will prevail. Asked during the first debate to outline "the lessons of Iraq," McCain said, "I think the lessons of Iraq are very clear: that you cannot have a failed strategy that will then cause you to nearly lose a conflict." A soldier's answer—but a statesman must have a broader view of war and peace. The years ahead will demand not only determination but also diplomacy, flexibility, patience, judiciousness, and intellectual engagement. These are no more McCain's strong suit than the current president's. Obama, for his part, seems to know that more will be required than willpower and force to extract some advantage from the wreckage of the Bush years.

Obama is also better suited for the task of renewing the bedrock foundations of American influence. An American restoration in foreign affairs will require a commitment not only to international cooperation but also to international institutions that can address global warming, the dislocations of what will likely be a deepening global economic crisis, disease epidemics, nuclear proliferation, terrorism, and other, more traditional security challenges. Many of the Cold War-era vehicles for engagement and negotiation—the United Nations, the World Bank, the Nuclear Non-Proliferation Treaty regime, the North Atlantic Treaty Organization—are moribund, tattered, or outdated. Obama has the generational outlook that will be required to revive or reinvent these compacts. He would be the first postwar American president unencumbered by the legacies of either Munich or Vietnam.

The next president must also restore American moral credibility. Closing Guantánamo, banning all torture, and ending the Iraq war as responsibly as possible will provide a start, but only that. The modern presidency is as much a vehicle for communication as for decision-making, and the relevant audiences are global. Obama has inspired many Americans in part because he holds up a mirror to their own idealism. His election would do no less—and likely more—overseas.

———

What most distinguishes the candidates, however, is character—and here, contrary to conventional wisdom, Obama is clearly the stronger of the two. Not long ago, Rick Davis, McCain's campaign manager, said, "This election is not about issues. This election is about a composite view of what people take away from these candidates." The view that this election is about personalities leaves out policy, complexity, and accountability. Even so, there's some truth in what Davis said—but it hardly points to the conclusion that he intended.

Echoing Obama, McCain has made "change" one of his campaign mantras. But the change he has actually provided has been in himself, and it is not just a matter of altering his positions. A willingness to pander and even lie has come to define his presidential campaign and its televised advertisements. A contemptuous duplicity, a meanness, has entered his talk on the stump—so much so that it seems obvious that, in the drive for victory, he is willing to replicate some of the same underhanded methods that defeated him eight years ago in South Carolina.

Perhaps nothing revealed McCain's cynicism more than his choice of Sarah Palin, the former mayor of Wasilla, Alaska, who had been governor of that state for twenty-one months, as the Republican nominee for vice president. In the interviews she has given since her nomination, she has had difficulty uttering coherent unscripted responses about the most basic issues of the day. We are watching a candidate for vice president cram for her ongoing exam in elementary domestic and foreign policy. This is funny as a Tina Fey routine on *Saturday Night Live*, but as a vision of the political future it's deeply unsettling. Palin has no business being the backup to a president of any age, much less to one who is seventy-two and in imperfect health. In choosing her, McCain committed an act of breathtaking heedlessness and irresponsibility. Obama's choice, Joe Biden, is not without imperfections. His tongue sometimes runs in advance of his mind, providing his own fodder for late-night comedians, but there is no comparison with Palin. His deep experience in foreign affairs, the judiciary, and social policy makes him an assuring and complementary partner for Obama.

The longer the campaign goes on, the more the issues of personality and character have reflected badly on McCain. Unless appearances are very deceiving, he is impulsive, impatient, self-dramatizing, erratic, and a compulsive risk-taker. These qualities may have contributed to his usefulness as a "maverick" senator. But in a president they would be a menace.

By contrast, Obama's transformative message is accompanied by a sense of pragmatic calm. A tropism for unity is an essential part of his character and of his campaign. It is part of what allowed him to overcome a Democratic opponent who entered the race with tremendous advantages. It is what helped him forge a political career relying on both the liberals of Hyde Park and the political regulars of downtown Chicago. His policy preferences are distinctly liberal, but he is determined to speak to a broad range of Americans who do not necessarily share his every value or opinion. For some who oppose him, his equanimity even under the ugliest attack seems like hauteur; for some who support him, his reluctance to counterattack in the same vein seems like self-defeating detachment. Yet it is Obama's temperament—and not McCain's—that seems appropriate for the office both men seek and for the volatile and dangerous era in which we live. Those who dismiss his centeredness as self-centeredness or his composure as indifference are as wrong as those who mistook Eisenhower's stolidity for denseness or Lincoln's humor for lack of seriousness.

Nowadays, almost every politician who thinks about running for president arranges to become an author. Obama's books are different: he wrote them. *The Audacity of Hope* (2006) is a set of policy disquisitions loosely structured around an account of his freshman year in the United States Senate. Though a campaign manifesto of sorts, it is superior to that genre's usual blowsy pastiche of ghostwritten speeches. But it is Obama's first book, *Dreams from My Father: A Story of Race and Inheritance* (1995), that offers an unprecedented glimpse into the mind and heart of a potential president. Obama began writing it in his early thirties, before he was a candidate for anything. Not since Theodore Roosevelt has an American politician this close to the pinnacle of power produced such a sustained, highly personal work of literary merit before being definitively swept up by the tides of political ambition.

A presidential election is not the awarding of a Pulitzer Prize: we elect a politician and, we hope, a statesman, not an author. But Obama's first book is valuable in the way that it reveals his fundamental attitudes of mind and spirit. *Dreams from My Father* is an illuminating memoir not only in the substance of Obama's own peculiarly American story but also in the qualities he brings to the telling: a formidable intelligence, emotional empathy, self-reflection, balance, and a remarkable ability to see life and the world through the eyes of people very different from himself. In common with nearly all other senators and governors of his generation, Obama does not count military service as part of his biography. But his life has been full of tests—personal, spiritual, racial, political—that bear on his preparation for great responsibility.

It is perfectly legitimate to call attention, as McCain has done, to Obama's lack of conventional national and international policymaking experience. We, too, wish he had more of it. But office-holding is not the only kind of experience relevant to the task of leading a wildly variegated nation. Obama's immersion in diverse human environments (Hawaii's racial rainbow, Chicago's racial cauldron, countercultural New York, middle-class Kansas, predominantly Muslim Indonesia), his years of organizing among the poor, his taste of corporate law and his grounding in public-interest and constitutional law—these, too, are experiences. And his books show that he has wrung from them every drop of insight and breadth of perspective they contained.

The exhaustingly, sometimes infuriatingly long campaign of 2008 (and 2007) has had at least one virtue: it has demonstrated that Obama's intelligence and steady temperament are not just figments of the writer's craft. He has made mistakes, to be sure. (His failure to accept McCain's imaginative proposal for a series of unmediated joint appearances was among them.) But, on the whole, his campaign has been marked by patience, planning, discipline, organization, technological proficiency, and strategic astuteness. Obama has often looked two or three moves ahead, relatively impervious to the permanent hysteria of the hourly news cycle and the cable news shouters. And when crisis has struck, as it did when the divisive antics of his ex-pastor threatened to bring down his campaign, he has proved equal to the moment, rescuing himself with a speech that not only drew the poison but also demonstrated a profound respect for the electorate. Although his opponents have tried to attack him as a man of "mere" words, Obama has returned elo-quence to its essential place in American politics. The choice between experience and eloquence is a false one—something that Lincoln, out of office after a single term in Congress, proved in his own campaign of political and national renewal. Obama's "mere" speeches on everything from the economy and foreign affairs to race have been at the center of his campaign and its success; if he wins, his eloquence will be central to his ability to govern.

We cannot expect one man to heal every wound, to solve every major crisis of policy. So much of the presidency, as they say, is a matter of waking up in the morning and trying to drink from a fire hydrant. In the quiet of the Oval Office, the noise of immediate demands can be deafening. And yet Obama has precisely the temperament to shut out the noise when necessary and concentrate on the essential. The election of Obama—a man of mixed ethnicity, at once comfortable in the world and utterly representative of twenty-first century America—would, at a stroke, reverse our country's image abroad and refresh its spirit at home. His ascendance to the presidency would be a symbolic culmina-tion of the civil- and voting-rights acts of the nineteen-sixties and the century-long struggles for equality that preceded them. It could not help but say something encouraging, even exhilarating, about the coun-try, about its dedication to tolerance and inclusiveness, about its fidelity, after all, to the values it proclaims in its textbooks. At a moment of economic calamity, international perplexity, political failure, and battered morale, America needs both uplift and realism, both change and steadiness. It needs a leader temperamentally, intellectually, and emotionally attuned to the complexities of our troubled globe. That leader's name is Barack Obama.

ACKNOWLEDGMENTS

For the better part of forty years (not that there was anything "worse" about the fifteen-year break I took to work successively for Jimmy Carter and *The New Republic*), I have been lucky enough to be surrounded and protected by the editorial staff of *The New Yorker*. Over the years the cast of characters has changed but the excellence of the performance has not. I give thanks to our managing editor, Kate Julian, and her assistant, Alexander Dryer, and to Pat Keogh and his production staff for finding me the extra time and space, respectively, I almost always seem to need on Fridays. At newyorker.com, I thank Blake Eskin and Trish Deitch. To all my colleagues—especially the fact-checkers and copyeditors whose invisible work gives the magazine its spooky aura of authority—I give thanks.

Speaking of authority, David Remnick, our editor in chief, and Dorothy Wickenden, our executive editor, are wonderful people to be down an organization chart from. I thank David for his support, patience, encouragement, and friendship. I thank Dorothy for hers, and also for hosting *The New Yorker*'s political podcast, on which, in conversation with the likes of Ryan Lizza, George Packer, Jeffrey Toobin, Jane Mayer, John Cassidy, Peter J. Boyer, Elizabeth Kolbert, and James Surowiecki, I seldom fail to have (or steal) a useful insight. Thanks, too, to Si Newhouse, for providing from on high the resources and the freedom for all this to happen.

Scott Moyers, my editor at The Penguin Press for *Politics* and now my champion at The Wylie Agency, and Ann Godoff, Penguin's president and publisher, made this book possible. Ann's colleagues, Lindsay Whalen and Tracy Locke, made working on it a pleasure.

Finally, my deepest gratitude goes to Virginia Cannon—my wife, my dearest friend, and the mother of our son. Also my editor, which I don't mean only in the sense familiar to readers of authors' nods to their spouses—"She's my best editor," et cetera (though she is that). I mean it literally: as a senior editor of *The New Yorker*, she is officially charged with the supervision and editing of a dozen or more staff writers, including, as it happens, me. In theory, combining corporate discipline with marital felicity should be hazardous to both. In practice— our practice, anyhow—it works beautifully. I can't imagine either life or work without her.

INDEX